JEAN GIRAUDOUX
The Writer
and His Work

JEAN GIRAUDOUX

The Writer
and His Work

GEORGES LEMAITRE

FREDERICK UNGAR PUBLISHING CO., NEW YORK

TO STEPHANIE

Acknowledgments

I wish to express my sincere thanks to Mme Christian Gaignault and to M. Pierre Brunel for the help they generously gave me in the preparation of this book and also to Mrs. Wynifred Lemaitre, Librarian at Wellesley College, for her unfailing kindness in providing me with invaluable aid and in making extensive research on my behalf.

Important fragments of an essay on Giraudoux included in my book *Four French Novelists,* which was published by the Oxford University Press in 1938, have been incorporated in the present volume. I wish to thank the Oxford Press for its gracious cooperation in that matter.

My thanks are also due to the Librairie Bernard Grasset, to the firm Ides et Calendes of Neuchâtel (Switzerland), and particularly to M. Jean-Pierre Giraudoux for their courtesy in granting me permission to quote passages of the works of Giraudoux for which they hold the copyright. The English translations of the quotations are my own.

I should like to repeat here the expression of my gratitude, which I have already mentioned in the preface of *Four French Novelists,* to the late Professor C.E. Fryer, F.R.Hist.S., to whom I am greatly indebted for much scholarly and friendly advice.

Georges Lemaitre

Contents

Two souls, alas! reside within my breast,
And each withdraws from, and repels, its brother.
One with tenacious organs holds in love
And clinging lust the world in its embraces;
The other strongly sweeps, this dust above,
Into the high ancestral spaces.
Goethe, *Faust*, Part One
from the Bayard Taylor translation

On opening a book, a reader says to himself:
"I am going to have a fine story."
I would like him to say, as he opens one of my books:
"I am going to get in touch with a living soul."[1]
Jean Giraudoux

℀ I ℀
From Peaceful Bellac
to Wartime Paris

Hippolyte Jean Giraudoux was born on October 29, 1882, in Bellac, a small town of fewer than five thousand inhabitants in the old province of Limousin. Although Bellac is of some antiquity, its history does not recall any special heroic deeds or important political events. It is picturesque enough, but no more so than a hundred other French provincial towns. The climate is harsh and damp, and in winter very cold. The surrounding country has some attractive scenery: the rolling hills are crowned with thick dark woods; patches of brown fields or green meadows deck the lower slopes; down in the valleys, brooks bubble over rounded pebbles and mossy stones. Yet an atmosphere of seriousness, almost of melancholy, seems to pervade the whole landscape.

For Giraudoux, however, Bellac is "the most beautiful town in the world."[2] Throughout his works he has never tired of expatiating on the quaint charm of his native place and the beauties of his native Limousin. Both town and province strongly influenced his personality and left an indelible stamp on his works. Giraudoux grew up in the peaceful atmosphere to be found in almost any secluded provincial town. From his early childhood he was well acquainted with the familiar types of a small old-fashioned French community: the pharmacist, the road surveyor, the tax

1

collector, the controller of weights and measures, and many varieties of inspectors, all deeply imbued with a consciousness of their own importance in the petty officialdom of France.

To those good people life did not present many complications or problems. Their ideas rested upon an old and firmly established yet mellow tradition. They had simple and definite notions of good and bad; their merits as well as their defects were moderate and normal; they led on the whole a well-regulated and well-balanced existence: "Small towns are not mirrors that distort. The prevailing qualities of life, its ebb and flow, were reflected in Bellac in such a well-ordered way and so patently that they were quite inoffensive. January was always cold, August always torrid; each of our neighbors had but one virtue or one vice at a time; we learned to know the world, as is fitting, by spelling each season and each sentiment separately. Each of the well-plastered houses in the street played, as it were, one musical note—avarice, vanity, gluttony; no sharps, no flats: no miser-glutton, no modest-wanton."[3]

Many of those *petits bourgeois* were undoubtedly open to ridicule. After all, however, they did not lack the essentials of life; they enjoyed their home town, their family, their occupation or their trade, in fact their whole existence, quietly, sincerely and honestly: "We tasted life . . . in all its fullness."[4]

In the Limousin countryside closely surrounding the little town and within the easy reach of even a child, Giraudoux learned to understand and appreciate Nature. Nature did not reveal herself to him in her most spectacular aspects. He was in contact with a subdued type of scenery whose charm depended essentially on seasonal impressions and fine hourly shades. From his native Limousin, Giraudoux derived a lasting taste for the disciplined lines of an old French landscape, with an acute awareness of the rarest and most fleeting elements in the play of light and color under a changing sky.

Giraudoux belonged to a very modest family. His father, Léger Giraudoux, was a small official in the service of the Department of Highways in Bellac. In 1889, however, unable to endure the damp climate of Bellac because of his arthritis, he obtained a transfer first, for a short time, to Bessines. Later he became the tax collector in Pellevoisin, a nearby small town that had a somewhat sunnier exposure. Six years later, in 1895, he moved to a similar position in the town of Cérilly. The picture of a sleepy provincial town that Giraudoux evoked so often under the name of Bellac probably combines the features of Bellac itself with those of Bessines, Pellevoisin, and Cérilly.

Family life in the Giraudoux household was pleasant and peaceful. Jean Giraudoux had little in common with his father, whom he respected as a good, honest man, but who tended to be somewhat sententious and pompous. He was much closer to his mother, *née* Anne Lacoste. She was a shy and sensitive woman, endowed with a great deal of innate refinement and imaginative fantasy. Her son seems to have inherited many traits of her character. Jean Giraudoux had a brother, Alexandre, two years older than himself. The two boys got along very well together and retained close and affectionate relations throughout their lives.

Giraudoux went to a series of local elementary schools successively in Bellac, Bessines, and Pellevoisin. He worked so well there and showed himself to be so bright that at the age of eleven he was granted a scholarship to pursue his studies at the lycée of Châteauroux. The latter, in the province of Berry, appeared to young Giraudoux as "the ugliest city in France."[5] The seven years that he spent there, however, were of crucial importance for the molding of his mind.

He was, by nature, of a much finer grain than most of his rather oafish schoolmates. He did not form any close friendships with any of them. He was definitely, though discreetly, aware of his intellectual superiority, and he took a perceptible pride in his scholastic achievements. His behavior, however, was so elaborately courteous that his successes never aroused in the other pupils any serious jealousy or hostility against him.

His instinctive reserve, even a certain aloofness, protected him against the roughest aspects of the life of a young boarding pupil in a French lycée at the end of the nineteenth century. The régime of a French lycée at that time was austere and stern but not truly oppressive, and the seven years that Giraudoux spent in Châteauroux were certainly not years of Dickensian misery. He must have suffered from loneliness, however, and, very much like a character in one of his novels who bears a strong resemblance to young Giraudoux himself, he was undoubtedly "often isolated and silent."[6]

He found in his work, however, a rich compensation for his

loneliness. Work was for him a source of unending, intense joy. Not only did he perform with zeal all the tasks that were required from him by his teachers, but he contrived all sorts of ruses in order to study incessantly, even during the periods of rest provided by school regulations, and against the wishes of the teachers themselves. "O work, beloved work," he wrote in reminiscence twenty-five years later, "thou who overthroweth shameful laziness! O work of a child, generous as the love of a child! It is easy, however watchful the teachers' supervison may be, to work unceasingly. In the refectory, while the mail was being distributed, since I never received any, I took advantage of the opportunity to review my notebooks. On Thursdays and Sundays, in order to avoid going to a walk with the other pupils, I used to slip stealthily into the study room . . . . During recesses between classes, I did not even trouble to conceal my book, but moved slowly round and round a pillar, according to the position of the supervising master, who was pacing up and down the courtyard. I used to get up every morning at five and joyfully retrieve from my desk a half-constructed composition, the scattered sheets of an essay."[7]

Giraudoux absorbed with eagerness all that his teachers were able to offer him. Latin, Greek, and French classical literature were then the fundamental subjects taught in French schools. He not only assimilated the linguistic husks of the classics, but also felt active within him the spirit that they are supposed to inspire. Every human thought or action, past or present, became tinged in his eyes with the splendid and noble glow of eternal beauty.

Giraudoux reviewed, under the transparent guise of one of his characters, his indebtedness to his first teachers: "I owed them a broad outlook on life and a limitless soul. I owed it to them that, when I saw a hunchback, I thought of Thersites, and when I saw a wrinkled old woman, I thought of Hecuba. I knew too many heroes to conceive of anything but beauty and ugliness on a heroic scale. . . . I owed to them my belief in those sentiments that one experiences within a sacred wood, during a night in Scotland, amidst an assembly of kings—a belief in mystic exaltation, in horror, in enthusiasm. . . . We knew by heart all the noble lines, all the sublime utterances. . . . How sweet is the sublime to a boy reading, after his lessons are done, in the ill-lighted study, while the thunder rumbles outside."[8]

This moral idealism, this heroic transfiguration of the universe was only one side of Giraudoux's mental development during his school years. At the same time, a rigid intellectual discipline was laid upon the docile student by the joint efforts of a score of teachers, all ardent devotees of *La Raison*. A strictly rationalist method, implying careful analysis of problems, precise accounts, symmetrical statements, clever distinctions, became, temporarily at least, a part of his personal way of thinking.

Later on, ironically apostrophizing an imaginary character who stands for one of his former teachers, Giraudoux referred to the professorial craze for explaining everything logically: "How sweet it was to tread the ground, how sweet to live—you declared— when you explained by reason everything that comes to pass! Those mechanical birds in the tower were singing by the grace of reason.... By virtue of reason, as soon as the winter fled, spring returned. And as long as the pole star looked blue, one was ready to die. How lovely the Seine looked in the neighborhood of Les Andelys when, by reason, it traces twelve curves, each of them containing a railway station and a church!"[9]

Yet, willy-nilly, and whatever his ultimate reactions may have been, Giraudoux was too good a student not to allow himself to be impregnated with the fundamental doctrine of his masters. Indeed, he bore the mark of their influence all his life.

After obtaining his *baccalauréat* in 1900, he was awarded a scholarship in a Parisian lycée—Lycée Henri IV—where he was to prepare for the entrance examination to the Ecole Normale Supérieure. He was soon expelled from that lycée for a juvenile prank, but he was accepted at once by another similar institution, the Lycée Lakanal. His mode of life there was not very different from that in Châteauroux. His studies were much more advanced and more specialized, but their general trend remained the same. He became particularly interested in Hellenic culture, which was to remain all his life a dominant element of his thought. He won first prize in Greek translation in a national contest, the Concours Général, held yearly among all the best qualified young scholars of France. He failed, however, to pass the extremely difficult entrance examination to the Ecole Normale in 1901 and was not accepted to that school until 1902. In 1902 and 1903, he did his military service, first in Châteauroux, then in Lyons and Clermont-Ferrand with the 298th Infantry Regiment; he was discharged with the rank of reserve sergeant.

Up to the time of his admission to the Ecole Normale Supérieure, the world of Giraudoux had been comparatively limited, simple, and clear. The only aspect of reality that he knew well was the plain and wholesome life of his native Limousin. He had returned there from school every year to spend the summer vacation with his family. He was deeply attached to his birthplace and he felt in perfect harmony with the small provincial towns where he had had the happiest moments of his youth. At the same time, he had acquired from his teachers a lofty moral ideal, an implicit trust in traditional logic and human reason, and also a thorough knowledge of the classics. Because the moral values he had learned to revere at school were in no way challenged by the environment that he knew, his mind was not troubled by anxious questioning or distressing doubt.

His experiences with the Ecole Normale brought about in him an abrupt and dramatic change in outlook. The Ecole Normale Supérieure on the Rue d'Ulm in Paris is officially a center of preparation for high university posts. In point of fact, although the majority of the *Normaliens* do become professors, the Ecole Normale has become to a large extent a training ground for intellectually outstanding young men who eventually scatter and frequently distinguish themselves in the most diversified fields — in literature, in politics, in diplomacy, and even in business. In spite of that diversity in their careers, most alumni of the Ecole Normale Supérieure retain in common an attitude called *"l'esprit normalien."*

L'esprit normalien is a rather baffling compound of seemingly unrelated and even often contradictory elements, which moreover may vary greatly from one man to another. All young *Normaliens,* however, have been subjected to an extremely rigorous process of selection and they are steeped in the best intellectual disciplines of French traditional scholarship. They are not always free from a certain tendency to show their learning through erudite and sometimes cryptic allusions to little known points of knowledge.

Perhaps in compensation, they are also inclined to display a curious intellectual flippancy, and they love to turn serious questions into jokes. Their attitude in this regard may range from light skepticism to caustic irony, but it is usually replete with imaginative fantasy and rollicking humor.

Many *Normaliens* possess great external brilliance. They like to juggle with words and with more or less logical paradoxes as well. Intellectual acrobatics are definitely among the favorite sports of the school. From time to time, life at the Ecole Normale is punctuated with outbursts of facetiousness, which have become famous throughout France under the name of *canulars normaliens*. They represent a generally complicated form of spoofing and are considered as most enjoyable when their perpetrators have succeeded in "pulling the leg" of a particularly pompous personage.

At the same time, the Ecole Normale is a hotbed of genuine idealism. Most *Normaliens* are imbued, as Giraudoux himself had been, with the noble ideas found in the books of the great writers of the past. In the secluded atmosphere of the school, three hundred young men, generally high-minded and keen, enrich one another through the mutual stimulation and challenge of their different aspirations, illusions, and dreams. Quite a few of them evince a contemptuous disregard for material interests, and they often live in an atmosphere of intense spirituality.

Those gifted young men have, as a rule, learned a great deal from books; but when they enter the school, they know little of actual life. Yet in many cases, the Ecole Normale provides them with unforeseen opportunities to contact the real world. More often than not, the inevitable confrontation between ideals and reality causes in them serious moral turmoils. Almost invariably, however, thanks to their exceptional inner resources, they emerge from these temporary crises with a better grasp of reality itself and an increased awareness of the value of their ideals. Giraudoux, who went through such a crisis himself, aptly summarized his own experience, as well as the experience of many of his schoolmates, in the conclusion of an essay on *L'Esprit Normalien*: "L'Ecole Normale est une école de réalisme spirituel."[10]

Giraudoux absorbed the finest as well as the most irritating traits of *l'esprit normalien*. He remained until the end of his life an idealist, although he never rid himself of a certain intellectual flippancy, an inordinate love for verbal acrobatics, and a persistent fondness of spoofing. The crucial event during that part of his life, however, was the impact on his tidy rational and logical mental world of a bewildering, disruptive new reality.

In the course of his first two years at the Ecole Normale, Giraudoux came into contact with an outstanding professor of German at the Sorbonne, Charles Andler. Partly under his influence, he decided to specialize in German literature. Those *Normaliens* who specialize in foreign languages usually spend some time in the country of their subject during their third year of study. They are granted a small stipend for that purpose. In the spring of 1905, Giraudoux, having received a modest scholarship, started his travels through Belgium, Holland, northern Germany, and finally established himself in Munich. There he worked on the manuscript of the *Festgesänge* by the Romantic poet Platen, having chosen the work for his dissertation for the Diplôme d'Etudes Supérieures in German. Very soon, however, scholarly research dwindled for him into almost complete insignificance. Infinitely more significant in his eyes was the twofold revelation that actual contact with life in Germany brought to him at that time.

He discovered in Germany a reality that was startingly different from anything that he had seen or studied in France. The orderly, practical, and somewhat tame environment that he had known in Limousin and the clear logical principles that he had learned from the classics had constituted so far the framework of his personal experience. Then, almost everything around him in Bavaria clashed with that experience. The Bavarian reality appeared to him as a bewildering medley of bizarre customs, colorful but strange cities, picturesque but unfamiliar landscapes. He had the disconcerting impression of being plunged, all of a sudden, into another world, another age: "I found myself in that epic period of the Holy Roman Empire which goes on living in Germany in the morning, while the Romantic period appears at noon, and the Sturm und Drang phase in the evenings and around the cities."[11] He was enthralled by that phantasmagoric spectacle and completely captivated, at least temporarily, by the charm of old Germany. On the other hand, he seems to have practically ignored modern Germany with its methodical efficiency, its sense of stern discipline, and its technological expertise.

At the same time he made another momentous discovery, the discovery of the poetic "soul" of Germany. He had certainly been prepared for that discovery by his academic studies under Andler in German Romanticism. But only a close and personal contact with the German people made him realize the existence in Germany of an approach to cosmic problems completely at variance with the thought process of the French. While the French could analyze and classify with rational rigor the facts, feelings, or concepts constantly surging in them or around them, the Germans were able, through instinctive, intuitive insight, to establish an intimate, almost mystic, communication with the core of the universe.

That revelation shook Giraudoux profoundly. He did not discard the classical ideal, founded on Greco-Roman culture and completed by French rational thinking which had been so far the basis of his spiritual life. At this point, however, that ideal appeared limited and fragmentary, leaving beyond its boundaries immense and rich domains that he longed to explore.

Meanwhile, Giraudoux had to face more trivial but imperative problems. His travel allowance had been very meager to begin with, and he was running out of cash. It happened that, just at that time, a fairly important French official, Eugène Morand, the Curator of Statuary Not on Exhibition at the Louvre Museum, was in Munich to represent the French government at an international art show. His young son Paul, who was later to become a noted and talented writer, had failed to pass the examination of *baccalauréat* a few months earlier and needed tutoring. Giraudoux became his tutor and very soon also his friend. After the Morands' return to France, Giraudoux secured a few other similar jobs, and he taught French for a while to the Prince of Saxe-Meiningen.

As much as Giraudoux admired and even loved German culture and German people, however, he was too much deeply rooted in French life and tradition to want to prolong his sojourn in Germany indefinitely. In the spring of 1906, he returned to Paris, after taking a long trip through the southern part of the old Austro-Hungarian Empire and the north of Italy.

In Paris, he received the Diplôme d'Etudes Supérieures in German and started officially his regular fourth year of studies at the Ecole Normale. His travels abroad and his contacts with "real life," however, had made him lose practically all interest in purely academic work. He obtained permission to live outside the school, and he took a lodging in a pension in the Latin Quarter. He renewed his acquaintance with the Morand family and in their circle met many influential and exciting personalities of the literary world and the stage. For many months he enjoyed all the aspects of life that Paris can offer to a young student, spending much more time in the cafés of the Boulevard Saint-Michel than in the lecture rooms of the Sorbonne. As a result, when he presented himself in 1907 to the very stiff competitive examination known as the *Agrégation,* which should have been the crowning of his studies at the Ecole Normale, he failed dismally.

He does not seem to have taken that failure dramatically. Thanks to the help of influential friends, he was given a chance to go to Harvard for a year as an exchange student. Nominally, he was supposed to pursue his studies in German, but the best of his attention was absorbed by the pageant of American life that was unfolding before his eyes. He made no serious effort, however, to understand the American way of life, still less to grasp the "soul" of America, as he had successfully done in the case of Germany. He was simply fascinated by the multifarious aspects of an immense and infinitely varied country, where everything that he saw appeared to him strange and often puzzling. He was particularly fascinated by the splendid creatures he met at Radcliffe and Wellesley College.

When Giraudoux returned to Paris in 1908, his friends noticed at once a great change in his appearance. He had been formerly notorious for his indifference to sartorial elegance and also for a certain provincial deficiency in social graces. After his contacts with the Harvard men, he had acquired a discreet refinement which was to remain a distinctive trait of his personality. Always nattily dressed, he showed a poise and an ease of manners that contrasted markedly with the occasional awkwardness of the student of yesteryear.

Officially, however, Giraudoux remained a student for two more years. He was still supposed to work toward the difficult degree of *Agrégation*, but his work became increasingly desultory and vague. Because he had completed his regular four years at the Ecole Normale Supérieure, he registered as an ordinary graduate student at the Sorbonne. Free from any type of supervision, he could lead an amusing and picturesque existence at the border of the academic world and literary bohemia. He rented a small apartment at No. 16 Rue de Condé, and he found great pleasure in decorating his lodging with various objets d'art that he chose with discriminating good taste in the numerous antique shops of Paris.

For a while, mainly in order to secure an adequate even if modest regular income, he dabbled in journalism. He became the secretary of Maurice Bunau-Varilla, the director of the important newespaper *Le Matin,* and he wrote a fairly large number of short stories for that paper. Those stories have, as a rule, little literary value and were for Giraudoux hardly more than potboilers. But he also attempted more serious literary composition. He published in several avant-garde reviews sketches of French provincial life that were collected in book form as *Provinciales.* Although the book was enthusiastically praised by a few Left Bank sophisticates, only thirty copies were sold in the first four years after publication.

Giraudoux was then twenty-seven years old. Partly on the advice of his friend Paul Morand, who had himself decided to enter the great French diplomatic school, the Ecole des Sciences Politiques, he made up his mind to introduce order into his rather disorganized existence, and to start a regular career.

Two different types of examinations guard the entrance of the French Foreign Service. One, fairly difficult and known colloquially as the *Grand Concours,* opens the way to important diplomatic posts, particularly in embassies. The other, known as the *Petit Concours,* is much easier, but leads only to secondary positions, especially in consulates. Giraudoux presented himself to the *Grand Concours* and failed, but he succeeded in passing the *Petit Concours* in June 1910.

This change of career does not seem to have markedly altered Giraudoux's mode of life for several years. He was assigned to the Political Bureau of the Foreign Ministry on the Quai d'Orsay with the rank of Elève Vice-Consul. In 1911, in view of his previous experience in journalism, he was placed in the foreign press section. He did not find his duties very absorbing, however, and he went on enjoying as much as before the amenities offered by the gay French capital.

He also went on writing short stories. Three were published under the title *L'Ecole des Indifférents*. Each one illustrated, under the guise of a fictitious character, a particular facet of Giraudoux's own personality. They presented a medley of whimsical reminiscences, pointed, clever remarks, poetic notations, and startling paradoxes. The book fared little better than *Provinciales* with the general public, but it established Giraudoux's reputation as a writer in a restricted group of Parisian literati.

Among them was a man who was later to play a decisive part in Giraudoux's life and career, Philippe Berthelot. Berthelot was at that time Head of the European Section of the Political Bureau of the Quai d'Orsay. He was an extremely capable diplomat and administrator, and also a great lover of literature and art. Paul Claudel, who was himself a diplomat and a poet, very probably drew Berthelot's attention to the budding young author who was working in his service. Berthelot found that Giraudoux was a very interesting young man—and also an excellent partner for his games of tennis. Soon Giraudoux became Berthelot's personal protégé.

Berthelot's friendship was of great help to Giraudoux at the beginning of his career. In those days, the French diplomatic corps formed an exclusive and almost closed little world. Its regular members often looked askance at people whom they considered as intruders—for instance, men who having studied to become professors tried to worm their way into the Foreign Service. For that reason, Giraudoux met with a few difficulties in his first years of work at the Foreign Office. But thanks to Berthelot's patronage and to his own personal tact—he was soon fully accepted by his colleagues and promoted to the rank of Vice-Consul at the end of 1913.

In the meantime, he had frequently served, temporarily of course, as diplomatic courier. This work enabled him to travel throughout Europe, carrying with him the mail pouch that contained classified documents addressed by the Ministry of Foreign Affairs to the French embassies in the great capitals of the continent, and also the confidential dispatches sent in return by the embassies to the Quai d'Orsay. Giraudoux always intensely enjoyed the novelty and the strangeness of the various colorful countries he had a chance to visit.

On the whole, during nearly a decade, from his departure to Germany in 1905 until the outbreak of World War I, Giraudoux led an extremely erratic but most enjoyable existence. The world was passing then through a phase that the French wistfully call *La Belle Epoque*. Life then did not seem to anyone either tragic or absurd. It appeared to most people as beautiful, easy, and mellow. Brutal national antagonisms were temporarily dormant; prosperity and security reigned almost everywhere; art and literature were flourishing abundantly; an atmosphere of gaiety, even of jollity, pervaded the teeming cities of Europe and America. Of course, ominous dark clouds were already perceptible on the distant horizon; but few people noticed them in the last brilliant glow of the great declining civilizations of the West. The old rules of moral decency were accepted, at least outwardly, by all, and a discreet veil of seemingly social decorum concealed the most unsavory aspects of the slowly deteriorating human condition. For a young man like Giraudoux the spectacle of that pageant was truly entrancing.

Normally enough, the aspect of that happy world that Giraudoux appreciated most was—the young women. A fictitious character in one of his novels who represents to a large extent the person of the author himself says: "Les jeunes filles seules m'attiraient."[12] He goes on expatiating on their charm, their pride, their ardor, their gracefulness. Paul Morand says that his favorite young feminine friends were Denise Rémon, Suzanne Lalique, Thérèse de Dreux, Suzanne Linzeler, and Mimi Toupié. Two other girls, who seem to have played a particularly important part in his life, were known only remotely to Giraudoux's friends as the young lady in blue and the young lady in pink. They have been recently identified and were named, respectively, Marguerite Bujard and Laure de Messey.[13] The nature of their relations with Giraudoux is not exactly known. That he was several times in love is more than probable, but that he never was deeply in love is practically certain. In Germany, in America, in France, he would enjoy the presence and the charm of a girl, but after a while he would pass lightly to another.

The social situation of the *jeunes filles* was then in a phase of uncertainty and change. The rigid framework of Victorian tradition that had formerly encased all young females 'in a moral corset of unyielding rules was breaking down everywhere. The near total freedom, however, which has recently swept away all the previously accepted standards of decent feminine behavior was not conceived then, even by the most liberal men, as a remote ethical possibility. In the early part of the century, therefore, the *jeunes filles* were allowed to take their first steps toward a thrilling even if somewhat perilous liberty.

They were often held back, however, by an instinctive fear of the new, uncharted land opening before them and also by a lingering inner reverence for the strict conventions that, in the past, had been considered as an imperative duty by their mothers. Thus arose an alternation in their behavior of audacity and restraint, of unexpected eagerness and disconcerting reticence that often seemed puzzling to masculine eyes, but that greatly enhanced their mystery and charm.

That ambiguous and intriguing type of *jeune fille,* which corresponded to a definite though temporary phase in the evolution of the modern world, left for many vears a deep imprint on Giraudoux's views of young femininity. For many years the challenging and alluring figure of a half-emancipated damsel served as a model for a variety of both timorous and adventurous maidens who graced Jean Giraudoux's best early novels.

That ambiguousness of the feminine situation was only one aspect of the great chasm then opening in Western culture. Until the end of the nineteenth century, Western man had generally conceived the reality surrounding him as a solid and rational entity. Then, almost at once, a series of scientific discoveries began to dissociate the elements of that reality into minute, separate fragments. At the same time, philosophical speculation started to dissolve the rational cement that had previously held its various component parts together. The conception of the structure of the universe that had prevailed in Europe since the Renaissance was challenged from all sides at once. The most firmly established beliefs in the moral and intellectual fields were assailed and, not infrequently, destroyed.

The end of the nineteenth century in France was marked by a mood significantly called *fin de siècle*. It blended a nostalgic admiration for a glorious past with the dark foreboding of an irremediable impending decadence. The gradual disintegration of all values, which was already discernible at the turn of the century, had not yet reached the disastrous proportions that it attained fifty years later. Yet, the progressive fragmentation of reality and the incipient breakdown of the old principles were keenly perceived by artists and writers such as Jean Giraudoux.

The apparent loveliness of the world and its continued propitious state at that time, however, prevented most of those young men from falling into a mood of gloom or despair. Thus there was simultaneously in Giraudoux a deeply rooted optimism and *joie de vivre* that enabled him to enjoy to the full the glittering spectacle of the world, and also the realization that that world was merely an assemblage of isolated units, magnificently juxtaposed perhaps, but devoid of general meaning and presenting in themselves no evident sign of fundamental unity.

This view of the world may explain in part an essential trait of Giraudoux's character that he himself has often called his "indifference." Because reality as he saw it contained nothing truly coherent and solid, how could he become firmly attached to any of its aspects? He therefore displayed a tendency to adopt an elusive, evasive, detached attitude toward life. That "indifferent" disposition of mind was probably innate in him, but it was certainly reinforced by the nature of the moral atmosphere in which he spent his formative years. In any case, it came clearly to the fore during the most disorganized period of his life, and it found a somewhat complacent expression in his book *L'Ecole des Indifférents*.

World War I did not markedly alter this rather casual outlook on life. At the beginning of the war the French General Staff had planned to attack the Germans in Alsace. The 298th Regiment of Infantry, in which Giraudoux served as a sergeant, was among the troops taking part in that operation. In August, 1914, those troops entered Alsace but met with little resistance from the Germans. Indeed, at the same time, the bulk of the German forces swept through Belgium and inflicted a severe defeat on the combined French and British armies near the cities of Mons and Charleroi.

The French and the British retreated hastily and established a new line of defense on the River Marne. All the available reserves were called by the Allies to reinforce their position there. The 298th Regiment was withdrawn from Alsace and, after a long circuitous march, was thrown into the Battle of the Marne. Giraudoux went into action on September 6 and distinguished himself through his conspicuous bravery, but he was wounded and evacuated to the rear on September 16, 1914.

Then began a long period of tedious treatments in various military hospitals—in Fougères, in Bordeaux, and in Pau. Although his wounds, caused by shell fragments in the groin and in the leg, were not very serious, his case was complicated by an intestinal ailment that delayed his recovery. He spent the winter of 1915 on furlough in Paris and led there, in spite of the darkness of times, a not too somber social life. In the spring of the same year, he was declared medically fit for active duty, promoted to the rank of lieutenant and transferred to the 175th Regiment of Infantry.

Almost at once that regiment was assigned to the operation that the Allies had launched in the Dardanelles, with the hope of reaching and taking Constantinople. Giraudoux was made liaison officer between the British and French elements of the Allied Expeditionary Corps. On July 21, 1915, he was slightly wounded in the hip by shellfire and once more removed from the fields of battle. His recurrent intestinal ailment left him for a long time so much weakened that he was in no condition to stand the strain of the rigorous life in the trenches.

He was not discharged from the army, however, but simply attached, under Philippe Berthelot, to the Cabinet of Aristide Briand, who was then Minister of Foreign Affairs of France. In July, 1916, Berthelot had Giraudoux included in a group of officers assigned to Lisbon to train the Portuguese army. The frolicsome tone of the letters that Giraudoux wrote then to his Parisian friends suggests that he hugely enjoyed this Lusitanian escapade.

After his return to France, thanks again to Berthelot's protection, he joined a mission of French military instructors at Harvard.

France and the French were very popular in America in those days, and when young, elegant Giraudoux—a twice-wounded officer, a dashing diplomat, and a writer to boot—arrived in the United States in April, 1917, he was received with open arms by Boston society. As in his first sojourn in America, he loved the external charming aspects of American life, but made no serious attempt to understand the deep inner values of American culture. On the other hand, he made startling progress in his acquaintance with young American womanhood.

The exhausting tempo of his professional and personal activities soon played havoc with his still precarious health. His old intestinal ailment reappeared, and he had once more to go to the hospital. After a few months he was sent back to France for further medical care. When he had sufficiently recovered, the military authorities transferred him to a prestigious elite corps, the 26th Bataillon de Chasseurs à Pied. At the same time, he received a very soft assignment at the headquarters of the French general staff in Paris. He was more often seen in the literary cafés of the Left Bank than in the office that he was supposed to occupy regularly. After the Armistice, he was first placed at the disposal of the Ministry of Foreign Affairs and then, some time later, finally discharged from the army.

Giraudoux's war experience provided him with enough material for three slender books published between 1918 and 1920: *Lectures pour une Ombre, Amica America,* and *Adorable Clio.* The usual war themes of heroism and horror, of destruction and death appear in them occasionally, but they are played, as it were, on muted strings, while the general tenor remains curiously nonchalant and even tinged with genial humor. Indeed the war had not been for Giraudoux a gruesome nightmare of mud and blood. Partly because of his persistent ill health, and partly thanks to Berthelot's protection, he had spent the greatest part of the four years of war far from the front lines.

When he was at the front, however, he did his duty remarkably well. He was twice cited for bravery, and in July, 1915, he received the Cross of the Legion of Honor for outstanding gallantry in action. Yet he never knew the endless months of misery and filth in the trenches that left a profound and tragic mark on so many men of his generation.

War appeared to him as a fantastic adventure, offering him

countless opportunities to make strange and stimulating discoveries: "What did the war mean to me? Awakenings, incessant awakenings."[14] This attitude explains the flippant epigraph of *Adorable Clio*: "Forgive me, O War, that, whenever I could, I have caressed thee."[15] The war did not bring about any marked deepening of Giraudoux's thought. On the other hand, it did not destroy or even damage his optimism, his lightheartedness, and his gaiety. At the end of the war, Giraudoux was still smiling appreciatively at the wonderful gifts of life.

One of the reasons for that happy disposition may have been that he came to know about that time a very beautiful young woman who was to play a most important part in the rest of his life. She was a young divorcée who had resumed her maiden name, Suzanne Boland. From her first marriage with an Army man, Colonel Pineau, she had a daughter, Arlette, who died while still comparatively young, and a son, Christian Pineau, who later became a distinguished politician and even at a certain time (1955) a Prime Minister of France.

Suzanne Boland had many friends in the artistic circles of Paris. Giraudoux met her for the first time in a painter's studio a short time before the war. They were about the same age, and their first casual acquaintance soon ripened into a close personal relationship. Giraudoux had been impressed at once by her liveliness, her striking elegance, and her strong personality. She herself has said that she was attracted to him by his intelligence, "a marvelous intelligence."[16]

She added that she also loved his fighting spirit, which evidently offered a challenge to her own combative instinct: "He was very stubborn and so was I. We never gave in to each other. He did not bear me any ill will on that account. Quite the contrary. Many times he repeated to me that if he had for me the highest regard, it was partly because I never let him have his own way with me."[17]

Giraudoux's courtship of Suzanne Boland was long and understandably stormy. They saw a great deal of each other during the war and were quietly married in 1918. Some time afterward, at the end of 1919, the birth of a son, Jean-Pierre, happily completed their family circle.

Giraudoux's marriage marked a definite turning point in his life. Until then, he had enjoyed the spectacle of the world as an artist and a dilettante, and he does not seem to have taken even his own career as a diplomat very seriously. At this point, being past thirty-six and having become the responsible head of a household, he changed his way of life almost completely. Setting earnestly to work he successfully passed the examination of the *Grand Concours,* which opened for him the gates of a high diplomatic career. In May, 1919, he was raised to the rank of Secretary of Embassy. Still in poor health, however, he obtained a leave of absence and went to rest in the town of Cusset.

Cusset is situated in the old province of Bourbonnais, near the famous resort of Vichy. In the past, Cusset had been renowned as one of the most important strongholds of the Dukes of Bourbon, but its strong fortifications have been pulled down for a long time and it has become a sleepy provincial town, not very different from Bellac or Cérilly. Jean Giraudoux's brother, Alexandre, who had become a physician, had established his medical practice there.

As Giraudoux's son, Jean-Pierre, later wrote: "It would be difficult to imagine two brothers as dissimilar and yet as close as Alexandre and Jean Giraudoux. My uncle, bossy and good-natured, fond of teasing, always truculent, sometimes using dirty words purposely to shock his wife . . . was dominating the family group. . . . My uncle was the earth, intensely present. My father looked as if he were made of air, light, suave, also fond of teasing but more sweetly than his brother, detached and always seeming far away."[18]

When their father, Léger Giraudoux, had reached retirement age in 1901, he and his wife went to live in Cusset in order to be near their son Alexandre. They bought a comfortable house there, and subsequently Jean Giraudoux often found a welcome shelter in his parents' home, particularly in periods of tension and stress.

At the end of 1919 and at the beginning of 1920, he remained there for about six months. Thanks very probably to the regular and quiet mode of existence that he led at that time, he recovered completely from his intestinal ailment. In April, 1920, he returned to active duty in the diplomatic service, but he was not at all anxious for a post abroad. Once more, Berthelot intervened in his favor, and he was attached to the Service des Œuvres Françaises à l'Etranger, the department of the Ministry of Foreign Affairs that supervises and fosters the development of French intellectual influence abroad. For four years, he acquitted himself of his functions there conscientiously and competently.

At the same time, he contrived to bring out a series of novels, *Simon le Pathétique, Suzanne et le Pacifique, Siegfried et le Limousin,* and *Juliette au Pays des Hommes,* which placed him among the major writers of France. His previous books had been somewhat lightweight. His new works, although written in the same vein, offered definitely more substance. *Simon le Pathétique* is an account of a sensitive adolescent's first view of the world, his early feminine flirtations, and his growing fondness for a lively girl called Anne, who has many traits of Suzanne Boland.

Suzanne et le Pacifique, the story of a young girl shipwrecked alone on a tropical island, looks at first like an entertaining variant of the adventures of Robinson Crusoe. The book also represents Giraudoux's first protest against the cult of efficiency and effort in our modern society. In *Siegfried et le Limousin,* Giraudoux linked in a fanciful setting some of his own spiritual experiences in Germany with the study of a question which, in the early 1920's, was among the greatest worries of the French people at large: What really lies at the bottom of the German soul? In *Juliette au Pays des Hommes,* the young heroine runs away from her small provincial home to go on a husband-hunting expedition in Paris. That rather thin plot provided Giraudoux with a pretext to develop some of his favorite ideas about literature and art.

Giraudoux was already well known in the professional literary groups of the capital. Thanks to his success as a writer, however, and thanks to the introductions given him by his ever faithful protector Berthelot, he could penetrate certain exclusive circles of old French nobility. While still a student he had become acquainted with Count Charles de Polignac, who always remained among his best friends. He then met other members of the same class. Giraudoux was only moderately snobbish, for a diplomat, but he felt very much flattered by the courteous attention he received from those refined aristocrats. Fully aware of their weaknesses, he was nonetheless captivated by their charm and the elegance of their manners. Eventually, he came to think that the tradition they represented was truly the flower of Western European culture.

A successful author, an established diplomat, and a happy head of a family, Giraudoux seemed to have reached stability at last. Then, all of a sudden, he found himself involved in a violent and bitter feud between powerful members of the Foreign Ministry. The foreign minister of France at that time was Raymond Poincaré. Poincaré had been President of the Republic during World War I, but after the expiration of his term of office he had returned to practical politics as a senator. He came originally from Lorraine. Like many Lorrainers, he had a stern and austere outlook on life. He was a man of perfect integrity and had the deserved reputation of being absolutely incorruptible. A lawyer by profession, he tended to take a legalistic attitude in all the problems he had to face. It may be added that, like many other natives of Lorraine, he had a deep distrust of the Germans, and he believed that firmness, even hardness, was the best policy for the French to follow in dealing with Germany.

His main rival, Aristide Briand, was essentially a shrewd diplomat. As such, he was very flexible in his approach to all political questions. He did not enjoy the same reputation of honesty as Poincaré. His beginnings in the political career had been marred by unsavory happenings to which his enemies had given wide publicity. Perhaps as a consequence, he was ready to understand human foibles and to accept, in ambiguous situations, practical even if sometimes equivocal compromises. In regard to Germany, he wanted to use moderation and patience, and his ultimate hope was that the two nations could one day be truly reconciled.

Philippe Berthelot had been for a long time associated with Briand, and he shared most of his ideas. His differences with Poincaré, however, seem to have been more a matter of personal incompatibility than of disagreement on political principles. Berthelot came from an old cultured Parisian family, and he was himself very much of a Parisian society man. He loved above all the company of young writers and artists. His views were always tolerant and broad, sometimes even bordering on cynical skepticism. He had played an important part, behind the scenes, as Director of the Political Bureau at the Quai d'Orsay, during the Paris Peace Conference that led to the elaboration of the Treaty of Versailles in 1919. In September, 1920, he had been promoted to the rank of General Secretary of the Ministry of Foreign Affairs. His influence had reached a peak when, in January, 1921, a financial scandal nearly shattered his career.

The most important French banking institution in the Far East at that time was the Banque Industrielle de Chine. After engaging in risky and questionable speculations on the fluctuating value of various foreign currencies, that bank found itself on the brink of bankruptcy. One of its directors was André Berthelot, Philippe Berthelot's own brother. Then, acting upon his own authority and without consulting Briand, who was then in Washington as the French representative at the Disarmament Conference called by President Harding, Berthelot took upon himself to send confidential telegrams to the French diplomatic representatives in the Far East, and also in London and New York, in which he said that the French government had decided to intervene and help the Banque Industrielle de Chine out of its difficulties. The news of that alleged forthcoming intervention leaked out and, when Briand returned from Washington, he found himself faced with a storm of accusations and criticisms. Philippe Berthelot resigned his position of General Secretary at once, but Briand went on bestowing on him publicly marks of his continued personal esteem.

At the beginning of 1922, Briand was forced out of office by his old rival Poincaré for reasons unconnected with the Banque Industrielle de Chine scandal. When Poincaré replaced Briand as prime minister and minister of foreign affairs, he took steps at once to have Berthelot summoned before a Conseil de Discipline. Berthelot had to answer the charge of having committed serious irregularities while in office. He was pronounced guilty and removed to the inactive list of the ministry. His disgrace was official and complete.

Giraudoux began then to write a book both to vindicate and avenge his protector and friend. Before he could finish it, however, Poincaré, fully aware of Giraudoux's hostility, had him assigned in 1924 to a post corresponding to his rank of Secretary of Embassy—in Berlin. In May, 1924, Poincaré fell from power and his successor, Edouard Herriot, who was a former *Normalien* himself, allowed Giraudoux to return to Paris; he was put in charge of the Service d'Information et de Presse at the Quai d'Orsay. Some time afterward, in April, 1925, Herriot was replaced as Prime Minister by Paul Painlevé, who took Briand as minister of foreign affairs. At once, Briand called back Berthelot, who resumed his position as General Secretary, but who never recovered his previous influence. In July, 1926, after several changes of ministries in the midst of a confused and chaotic political situation, Poincaré and Briand came to a tacit understanding: Briand would remain in charge of the foreign affairs ministry, where he could pursue his cherished policy of reconciliation with Germany, while Poincaré would concentrate his attention on the rehabilitation of French finances, which were then in a state of extreme disorder.

Just then, Giraudoux published *Bella,* at which he had been working for some time. It contained a most flattering portrait of Berthelot in the character Dubardeau and a most unflattering characterization of Poincaré in Rebendart. *Bella* also made a number of vicious attacks—naturally under fictitious names—on some of Giraudoux's colleagues at the Quai d'Orsay, for whom he evidently felt no love. The virulent diatribe was eagerly read by the general public, most of whom were trying to guess the identity of the persons who had served as models for the worst villains portrayed in the book; this questionable curiosity contributed greatly to its success.

Bella was most unfavorably received at the Quai d'Orsay, virtually ruining Giraudoux's prospects of a brilliant diplomatic career. Most of the diplomats resented the actions of one of their number who, in airing his personal grievances, had brought into the open and spread before the public's eye their internal intrigues and squabbles. Berthelot himself felt more embarrassment than gratitude. He was not happy at having his dubious dealings with the Banque Industrielle de Chine recalled even indirectly. Furthermore, he did not wish to be drawn into a new conflict with the powerful and dangerous Poincaré. As for Poincaré himself, the attack missed fire, because the book came out precisely when he was putting an end to a disastrous system of inflation and was being hailed all over the country as "the savior of the franc."

Giraudoux realized that he had aroused the ire of many of his colleagues. Without waiting for possible reprisals, he started discreet and informal negotiations with his superiors. Soon a compromise was reached between them: Giraudoux himself asked officially to be placed "*hors cadre*"; that is to say, he would no longer belong to the regular diplomatic staff of the Quai d'Orsay. His request granted, he was appointed to the committee in charge of the evaluation of the damages sustained by the Allies in Turkey during World War I, a relatively unimportant assignment.

Giraudoux's office was no longer in the prestigious building of the Quai d'Orsay but in a modest, unimpressive house on the Avenue Malakoff. He worked there at obscure but not too demanding tasks for about eight years, and his life was not profoundly disturbed by those events. Having entered the Foreign Service almost by accident, he had never occupied really important positions. He was careful, however, not to terminate his connections with the official diplomatic circles, where he always retained useful personal friendships.

Giraudoux's private life was particularly happy during that period. He lived with his family in a cosy and comfortable apartment at No. 8 Rue du Pré-aux-Clercs, in a very old district of Paris, on the edge of the Latin Quarter. That district has a rich historical atmosphere, but its buildings are somewhat antiquated and the streets are dark and narrow. Suzanne Giraudoux said: "It was very pretty, but abominably depressing. I hated that district. But Jean loved it and did not want to leave."[19] In spite of that minor disagreement between Giraudoux and his wife, their marriage was at that time perfectly harmonious. Moreover, Giraudoux doted on his young son: "What a charming father he was when Jean-Pierre was a child! He played with him and took him for long walks. He displayed such a pride in him that it was really touching."[20]

Completing this picture of domestic happiness, France was passing through a phase of optimism and hope. The policy of reconciliation with Germany initiated by Briand had culminated, on October 16, 1925, with the signing of the Treaty of Locarno, and for several years the "spirit of Locarno"—a spirit of mutual understanding and friendship—officially pervaded the relations between Germany and France. Furthermore, the monetary and economic crises that had shaken all the nations of Europe immediately after World War I had been settled successfully, and the West had entered an era of seemingly boundless prosperity and expansion.

Under those circumstances, Giraudoux published another novel, *Eglantine*. His mood here, however, was very different from his attitude in *Bella*. *Eglantine* contained no trace of bitterness. The general subject of the book—a comparison between the culture of Western Europe and the mentality of the people living in the Middle East—may have been partly inspired by Giraudoux's recent diplomatic appointment, but even though Giraudoux clearly expressed his preference for the West, his views never were presented in an aggressive manner.

The political situation in Europe soon began to deteriorate markedly. In spite of the prevailing general prosperity, the Nazi party was making spectacular progress east of the Rhine, and Chancellor Stresemann's policy of understanding with France was under violent attack. French public opinion had hoped, after the Locarno Treaty, to see a liquidation of the age-old Franco-German feud and had begun to look on the Germans as partners rather than enemies. Soon, however, the French were again seriously alarmed and puzzled by the vagaries of their neighbors' emotional moods.

In 1922 Giraudoux had attempted to explain those moods in his novel *Siegfried et le Limousin*, but at that time the French were still steeped morally in a warlike atmosphere and failed to understand Giraudoux's message. In 1927, Louis Jouvet, a producer and actor with a keen understanding of the French public, urged Giraudoux to give him a stage version of his old work. Giraudoux accepted, although without much enthusiasm at first. "We were so much persuaded both he and I," said Suzanne Giraudoux, "that it would not succeed that at the rehearsal we felt no emotion whatever."[21]

The play *Siegfried*, presented for the first time on May 3, 1928, succeeded beyond all expectations. It revealed to the public that Giraudoux was an outstanding dramatist, and made Giraudoux himself aware that he was much more gifted for the technique of the theater than for that of the novel. From then on, although he still composed a few novels occasionally, he dedicated the best of his energy to the stage. After *Siegfried, Amphitryon 38* was a subtle and clever variation on the eternal themes of feminine fidelity and fickleness. Suzanne Giraudoux said later: "It was the image of the happy couple that we were in those days."[22]

Giraudoux's happiness was marred in the following years by a series of problems having complicated and interlocking causes. One of them was undoubtedly that he entered his fiftieth year. Although he retained a remarkably youthful appearance, he experienced, as is only normal, all the psychological as well as physiological difficulties that this phase of life almost inevitably implies. Those difficulties, however, took a peculiar form in him. He frequently indulged in "fugues" away from home. He would disappear sometimes for fairly long periods without letting anyone know where he had gone. "Sometimes he would leave me for several weeks," said Suzanne Giraudoux. "Where was he? What was he doing? You can imagine my feelings."[23] The novels *Aventures de Jérôme Bardini,* written at that time, and *Choix des Élues,* composed a little later, have as their essential subject the theme of the fugue.

Giraudoux's marriage was no longer happy. Their son Jean-Pierre has mentioned the "innumerable scenes"[24] that took place in the family. He said that his mother was "totally pessimistic, almost neurotic. . . . Sorrow without cause, overflowing and tumultuous unreasonableness expressed themselves through my mother. There was something powerful and sublime in the rejection of happiness undertaken by Suzanne Giraudoux."[25]

Then more delicate problems arose from Giraudoux's continued fervent admiration of young womanhood. Jean-Pierre Giraudoux said that his father had not many liaisons but that they lasted a very long time.[26] Suzanne reacted violently to that situation, and Giraudoux's home, formerly so pleasant, soon resounded with the impassioned utterances of his irate spouse. She said herself: "I have frequently found in the dialogues of his plays an echo of our conversations, of our quarrels. Even the frightening threat of Ondine: 'If you are unfaithful to me, you will die' is not foreign to me."[27]

Much later, Jean-Pierre, summarizing the complex relationship

between Giraudoux and his wife, said that his "father remained
attached to a woman [Suzanne] whom he had undoubtedly loved
more than any other, perhaps because she possessed as much
charm as he did, perhaps because she felt for him a passionate
love which faded away only ten years after his death and the violence of which overwhelmed his weakness."[28]

This passage may explain the startling change that took place
at that time in Giraudoux's views on women. In the past he had
shown in his works mainly sweet and and light-headed young
girls. Most of the tense females appearing in his later plays are
made of definitely harder and sterner stuff: "If Jean has conceived
so many violent women," said Suzanne, "he owes it to me."[29]

At the same time, Giraudoux was deeply affected by disheartening developments taking place in France and abroad. In France,
a succession of nauseating scandals—the Marthe Hanau affair,[30]
the Oustric affair,[31] the Stavisky affair [32]—revealed the extent
of the venality and corruption prevailing in high French political
circles. Because of his close connection with those groups, Giraudoux undoubtedly learned even more than the general public
about the clandestine collusions between certain barons of finance
and the politicians in power. He thus discovered an unsuspected
underground where graft, bribery, larceny, and even associations
with gangsters were common and regular practices. Until the
end of his life, he remained haunted by the depths of foulness
and evil into which he had peered.

European political problems were also taking a critical turn.
The death of Stresemann in 1929, in the midst of growing discontent and distrust, had left little hope that the Germans would
pursue his policy of reconciliation with France. After the onset
of the Great Depression, the triumph of Hitler at the 1930 elections
in Germany practically sealed the doom of the Weimar Republic.
Briand himself died in 1932, a defeated man, having lost for a
long time any real influence on French foreign affairs, and having
dismally failed in his efforts to secure world peace.

The cumulative effect on Giraudoux's mind of the psychological
troubles linked with middle age, of the emotional strain resulting
from very serious marital difficulties, and of the intense concern
that he felt about the disastrous evolution of French and German
politics, brought about in him a severe crisis which completely

altered his moral outlook. That phase of Giraudoux's life is often referred to as the "1932 crisis." The crisis actually extended over several years—years that were generally marked by pessimism and sadness.

Even these years, however, were not uniformly blanketed with gloom. Giraudoux's fundamental optimism sometimes pierced his melancholy. The most remarkable manifestation of that occasional reappearance in Giraudoux's middle years of his past youthful fantasy and gaiety is the charming comedy *Intermezzo*, written immediately after the failure of one of his most depressing plays, *Judith*. *Intermezzo* represents a vein of light, cheerful inspiration that was never completely destroyed in Giraudoux's mind, but that was seldom apparent during his years of crisis. On the whole, that crisis gave his thoughts, which had often been somewhat superficial, an entirely new density and strength. Under the influence of his altered mood, he acquired a sense of the deep, tragic element in the human condition. Furthermore, he came to believe that that tragic element was determined by an ineluctable fate.

In 1934 Giraudoux's life took a new turn. The resentment aroused at the Quai d'Orsay by the untoward publication of *Bella* had largely faded away with the passing of time. His spectacular success as a dramatist had added a new luster to his name. After the triumphal success of *Siegfried* in 1928, he had been given a promotion to the rank of Councilor of Embassy, although he was maintained "hors cadre." Later when he asked to resume a more regular diplomatic career, his request received a friendly consideration. Although he was of course not asked to work at the Quai d'Orsay itself, after some protracted unofficial negotiations, he was appointed Inspector of the Diplomatic and Consular Posts Abroad.

This position was completely to his taste. It enabled him to gratify his old longing to travel—and his more recent desire not to be frequently at home. He kept his permanent lodging in Paris, however, having recently given in to his wife's insistence on moving from the Rue du Pré-aux-Clercs apartment to a new residence at No. 89 on the Quai d'Orsay, near the Ministry of Foreign Affairs, a superb location overlooking the Seine. Its wide French windows opened on an impressive panorama of half the city of Paris. The interior, decorated with light, harmonious colors, was very elegant, although perhaps somewhat formal and cold. "It was I, yes I alone," said Suzanne Giraudoux, "who made all the arrangements in this apartment. . . . [Jean] left to me the care of fixing everything."[33]

For four years Giraudoux spent a great part of his time roaming throughout the world. In 1935 he visited first Poland, then the West Indies, then the United States. In 1936 he returned to America. In 1937 and 1938 he took a long trip around the world, staying for a few months in the Far East, then in the South Pacific, and later in the Middle East. Those journeys, however, did not bring him the exhilaration that he had experienced in his youthful travels. His long tours were prompted only to a small degree by the desire to discover and enjoy the most colorful aspects of the world. Traveling meant essentially for him a flight from painful or irksome problems, which seemed to follow him wherever he went.

One of the most harrowing problems that the men of his generation had to face was posed by the menacing attitude of Nazi Germany. When Hitler officially became Führer of the Third Reich in 1933, a feeling of dread gripped all the diplomats of Europe. When on March 16, 1935, he announced that Germany was launching a full rearmament program, and when hardly more than a week later, on March 25, he denounced the Locarno Treaty, which had been considered as the cornerstone of Franco-German peace, the French people sensed that they were drifting inevitably toward a catastrophic war. Giraudoux, who had always been able to compose his plays with incredible speed, wrote at that time a poignant drama, *La Guerre de Troie n'aura pas lieu*, in which he expressed an agonizing premonition of the disaster to come.

The feelings of anguish that the French people at large experienced in the years preceding the World War II were compounded in the case of Giraudoux by personal problems. Suzanne Giraudoux summarized the most serious of these difficulties as "the eternal problem of the misunderstandings between two human beings who loved each other and inflicted pain on each other."[34] These misunderstandings had become so grave that, according to Jean-Pierre's testimony, Giraudoux earnestly considered, during the summer of 1936, asking his wife for a divorce.[35] In his novel *Combat avec l'Ange* Giraudoux portrayed a neurotic woman who rejects the best chances of happiness offered her by life. His play *Electre* combined the presentation of an imperious and violent woman with the haunting evocation of a set of catastrophic events implacably imposed on man by fate. Another play, *Ondine*, illustrates the tragic inability of two married people to reach a deep understanding and their no less tragic power to inflict untold suffering and misery on one another.

Also at this time Giraudoux gave several lectures at the Université des Annales, a private institution catering mostly to cultured society men and more particularly to society women. Two of his lecture courses have left important traces in Giraudoux's work. A book based on his lectures on La Fontaine was published under the title *Les Cinq Tentations de La Fontaine*. Giraudoux also gave a series of lectures on contemporary France with suggestions for urgently needed reforms in the social, political, and administrative structures of the country. Those very successful lectures showed that Giraudoux, who had not yet shaken off the reputation of frivolity attached to his name, was also capable of earnest thinking about the practical problems of the period. He offered the essentials of his views on those problems in the book *Pleins Pouvoirs*.

When the war broke out, Giraudoux was called by the Daladier Ministry and made head of the central office of French wartime propaganda, with the title of Haut Commissaire à l'Information. At first, he seemed reasonably well qualified for that position. He was reputed to be an expert on Germany; his book *Pleins Pouvoirs* had shown that he had a sound grasp of practical affairs; as a playwright, he had proved his ability to hold the attention of the public.

Giraudoux, however, had little aptitude for administrative work, and he was not in the slightest degree a bureaucrat. He soon discovered that the Hôtel Continental in Paris, where the Service de l'Information had been established, was a hotbed of the worst type of bureaucracy; it must be said that Giraudoux made scarcely any effort to clean up that morass of inefficiency and confusion. Not unfrequently, when a staff meeting was scheduled, he would slink away through a back door and let his subordinates and colleagues discuss without him unimportant, but also sometimes important, points of propaganda policy. The broadcasts that Giraudoux himself made on the radio disappointed all but his most fervent admirers. His addresses were studded with learned classical allusions, with pointed, witty remarks, and with sparkling, elegant paradoxes. His beautiful style could delight an audience of sophisticates at the Université des Annales, but it could not reach the plain man in the street. Even his son had to admit: "His speeches are graceful and noble, too graceful for the war, too noble to be effective."[36] And the rough soldiers at the front, who were awaiting in deep anxiety the attack of the German military juggernaut, expected from their leaders more than verbal quips and intellectual somersaults.

At the end of March, 1940, when Daladier was replaced as Prime Minister by Paul Reynaud, the Haut Commissariat à l'Information was transformed into a Ministère de l'Information and Giraudoux was released from his duties. Soon afterward, the French front collapsed and in June, 1940, the German troops swept across France. For a while, understandably enough, Giraudoux's main concern was for his son Jean-Pierre, who had left the disintegrating French army and had reached first Spain, then Portugal. Giraudoux and his wife managed to drive together as far as Lisbon, but when they arrived there Jean-Pierre had already joined de Gaulle in London.

Giraudoux returned to France and found that Marshal Philippe Pétain had established a reasonably stable government in Vichy. Giraudoux went to Vichy and accepted a post as Curator of Historical Monuments. When he discovered that the Vichy government was drifting rapidly toward a policy of close collaboration with Nazi Germany, he resigned his position and withdrew to Cusset.

A definite physical change in Giraudoux became clearly noticeable at that time. Until then, even in his late fifties, he had been remarkably alert, active, and spry. Then he suddenly began to look tired and worn. This change may have been merely the external sign of the normal decline in strength brought about by advancing age, or it may have resulted from the intense moral stress to which Giraudoux was subjected after the defeat of France, or from a hidden incipient disease. All of these factors may have been involved, to various degrees, in the obvious deterioration that took place in him. In any case, this last phase of his life was marked by a general decline both in his vitality and in his once buoyant spirit.

Even though he was frequently in a depressed mood, he also occasionally displayed a resurgence of his former deeply rooted gaiety and gusto for life. The works that he produced during that period therefore offer a curious alternation between dark pessimism and total trust in beauty and joy.

Causes for pessimism were not lacking. French morale was at its lowest ebb. In the wake of an unprecedented, crushing defeat, and under a brutal enemy occupation, the worst latent traits of human nature, cowardice, trickery and greed, flourished everywhere in France. The poor suffered incredible hardships while a few war profiteers insolently displayed their newly acquired wealth. Intrigue and corruption were rampant in the highest business circles, and the official government of Vichy was groveling before the victorious Nazis. A few examples of dignity and a few acts of heroism could be cited to relieve that otherwise disheartening picture, but they were neither numerous nor conspicuous, at least during the first two years of the war.

Giraudoux spent practically all his time, during those two years, in his retreat at Cusset. Only occasionally did he come to Paris, occupying there a modest room in the Hôtel de Castille, on the Rue Cambon. Although he never joined any Resistance movement, he was secretly accumulating an enormous documentation on the abuses and the crimes committed by the German occupation troops in France. From the end of 1942 on, partly in order to pursue that work more efficiently, and partly to avoid the growing and soon almost unbearable family tensions, he established himself almost permanently at the Hôtel de Castille.

During the war Giraudoux wrote four very uneven plays, *L'Apollon de Bellac, Sodome et Gomorrhe, La Folle de Chaillot,* and *Pour Lucrèce. L'Apollon de Bellac* is a short comedy brimming over with a feeling of confidence in the beauty of life. The cheerful and fanciful spirit pervading the play at first seems a throwback to the type of inspiration that had produced *Intermezzo.* In fact, however, that source of inspiration had never altogether dried up in Giraudoux's mind. It had been temporarily overlaid by cares and sorrows, but it gushed forth again, although with much less originality and charm.

Sodome et Gomorrhe is one of the most savage indictments of marriage ever written in French. Suzanne Giraudoux acknowledged that many of its episodes had their origin in the situation of the Giraudoux household. After stating that her husband usually talked to her about his various literary projects, she added: "Only for *Sodome et Gomorrhe* he said to me practically nothing at all. He felt a sort of shame to speak to me about it, perhaps because one finds in that play so many things that come from us."[37]

La Folle de Chaillot offers a picture, almost in black and white, of Giraudoux's own optimistic and pessimistic views of life. On the one hand, he showed unfathomable abysses of degradation and wickedness, but on the other he proclaimed his faith in the ultimate triumph of honesty. Giraudoux was unable to revise his manuscript of *Pour Lucrèce* before his death. Probably for that reason, this work does not offer the same dramatic tightness as his other plays.

Giraudoux also left unfinished the manuscript of a work dealing with the reforms that he believed should be made in the institutions of France. It was meant to complement the recommendations formulated in *Pleins Pouvoirs.* The fragments of that work were collected and published after his death in *Sans Pouvoirs.*

Giraudoux's health had been visibly impaired for several years. Almost constantly feverish, he suffered every winter from severe bouts of bronchitis. When his mother died at ninety in Cusset on November 2, 1943, the people present at the funeral were struck by his emaciated appearance. He seemed, however, still full of creative energy when all of a sudden he became very seriously ill. He was transported from the Hôtel de Castille to his old home on the Quai d'Orsay, where he had not lived for a long time. He died there on January 21, 1944, in the throes of torturing internal pains at the age of sixty-one.

A certain amount of uncertainty still prevails about the direct cause of his death. The rumor spread at once that he had been poisoned, perhaps by the Gestapo. Later it was said that he had died of uremia. Recently the hypothesis of a mysterious poisoning has been revived, although without proof.[38] Jean-Pierre Giraudoux believes that his father was the victim of accidental food poisoning: "He was not poisoned by the Germans, as it has been sometimes believed, but by an organic substance perhaps associated with the bad quality of the food available at that time."[39]

Giraudoux's unexpected death caused much commotion in the French theater, but it drew hardly any notice beyond it. Tremendous military and political events were taking place just at that time throughout the world, and very few people noted the passing away of a man who was still widely considered as an amateur diplomat and a whimsical entertainer. Many later discovered that, behind Giraudoux's entertaining whimsies, lay a complex and rich view of life and an original conception of the modern world.

Do you remember the day when you ordered me
to choose between the stoic and the epicure
and I couldn't obey you, because I loved both?[1]
Jean Giraudoux

❧ II ❧
Ideals and Reality

The crucial event in Giraudoux's life during his formative years
at the Ecole Normale Supérieure was his encounter with German
culture and reality. That event not only dislocated all his previous
plans to follow a university career, but also revealed to him a
view of the world utterly at variance with the fundamental values
that he had so far accepted unquestioningly.

During his school years Giraudoux had become imbued with
a clear and noble conception of existence, either derived from
the works he had studied or infused in him by the eloquence of
his idealistic instructors. He was to cherish that "vision splendid"
all through his life, clinging to it in spite of all its apparent opposition to reality. On the other hand, with and after his German
experience, Giraudoux became alive to the presence of an external
world that was richly colored, variegated, enormous, often in-
explicable and disconcerting, voluptuous or crude, but always
of engrossing interest.

He enjoyed that reality, accepted it as it was and gave it his
most sincere allegiance. A moral conception of life, however,
and an intense perception of reality cannot exist side by side in
separate and distinct compartments, as it were, without ever com-

35

ing into contact—and conflict. All Giraudoux's work bears witness to that conflict.

On the whole, Giraudoux's case is not an exceptional or even an uncommon one. The majority of men find themselves at one time or another in the same mental dilemma, torn between a revered ideal and an overpowering reality. This condition accounts for the general appeal of Giraudoux's writings. His originality lies to some extent in the special terms in which his problem was set—in the peculiar form of the ideal that he nurtured and in the sort of reality that he encountered. He displayed the true originality of his thought and art, however, essentially in the way he disposed of the problem itself.

Giraudoux's ideal, at least at the early stage of his mental evolution, comprised several distinct aspirations and tendencies. The most obvious was a constant preoccupation with moral ends and purposes. "In my opinion," he said, "the aim of a book, the dominant idea of an author when he writes a book, ought to be a moral idea."[2] The basic principles of Giraudoux's views on morals were inspired mainly by Greco-Roman classical thought. They rested on the solid foundation of definite and fixed values, accepted once and for all for their own sake, without any reference to a superior absolute.

These values implied the unconditional affirmation of the noble and the beautiful, not as superhuman archetypes, but as irrefragable human truths. No hope of reward, no fear of punishment were attached to them in any way, according to Giraudoux, either in this world or beyond the grave. For him they were solely the earmark of man's personal dignity and integrity.

Out of a sense of sheer self-respect, Giraudoux rejected everything underhanded, degrading, mean, and low. He loved and praised all the high sentiments, such as patriotism, generosity, abnegation, devotion, disinterestedness. The notions of good and evil have a positive meaning for him. His idea of goodness, however, does not conform to the Christian ideal of virtue. He is not overfond of such weak and humble feelings as pity: "Pity is what takes the place of love in selfish people."[3]

A certain amount of hardness, of pride, of tension appears in his ideal. The Stoicism of the ancients certainly exerted a determining influence on his aspirations: "There is a philosophy that

I have always appreciated and that is the philosophy of the Stoics."[4] The word "sublime," which so often recurs in his writings, most adequately describes the goal toward which he constantly strives.

The striving after the "sublime," however, does not entail any extraordinary or supernormal achievement on Giraudoux's part. It is simply an endeavor to consider the world as it ought to be. In a well-regulated universe, everything should be in its proper place. Giraudoux had been imbued with the classical idea of a sovereign order ruling the whole world; the existence of that order had acquired in his mind the force of a logical postulate. He did not conceive that order as an arbitrary dictate imposed on nature from the outside, say by a Creator, but as the expression of eternal reason within nature itself. The influence of French classical rationalism is easily discernible in his belief that logical rules and laws constitute the framework of reality and that, through the understanding of those rules, the whole working of the universe becomes obvious, simple, and clear.

Giraudoux must have perceived, even long before he left college, that in real life things are not always as they should be and that the supposed sovereignty of reason does not actually control the world. This conception, however, at once moral and rational, was so noble and satisfying that he retained it against all the contradictions of brute facts. In a variant of the play *Amphitryon 38*, Jupiter asks Amphitryon: "Have you, in your own life, obeyed those laws of axiom and syllogism?" The noble Amphitryon answers: "Yes, and I shall always obey them. They are the basis of human dignity."[5]

Giraudoux had to admit to himself that a sublime moral ideal and a logical rational order in the world may be, to a certain extent, beautiful figments of the imagination; yet they are instinct with tremendous spiritual force and therefore they deserve to be carefully preserved. If treated as mere convenient fictions, they will lose their efficacy as motives of behavior, but they can very well be surrounded with a poetic, fanciful atmosphere—in fact they cannot survive without it.

Because Giraudoux believed that humanistic values have to be protected from the corrosive action of reality, he deliberately wrapped them in the aura of free, airy fancy that they require—

"la fantaisie qu'exigent les humanités."[6] He did not lose them in fantasy, however; rather he wished to transpose and transfigure them, as human actions may be transfigured in poetry.

Thus the "ideal" of Giraudoux, as he conceived it in the early part of his life—with its triple aspect of sublime moral aspiration, rational, logical discipline, and imaginative fancy—can be understood as a perfectly coherent and normal growth. Its roots are deeply imbedded in classical culture, but its luxuriant foliage, springing from Giraudoux's poetic personality, has too often concealed the essential unity of the different and divergent shapes that it presents.

The ideal was conjoined in Giraudoux's mind with a whole set of plain and humble impressions that he garnered in his youth within his family circle and in his province of Limousin. The elements of this provincial experience were, as a rule, simple and matter of fact. They were made mostly of the sights, noises, and smells of a friendly little town. Thus Giraudoux calls up the scene of the good people hurrying to their business or gossiping in a café, the bustle in the street, and the far-off sounds from the surrounding countryside. "On market days, I had only to turn in my chair to shut out the sight of the marketplace and see before me the empty countryside, denuded of its flocks. I had acquired the habit of making this half turn on every occasion, directing my glance from the parson, perhaps, or the sous-préfet, as each passed by, over to the hills with their emptiness and silence. . . . It was scarcely more difficult to change the kingdom of sounds. I had but to change windows. From the side facing the streets, one might hear children at a game of trains, or a phonograph . . . or the noise made by the ducks and the young goats being borne off to the kitchens. . . . From the side looking toward the mountain, came the sound of the real train and of animals whose bellowing and bleating could be guessed at in the winter, before they actually reached the ear, because of the white cloud of vapor about their muzzles."[7] All those unpretentious details possess a strong pungent quality. The little world they constitute is charged for Giraudoux with a thousand personal memories, all very homely and yet deeply affecting.

No clash occurred in Giraudoux's consciousness, between the high ideals inculcated in him by his masters and the plain reality he perceived at home. The people whom he knew there shared with his idealist teachers, though naturally on a more earthly level, a respect for the essential principles of honesty and human decency. Within the narrow limits of their practical experience, they considered the world intelligible and clear. Generally, within the respective spheres of judgment and interest, the professors of Greek under whom he studied in Châteauroux and Paris conveyed to him the same moral law as the housemaids with whom he talked in the modest Giraudoux household. That coincidence gave young Giraudoux a reassuring sense of complete spiritual unity.

That unity was suddenly shattered when he left the secluded logical world of the scholars and the limited coherent world of his province. He was profoundly dismayed, as he faced the world at large, by the discrepancy between the orderly pattern he had been taught, both at school and at home, to expect in life, and the confusing, bewildering medley of uncoordinated impressions that soon assailed him from all sides: "I do not find in life anything that my masters and my maids have described to me."[8]

Giraudoux rapidly learned to enjoy the brilliant and picturesque world that was opening before his eyes. To his enraptured gaze unfolded a glittering pageant of new faces, strange customs, outlandish manners, unfamiliar tongues, unexpected adventures. In that intricate maze of apparently unrelated events he could not trace the logical sequence of cause and effect. Without warning, good would turn into bad and vice versa. Giraudoux had difficulty in gathering a general impression of any kind. Reality, as it revealed itself to him, was composed of small fragments, richly colored, but all of them self-contained and hard. Everywhere ambition, voluptuousness, pain, jealousy, love, selfishness, passion were parceling mankind out into separate and intense emotional units.

Giraudoux welcomed the variety of impressions that the world was offering him. All the aspects of reality—material or spiritual, familiar or strange, high or low—appeared to him as equally worthy of eager, personal interest. All the gifts of nature were accepted by him as integral parts of the wonderful experience that is life on earth. Yet Giraudoux never indulged in any outburst of passion, and he did not display an exclusive enthusiasm for any of the objects of his enjoyment. He tasted their flavor, but always with discretion and restraint, so that his attitude sometimes seems curiously casual and unconcerned.

Such an outlook precluded any attempt, any desire even, to penetrate beneath the surface of things. Giraudoux is loath to drill inquisitive holes into reality, from fear of detracting from its charm and dimming its brilliance. Giraudoux always surveys the world around him with deliberate superficiality. The remark of one of his characters might easily have been made by himself: "I find the surface layer of the world is quite thick enough. To me every living thing and every object assumes reality more from its color than from its skeleton."[9]

As noted, this view of the world, which remained almost unchanged in Giraudoux's mind until the late 1920s, corresponded to a definite phase in the development of modern civilization. It has a striking counterpart in the style of the great French painters who flourished during Giraudoux's formative years. The works of Maurice Denis, Pierre Bonnard, and above all Edouard Vuillard, offer the same joyful approach to life, the same fragmentation of external appearances, and also the same comparative superficiality.

Although Giraudoux's general view of the world, in the first part of his life, tallied with the views of a number of other men steeped in the same moral atmosphere, certain other deeper and more personal ideas began to appear here and there even in his very early works. These ideas were undoubtedly implanted in him by his studies in German Romanticism, but they developed because they found in his inner consciousness a fertile ground in which they could germinate and grow.

The first evidence of that development in Giraudoux's thought was his tendency, usually very discreet and often tinged with humor, to place a small, almost insignificant detail of human experience in the overwhelming context of the totality of the universe. Not unfrequently, under the cover of a poetic metaphor, he would pass, as if in play, from a minuscule everyday incident to the hugeness of the Cosmos, hinting at the existence between them of a definite correspondence and a profound harmony.

Certain German Romantic poets had presented very similar ideas in their works. Many of them conceived of the universe as a Great Being, which was instinct with a superior life. The visible aspects of our world were nothing but the contingent parts of that Being. The role and the value of those parts — and therefore, among other things, the meaning of our own selves — could be understood only in relation to the whole of that animated Cosmos. According to them, the essence of the Cosmos was accessible through contemplation in a semi-hallucinatory state. That state could be reached only by inspired initiates, who had first to rise above the trivialities of everyday life and give up the petty cares and worries that chain the ordinary man to pedestrian tasks and thus prevent him from soaring into the spiritual Infinite.

Giraudoux was certainly influenced by these ideas. They provided him with a half-poetical, half-mystical ideal that formed a deep substratum to his otherwise shallow views of the world. The German Romantic poets, of course, earnestly believed in those unprovable concepts. Giraudoux's thought, on the other hand, seems to have been flitting from one aspect of those theories to another. He was evidently reluctant to accept fully certain metaphysical and esoteric assumptions that they implied. His persistence in alluding to them, however, even vaguely, even with a smile, shows the importance that they progressively acquired in his mind.

As time went on, Giraudoux became more and more convinced that the core of the creation is a superior living entity, which he frequently calls the soul of the universe. This all-encompassing entity is the source of all the particular human experiences — sensations, perceptions, emotions, feelings, and ideas. Each of those experiences reflects only a small facet of the universe, but a profound harmony unites them and binds them to the totality of the Cosmos as well. We can observe only scattered similitudes between objects, qualities, or persons, but those similitudes point toward much deeper affinities.

Those correspondences link parts of the world that at first sight appear remote and unconnected. The meaning and value of those various parts, however, are revealed by the harmonious conjunctions existing between them. In fact, they cannot be truly appreciated and enjoyed unless these connections are seized intuitively by man through his power of poetic insight: "Great similarities are splashed across the world and show their light here and there. They bring together what is small and what is immense. From those alone come any longing, any spiritual force, any emotion. You will say that I am a poet? Well, probably I am because they alone strike me."[10]

The real value of things and their meaning within the universe, as disclosed by their secret correspondences, cannot be investigated by intellectual analysis. Man cannot rationally grasp the whole ensemble of the cosmic harmony. Human intelligence is oriented toward the practical. It brings man information about the pleasant and the painful, the useful and the dangerous. It is not meant to delve into mysteries beyond the scope of his material existence. In fact, the use of logical reasoning will prevent him from having access to the soul of the universe, which can be reached — so at least Giraudoux believes — only through imaginative fancy, poetic humor, and illuminating intuition.

Man, however, insists on using his intellect beyond its range and purpose. Thus he has become guilty of the offense that Giraudoux calls the "original sin." Giraudoux's idea of the original sin has only a remote and allegorical relation to the doctrine of the Fall of Man as presented in Genesis. The biblical text states that Adam was expelled from the Garden of Eden because he disobeyed the Lord, ate the fruit of the Tree of Knowledge and thereby forfeited his paradisial destiny. Giraudoux retained from that myth the idea that evil inevitably befalls man when he pridefully asserts his independent personality and when he indulges in a pernicious quest for knowledge.

Man is inordinately proud of the power that his acquired intellectual knowledge has secured for him in practical achievements. Through his pride, he has separated himself from the rest of the world and has thus created a discord in the universal harmony: "The soul of the world breathes through the nostrils of a horse and the gills of a fish. But man wanted to have a soul of his own, and he has thus rent apart the universal soul."[11]

Instead of welcoming the totality of the human experience on earth as it is, instead of accepting his own simple specific destiny, man craves artificial gratifications that are beyond his natural needs. In order to obtain them, he concentrates his efforts on unnecessary tasks, which may bring him a measure of physical comfort, but which make him lose sight of the spiritual role he should play in the universe—and thus he fails dismally in his pursuit of happiness.

Of course, man claims that, by setting himself apart from the rest of the universe, he is merely making use of his right to be a man. Giraudoux, commenting on the works of the great Romantic poets, states that their essential merit is that they brought the "message of the Rights of the Universe which was to abolish the Rights of Man."[12]

The whole of the universe infinitely transcends the puny presence of man, and man has to pay a heavy penalty for the "sin" he has committed when he separated himself from the rest of the cosmos. He cut himself off from every contact with the spiritual core of the creation and thus became unable to find any superior meaning for his life on earth. As a result, spending as he does the best of his energy on senseless activities, he is sinking slowly into misery and despair. To make matters worse, he still retains a deep hankering for the "Paradise lost" of real personal fulfillment, which remains irrevocably beyond his reach.

A few exceptional human beings are somehow exempt from the "original sin" and from the curse blighting the lives of ordinary men. The chosen few—among whom, naturally, is Giraudoux himself—who enjoy that privilege are those who are not separated from the soul of the universe. "I still live," says Giraudoux, "in that interval which separated the creation from the original sin. I have been excepted from the universal curse."[13]

He explains how a direct and spontaneous perception of the universe—free from the distortions caused by intellectual interpretative reasoning—enables him to see the world with a complete freshness of outlook: "I see the age-old furnishings of the world as Adam saw them, the trees, the pools without their first stains and its modern furnishings, the telephone, the cinema . . . in all their divinity."[14]

What, then, will be Giraudoux's aim and purpose in life? He compares himself to a Messiah and wishes to save mankind from its original sin. He wants to make men realize that they can regain a blissful vision of the world if they accept their oneness with the cosmos—the cosmos that has remained free from the purely human malediction: "I alone can see here and there the beings, the insects, the sunspots which—each one in its own category—have had the same fortunate fate that I have, and which are not subjected to the curse. I am a little Messiah by virtue of the sunspots."[15]

Such a messianic claim would be downright preposterous if put forward seriously. Giraudoux, however, takes care to wrap it in an atmosphere of humorous and ironical pleasantry. Nevertheless, Giraudoux undoubtedly had fairly set views about the type of life that a man should adopt in order to be "redeemed" from his obvious present distress. Starting with the assumption that a profound harmony reigns throughout the world and that that harmony is expressed in a network of secret correspondences between the various components of the cosmos, Giraudoux came to the conclusion that, if a man ignores these correspondences and consequently fails to conform to the rules of the cosmic harmony, he inevitably fails also to play the part assigned to him in the creation and therefore represents a disruption of the general order.

According to Giraudoux, when a man disregards that order and pursues obstinately selfish aims, when he forsakes the simple, spontaneous enjoyment of life to achieve spectacular personal success, he almost always misses his proper role in the world. For this reason men who are called "Very Important" or even "Great" more often than not lead utterly disjointed or tragic existences. A man's life should not be cluttered with an unnecessary abundance of material goods, or encumbered with puny or ponderous ambitions and schemes. Such preoccupations, whether trifling or grandiose, are clear marks of a cleavage between the individual and the soul of the universe. They are evil and bring regularly in their train restlessness, discontent, and misery.

Giraudoux believed that if man is to be in harmony with the universe, he must gleefully accept the totality of the human experience on earth and adapt himself to his particular condition, whatever it may be. One of Giraudoux's best-balanced and happiest characters says: "Of all people I know, I am the one who endorses and loves his destiny best. There is not a single vicissitude in human life that I do not accept, from birth to death."[16]

The modest, unpretentious, unassuming persons have a much better chance to play perfectly the role assigned to them by fate than the men whose mind has been warped by the arrogant belief that they can themselves shape the course of their existence. In any case, Giraudoux's predilection for the former is obvious. That predilection does not come from a Christian love for the meek, but from an intuitive feeling that only a wholehearted acceptance of one's situation in life, however humble, can bring about a close union with the general order of the cosmos.

For about twenty years Giraudoux was content to let the four main elements of his early experience and thought coexist in his mind. They were: a deeply rooted trust in the solid structures of the classical ideal; a nostalgic attachment to the quiet reality of provincial life; an intense curiosity about the magnificent, motley pageant of the world at large; and a sincere longing for an inspiriting union with the soul of the universe. These elements corresponded to the various forms of the ideal he had conceived and of the reality he had encountered, but they did not constitute a coherent, consistent whole. In many instances they even contradicted one another.

Giraudoux never attempted to solve those contradictions or to organize his ideas into a system. For him the building of a system was a vain exercise. The various aspects of the ideal and reality simply cannot be made to dovetail. Their differences did not cause in Giraudoux, as a man, any metaphysical anguish whatever, and the aesthetic value of the rich contrasts that they created was for Giraudoux, as an artist, an unending source of delight.

Even if the various forms of the ideal and reality that were present in Giraudoux's mind remained distinct and in some ways incompatible, they nevertheless constantly mingled with one another. Giraudoux took pleasure in underlining—but always discreetly—their interplay by pointing to subtle resemblances and unsuspected affinities. He suggests, as if in play, parallelisms, equivalences, similarities.

His suggestions are usually original and new, and they possess an illuminating or at least challenging value. They are not, however, founded on careful and serious analysis. They are presented in an atmosphere of poetic fancy, playful gaiety, waggish humor, sometimes even merry facetiousness. They bear witness, above all, to the optimistic, happy mood that long pervaded all of Giraudoux's thoughts and works.

This happy outlook was completely altered in the early 1930s, when Giraudoux reached the awkward period of middle age. He seems to have realized then that the world was not after all the jolly playground that he had once fancied it to be. Personal elements certainly played a part in the development of that moral crisis. The malodorous miasmas of corruption and scandal that poisoned the atmosphere of France at that time were also probably among the determining factors that brought about a dramatic change of orientation in his views. The success of his plays had given him a brilliant position in the world of letters. Yet, although he found himself, as it were, on an island of security and fame, he could not but sense waves of distrust and disgust all around him.

Giraudoux, who believed in the essential harmony of the universe, became more and more aware of the estrangement of man from the world in which he lives. The works that he composed in the second part of his career emphasize the constant breaks in the rhythm of the universe caused by the mere presence of man. Occasional mentions of such breaks had not been absent from his previous works. In the past, however, he had wanted to see mainly their liberating or stimulating consequences. Later he perceived the tragic moral results that they implied.

One of Giraudoux's most representative characters is shown in a state of dismay when he feels that the harmonious relations he had established with the rest of the cosmos are suddenly put in jeopardy: "He had the feeling that he was not 'on time' in regard to the rest of the universe and that he was, somehow, behind hand in his relations with every being, every animal, every object."[17]

In the end, Giraudoux seems to have wondered if man could ever achieve a real union with the cosmos. Was not the very existence of man's personality a discordant note in the complicated counterpoint of the universe? Because man could be at peace with himself only if he was also in harmony with the world, mankind might well be condemned — for lack of that harmony — to be prey to incessant conflict and anguish. Thus Giraudoux who, when he was young, tended to view life as an amusing and amiable joke, came, when he was older, to consider it as a stark tragedy.

Evidently in relation to that change of moral attitude, Giraudoux developed, during the last twelve years of his existence, a new and somber theme — the disgust that a sensitive man experiences at the contact with reality. That idea had been implicitly contained, although under a much more attenuated form, in certain passages of his previous works. It was presented clearly for the first time in *Aventures de Jérôme Bardini*. Bardini leaves his home, gives up his regular occupation in France, and goes to America. His flight is explained and partly justified by the nauseating feeling created in him by the very sight of the world as it is: *"une nausée à l'idée de la création."*[18]

Veiled allusions to that feeling appear more and more frequently in Giraudoux's subsequent books. In *Combat avec l'Ange*, even the following is said: "Existence is a terrible degradation."[19] Evidently, as years passed, existence itself became more and more distasteful to Giraudoux. More and more, he felt that the high principles which he had cherished in his youth, and which he still considered as being alone able to confer on man's life an eminent dignity, were constantly challenged by facts.

In the past, he had handled lightly, sometimes jokingly, these clashes between reality and the ideal. Later he saw in them the very essence of the human drama. The human lot seemed irremediably sullied and tainted by the contamination of everything that is low, mean, and vile in the world. Until the very end of his life, however, Giraudoux went on fighting desperately to maintain high and firm, above the mire of facts, the ideas of integrity, justice, and honor.

The tragic outcome of that fight for the ideal against the besmirching influence of facts is seen in Giraudoux's last play, *Pour Lucrèce*. The heroine of that play, Lucile, is assailed by an incredible succession of infamous machinations, plots, and lies. She is led to believe that she has been violated by a rake called Marcellus. Has she been guilty of any imprudence, any folly, any crime to deserve such persecutions? Her only crime has been to refuse to lower herself and accept the base compromises that are demanded by life on earth — a life that she now despises utterly: "I am not going to die betraying my crime, my unforgivable crime, my contempt for life."[20]

Lucile, a pure woman, prefers to die rather than be defiled by the ignominies of existence. After she has committed suicide, her death is explained as follows: "Indeed you have been raped. Not by Marcellus, however ... but by the stupidity of men, the coarseness of men, the wickedness of men. Those evils were revealed to you all at once. That was too much for you. Sweet as you were, you had to die."[21]

Lucile, however, did not die defeated. Her death itself is an ultimate protest against the ugliness of reality. It represents her last fight, a victorious fight, to avoid being dragged down from the high peak of the sublime ideal that she had reached effortlessly in her youth. When she "appeals" from the apparent condemnation passed on her by the real world, because of her intransigent attitude, one finds in her words an echo of Giraudoux's own protest when he was still holding on to his ideal, in spite of the blows and buffets inflicted on him by a hideous reality. "My appeal ... I hold it from a little girl who had my name, who was my age, and who had taken the oath, when she was ten years old, never to accept evil, who had taken the oath to prove by her death, if necessary, that the world is a noble place and that men are pure. This earth has become for her empty and vile. This life is no longer for her anything but degradation. But it does not matter. In fact it is not true, because she keeps her oath."[22]

The resolve to withdraw into death so that the value of the ideal can be rescued from the threat of destruction by reality—as exemplified by Lucile's suicide—corresponds to the ultimate stage in Giraudoux's own evolution of thought in the face of that problem. In his youth, his reserve toward his schoolmates had been a process of defense against their perhaps good-natured but aggressive coarseness. Somewhat later, when he became acquainted with the motley, mad world at large, he instinctively realized that a deliberate aloofness was the best means to protect the high principles that he revered from the dissolving action of the raw facts that he encountered everywhere.

Furthermore, as he found in many instances that disjointed world supremely attractive, he soon discovered that an elusive attitude was the best way to avoid being captured and enslaved by its blandishments: "The most beautiful things approach us, ensnare us and make us prisoners. Happiness is as possessive as a legitimate wife."[23]

He tasted the pleasures of life appreciatively, but at the same time a certain evasiveness on his part enabled him to remain free from too close entanglements with a cloying reality. Thus by cultivating a general "indifference" he could both enjoy the most charming, even if sometimes morally dubious, aspects of the world and at the same time keep his personal integrity intact. After World War I, however, he became the head of a family and simultaneously found himself engaged in the occupations and preoccupations of a regular career. The casual and nonchalant "indifference" that had protected him in the past proved inadequate to liberate his spirit from the coils of petty and often contemptible material interests that were winding themselves sedulously and inexorably all around him. To free himself, at least temporarily, he had to resort to flights from the real.

At first those flights were purely imaginary and took the form, for instance in *Suzanne et le Pacifique,* of fanciful daydreams. Later on, however, he became hauntingly aware that the bulk of man's practical, real life — at least as he saw it — was composed of small worries, mediocre ambitions, bureaucratic chicaneries, relentless struggles for success, pointless efforts, and constant strains. In the long run, those trivialities absorb and often destroy everything lofty and truly fine in the human soul.

Giraudoux then indulged, particularly during the period of his major personal crisis, in temporary though never protracted fugues. For a while the theme of the fugue became one of the main sources of his literary inspiration. *Aventures de Jérôme Bardini* and *Choix des Élues* represent the culminating points of that phase of his life and thought. As time went on and as Giraudoux's environment increasingly deteriorated — particularly during World War II — he came to believe that the maintenance of man's spiritual ideal was possible only through a withdrawal, perhaps a total withdrawal, from the irremediably tainted world of reality.

Thus Giraudoux's detachment from reality appears under one form or another at each stage of his moral evolution. It has nothing to do with the more or less morbid "alienation" from the world that has been experienced by many members of the generation that reached manhood after Giraudoux's death. It does not correspond exactly either to the condition generally understood as "escapism." It is true that, to a certain extent, the desire to avoid unpleasant contact with facts or situations that he considered obnoxious or irksome played a definite part in his attitude of withdrawal. Giraudoux did love life, however, and until the end he continued to proclaim, at least intermittently, that the world is beautiful.

He was not a frightened or defeated man. He was not a coward. He did not shrink from difficulties and hardships. His detachment was not so much a negative escape from annoyance as a positive step taken to preserve the most valuable elements of the spirit from defilement. Because the noble classical principles of morality that were so precious to him could not find their place in the modern world, he would save them by keeping them at a distance from the real. Because he could not soar toward the mystic heart of the universe when fettered by the thousand miserable minutiae of existence, he would release himself from daily life. He could therefore reach, if only in half-dream, the marvelous realm of the world before the Fall. Thus he would describe the fugue of one of his characters as "an excursion into Paradise lost."[24]

The whole notion of detachment or withdrawal from reality that is so much in evidence in all of Giraudoux's works must be considered essentially an antidote against certain noxious aspects of the world, contact with which might prove fatal to all that makes life worth living. Detachment is for Giraudoux the indispensable condition of the survival of the ideal; and it therefore becomes almost identifiable in some ways with at least some facets of the ideal itself.

The notion that withdrawal—even under its attenuated form of "indifference"—may be considered an aspect of the ideal is illustrated in a small episode of *Suzanne et le Pacifique*. Suzanne, after spending five years alone on an island, is brought back to the society of men. Then she falls in love with mankind: "I was in love with everybody. That vague indifference that we experience for other men, my solitude had set it one tone up, and it was now beginning with love."[25] This passage does not mean that, in reaction to years of loneliness, Suzanne was ready to fall in love with anybody, but that indifference itself, when carried to a high point, reaches the level of love.

On the whole, it can be seen that the relatively clear and distinct forms of ideal and reality that had characterized the development of Giraudoux's thought during the first part of his life were
later complicated—notably after his 1932 crisis—by two important
moral factors that altered and obscured them intermittently.
Those two factors—a growing repugnance toward sordid reality
and a feeling that a detachment from reality could alone safe-
guard the values that are the basis of the dignity of man—were
not without precedent in his early works. They became pre-
dominant, however, only after life had played havoc with Giraudoux's original youthful optimism.

But they did not obliterate the pattern of thought that had
constituted the framework of his mind for years. Until the end
of his life, he continued to trust the high principles that had been
inculcated in him by his masters; he retained a wistful memory
of the quiet and wholesome reality he had known in his provincial
Limousin; he showed a vivid interest in the spectacle of the world
at large; and he remained convinced that a union with the universe was the true way to spiritual salvation, at least for those
whom he sometimes called the elect.

Giraudoux's late disgusted rejection of the actual concept of
existence, and his final belief that a withdrawal from a corrupt
reality is the best way to keep the ideal intact, did not abolish
his previous views on the relations between ideals and facts.
They were only superimposed on them, as it were, and thus
created for the uninitiated reader a general picture of sometimes
disconcerting, and even almost bewildering complexity.

Indeed, although the notion of dualism—ideal and reality—
constitutes a good guiding thread for the exploration of the
labyrinth of Giraudoux's emotions and ideas, it does not make
that exploration a perfectly simple matter. Sometimes the reader
faces in Giraudoux's works straight lines and broad vistas;
more often he encounters winding bypaths, intricate twists and
turns, and even deceptively inviting blind alleys.

The various elements of Giraudoux's art alternate and overlap
one another constantly. He never attempted to organize his
views systematically. He placed no faith in systems, and he
found ironical amusement in the lucubrations of the philosophers.

He had nothing but mockery for the pedants "who claim to discover the reasons of what takes place on earth and to discover the keys to the mysteries of the heavens above."[26]

Thus the writings of Giraudoux offer a strange medley of ideas, emotions, sensations, images, metaphors, symbols that are sometimes related and sometimes opposed to one another, but also sometimes conjoined by sheer accident. They appear, disappear, reappear, and are tossed back and forth as in a dizzy game of battledore and shuttlecock. In many ways, his work resembles a curious daydream, in which fragments of reality are viewed in all their original freshness and are surrounded by a sublime, mystic, or simply evanescent atmosphere. The complicated figures drawn are sometimes merely a joy to the eye; sometimes also, like so many hieroglyphs, they hold a secret message. Very often those hieroglyphs are difficult to decipher and they are usually open to different interpretations.

Giraudoux evidently rejoiced in all these possibilities and variations. He was not anxious to solve the antinomies between the various forms of the ideal that he conceived and the various aspects of the reality that he saw. He was primarily an artist and a poet, and he was captivated by the fantastic spectacle that was brought into being by the interplay of reality and the ideal. As Giraudoux's son aptly remarked: "Why did Jean Giraudoux offer, while keeping away from any philosophy, a characteristic and essential element of contemporary sensibility and thought? . . . It is sometimes wisdom not to try to discover with artificial preciseness the secrets of the universe, which should be only lyrically celebrated and transfigured."[27]

What I am chiefly to be credited with is the publication
of that newspaper which gives detailed news,
not of men themselves, who are by definition
unchangeable, but of everything that in relation
to them is ephemeral, that is to say, the seasons,
the feelings, and the elemental wonders of the universe.[1]
Jean Giraudoux

❧ III ❧
The Novels and Stories of Giraudoux

In the absence of any definite and systematic trend in the development of Giraudoux's thought and art, his various works—novels,
plays, essays—can best be understood by following the vagaries
of his imagination. The material of his works was obviously
drawn to a large extent from emotions and episodes of his own
existence, as his son Jean-Pierre noted: "He was painting himself in his works, much more in his theater, where he had to impose a discipline to his verve, than in his novels which, however,
are almost autobiographical, but in which his taste for paradox
sometimes carried him beyond his own experience."[2] In all his
works, the autobiographical data are steeped in a poetical atmosphere, and yet they remain quite recognizable in their new
guise. In that respect—in spite of many quite obvious differences
—his process of poetic transposition of bare facts is not unlike the mode of approach to life found in Goethe's famous *Dich-
tung und Wahrheit.* An intimate blend of "poetry and truth"
forms in Giraudoux as well as in Goethe an ambiguous ensemble
that is always challenging, at times baffling, but on the whole
singularly appealing.

When he was very young, Giraudoux composed short stories,

such as "Le Dernier rêve d'Edmond About."[3] These juvenilia are of little interest as a rule. His first noteworthy literary attempts were tales that he wrote between 1908 and 1910 for the newspaper *Le Matin*. They were later collected under the title *Contes d'un matin*. Most of them are built around cases of obvious misunderstanding and end with a surprise, after the manner of the tales of Maupassant.

In one of the best of them, "Guiguitte et Poulet," a young man falls in love with a girl whom he believes to be virtuous and honest. As a matter of fact, she is an experienced thief. But she falls in love with him because she thinks that he is honest and decent and, lo and behold, he also is a thief. In such a simple anecdote, the too perfect symmetry of situations may entertain the reader, but it leaves him with an impression of contrived artificiality. The characters, moreover, are sketchily drawn, and the style, though vivid, remains on the whole undistinguished. Giraudoux was still in his literary novitiate.

In *Provinciales*, Giraudoux's inspiration was rooted in the firm ground of a familiar reality that he knew well: the life of modest, middle-class people, at the turn of the century in a small town of Limousin. Seven thumbnail sketches depict minor events that unfold in that particular setting. Most of them are seen through the eyes of a sensitive boy of ten. In spite of a certain monotony in the atmosphere of those homely scenes, the style of Giraudoux, by turns realistic, poetic, and ironical, confers on them real originality and charm.

The subjects are uncomplicated yet varied. For instance, "De ma fenêtre" describes a little boy's vague imaginings, when he is kept indoors by some childish ailment, about the good folks he sees through his bedroom window. "Sainte Estelle" is the story of a local religious visionary and of a solemn procession organized in her honor. "Printemps" and "Nostalgie" are small but delicate vignettes which evidently transpose Giraudoux's own wistful memories of his early impressions of beauty in his provincial hometown. "La Pharmacienne" tells of the wiles and maneuvers of a respectable matron and her two marriageable daughters to entice the road surveyor away from the pharmacist's wife, whose charms set all the masculine hearts aflutter.

L'Ecole des Indifférents strikes a much more personal note.

Outwardly, the book presents, like *Provinciales,* a series of unconnected short stories. In fact these stories form a composite portrait of Giraudoux himself—of Giraudoux seen from three different angles, as if he were reflected in a large triple mirror. With humorous and disarming frankness, he chose to look at himself from three angles revealing his least flattering aspects. He admitted, with an amused smile, that he was selfish, that he was lazy, that he was weak-willed. These three defects are embodied in the book, respectively, by three fictitious and complementary characters, Jacques l'Egoïste, Don Manuel le Paresseux, and Bernard, le Faible Bernard.

The three facets of Giraudoux's personality are united by their common quality of "indifference"—that is to say by an instinctive reluctance to come to grips with the real. At times, of course, a close contact with reality is inevitable, but that very closeness impairs the delicate beauty of the world: "When an object shines and attracts me, if I come close to admire it, if I bend my head over it, if I breathe. . . . Is it for that reason that it gets tarnished?"[4]

To preserve the freshness and the charm of the best things, one would be wise, says Giraudoux, to adopt a certain nonchalant aloofness toward them. A slight, discreet withdrawal from the world allows one to enjoy the world itself to the full. *L'Ecole des Indifférents* is brimming over with joy and love of life; but it also shows the "indifferent" detachment of Jacques, Don Manuel, and Bernard, as they move in the various places—Paris, Harvard, and a small town in central France—where Giraudoux himself had tasted the most delightful pleasures of his youth.

There is a very tenuous plot in each of these stories. In every case the plot provides a loose connection for clever sketches of small humorous scenes, rambling remarks about life and love, pieces of witty dialogue, irreverent jokes, and poetic notations of fleeting aspects of nature. In the background, one can perceive the graceful silhouettes of alluring yet elusive *jeunes filles.* All these elements are evidently parts of Giraudoux's own experience. Even though their original traits have been trasnformed, they retain a vibrant quality that only life can give.

Giraudoux's war books, *Lectures pour une Ombre, Amica America* and *Adorable Clio,* form an interlude in the development of his early works. Because of the nature of the subject, they differ somewhat from his previous writings. Their general tone, however, does not mark a break in the continuity of his art and thought. *Amica America* is a rather cheerful record of Giraudoux's mission to the United States. *Lectures pour une Ombre* and *Adorable Clio* consist of short sketches, some of which, like "Retour d'Alsace" and "Adieu à la Guerre," had been published separately.

In spite of the inevitably somber color of the background against which these sketches are drawn, Giraudoux's continued detachment and inveterate playfulness impelled him to insert, even in the midst of rather grim pictures, light touches of irony and humor. He never gave a full description of the horrors of war. He portrayed its familiar aspects without any particular emphasis, yet with a true ringing note that could be only sounded by one who knew. Sometimes he mentioned the elevating and purifying effects of danger. At other times, he could not help showing a disconcerting flippancy about the war, almost akin to the attitude of a schoolboy enjoying a tremendous lark.

Immediately after the war, and again in the frolicsome and mischievous mood of a schoolboy on a holiday, Giraudoux published a parody of parts of the *Odyssey* entitled *Elpénor*. Elpénor was one of the sailors of Ulysses and one of the most insignificant characters of Homer's epic. Because practically nothing is known of Elpénor's thoughts and actions, Giraudoux was free to present his life and personality exactly as he pleased. In the midst of an almost intemperate flow of unbridled imagination, he found a chance to demonstrate through pleasantries the junction between the classical ideal and modern reality that was one of his principal preoccupations.

In *Elpénor,* he filled the more or less bare framework of a classical tale with the richness of our contemporary experience. He engaged unhesitatingly in the most outrageous anachronisms in order to infuse life into the stiff figures of a remote Greek legend. Not only Elpénor, but also Ulysses, the Cyclops, the Sirens, from being pure classical entities, become warmly human and akin to us. *Elpénor* is a slender book, but not at all negligible. It blends a jocularity often reminiscent of the *canulars* of the Ecole Normale Supérieure with a genuine feeling for the old Hellenic myths and also an acute, loving sense of the real.

In a completely different vein *Simon le Pathétique* recalls the type of inspiration that had made Giraudoux write *L'Ecole des Indifférents*. In fact, the bulk of *Simon le Pathétique* was written before the war, and parts of it appeared in the newspaper *L'Opinion*. The outbreak of hostilities interrupted its publication. Throughout the war, Giraudoux worked intermittently at it, completely remodeling his manuscript. In 1918, a new version appeared without attracting much attention from the general public. A second, revised version of the book was issued in 1923, but the final text, still further revised, did not appear until 1926.

Like *L'Ecole des Indifférents, Simon le Pathétique* is based on definite autobiographical memories. It begins with the retrospective presentation of an adolescent's view of the world in the small town of Bellac. That adolescent, Simon, is the somewhat idealized double of Giraudoux himself when young. He possesses a singularly sensitive soul. The appellation "pathétique" ought not to be taken as having its usual meaning in French or English. Giraudoux retained here the Greek etymological connotation of the word, which is "feeling intensely."

Young Simon is shown applying himself with his whole heart to his studies in a provincial lycée. The classical humanities arouse in him a generous enthusiasm. After a while, however, he is struck by the mediocrity of his teachers, who see in the lessons of the past not a philosophy of life, but a pretext for notes and lectures. The young man, disillusioned at the prospect of becoming himself one day the victim of such intellectual atrophy, emancipates himself from college and books. He sallies forth into the world.

Then follows an episode that is handled sarcastically, contrasting sharply with the generally friendly and even tender tone of the rest of the book. It corresponds to the phase of Giraudoux's life when he was Bunau-Varilla's secretary. He depicts the latter, under the name of Jacques de Bolny, in a cruelly realistic portrait.

The scene is soon occupied, however, by a bevy of winsome *jeunes filles,* and the second part of the book is filled with stories of Simon's friendships and flirtations with Gabrielle, Hélène, Geneviève, and Anne. Eventually, and particularly in the late versions of the book, Anne—who greatly resembles Suzanne Boland—takes precedence over the others in Simon's heart and mind. The variations and vagaries of their reciprocal fondness, their waverings, their misunderstandings, their quarrels, their reconciliations, their measured audacities, their prudent retreats are presented in detail, but always in a tactful, restrained even reticent manner. Their mutual attraction seems about to blossom into a stronger attachement until one day Anne comes to Simon with the great news that she is engaged to somebody else.

Suzanne et le Pacifique is a variation on the theme of Robinson Crusoe. An Australian newspaper holds a competition in which prizes are offered for the best maxim on boredom. The first prize, a trip around the world, is won by Suzanne, a girl from Bellac, with the following entry: "If a man gets bored, give him excitement; if a woman gets bored, hold her back."[5] Suzanne sets out on her trip, first going to Paris, where she meets Simon (le Pathétique) and his friend Anne. Then she sails from St. Nazaire across the Atlantic, through the Panama Canal, to the South Seas. During a storm in the middle of the Pacific, the ship sinks and, out of all the passengers and members of the crew, Suzanne alone is saved. She clings to a raft and is cast on a small desert island.

The original Robinson Crusoe, marooned in somewhat similar circumstances, had set immediately to rearrange the order of nature. "That Puritan, although certain that he was the Providence's particular plaything, did not put his trust in Providence for a single minute. For eighteen years, he was busy all the time fastening strings, sawing stakes, nailing planks. . . . He had to have a table to eat from, a chair for writing, wheelbarrows and ten different types of baskets . . . three varieties of sickles and scythes and a sieve and grindstones and a harrow and a mortar and a sifter. . . . So much so that one would have liked to say to him: 'Now sit down; lay aside your gun, your parasol and your stick. . . . Don't work three months to make a table — just squat. . . . That tree that you want to cut so as to plant barley, shake it, it is a palm tree; it will give you your bread ready baked. And that one you are pulling in order to sow peas — gather those yellow snakes growing on it, called bananas.'"[6]

This is in fact what Suzanne does. Giraudoux draws a most humorous and whimsical picture of Suzanne's lazy and happy life in the bountiful bosom of tropical nature. Her dream island is populated only by myriads of colorful birds. Later, impelled by curiosity, she swims to another nearby island and finds it crowded with unfriendly, chattering monkeys. She also discovers the pitiful remnants of the work performed by a man — evidently long dead — who had also been shipwrecked and had consumed his strength foolishly following Robinson Crusoe's example of strenuous, exhausting effort. Suzanne, being wiser, returns to her Eden of facility and ease.

After a while, however, a carefree life in the midst of plenty grows tedious. Suzanne longs for the human traits that in Europe have been stamped upon raw nature by age-old civilizations. She fabricates makeup for her face. Being a woman, she misses sin. Because it is difficult to achieve a full-grown sin all by oneself, however, she resorts to her European memories for a fresh and abundant supply of it. "I would take the recollection of one day in Europe from the time of rising to the time of going to bed, sure that I would have only to tilt it, to shake it, just as if it were a prism, in order to have sin appear."[7]

She writes letters to Simon and also writes Simon's supposed replies. Further, she begins to give names to different parts of the island, names drawn from the little district of Bellac and from the cultural history of France. The French Academy and French literature provide her with scores of names, from Racine to Paul Claudel, and she finds plenty of bizarre applications for them. The island soon seems quite human and thoroughly habitable, and Suzanne enjoys complete happiness and balance there.

She keeps up the game until one day an English ship puts in at the island, picks her up, and brings her back to Europe. When she sets foot on French soil and is again face to face with real French people and French surroundings, she is overcome with emotion. This extravagant but delightful tale ends abruptly with the unexpected words of a new and unexpected character, the embodiment of reason and common sense, which now comes into play: "I am the Controller of Weights and Measures, Mademoiselle. Why are you crying?"[8]

Notwithstanding the fanciful development of the plot and quite apart from Giraudoux's evident enjoyment in the romantic atmosphere of the South Seas — an enjoyment shared by the reader — *Suzanne et le Pacifique* is replete with significant intentions. In the first place, it represents a definite reaction against the aggressive and contentious attitude toward life symbolized by Robinson Crusoe. Giraudoux has little sympathy for those who attempt by hard work and sheer obstinacy to force their will on a reluctant reality and thus become separated from nature. Giraudoux does not believe that nature is hostile to man. He enjoys it as he finds it and tries to effect a complete union with it, as Suzanne does in her island.

Nevertheless, stark reality is for him only the raw material of life. Reality by itself is shapeless and meaningless. Reality must be fitted within the framework of human ideas and culture. For this reason Suzanne applies the forms and outlines of French civilization to the abundant and simple products of tropical nature that Providence hands to her. As she remarks when she leaves her island: "In the foliage, in the slopes of the hills, there was that harmony which forty million French people have just succeeded in imposing on their mountains and their forests."[9]

The problem of the adaptation of reality to a set of elaborate ideas and principles is found in many of Giraudoux's writings, but he does not treat this problem seriously here. He is content to state his general position, leaving the adjustment of details to the vagaries of an exuberant imagination. The last words of the book — which are put in the mouth of that worthy official, the Controller of Weights and Measures — are a warning that all dreams come to an end, just as Suzannes's did.

Juliette au Pays des Hommes develops no particular theme and does not exhibit the same originality and boldness of conception as *Suzanne*. Juliette, a young woman from a small town in central France, is about to marry Gérard, a young man of the district. She loves him, after a fashion, but she longs to see something of the wide world spreading beyond the limits of her little province. She keeps a diary in which she has noted down the names and addresses of all the possible husbands who have crossed her path in the last few years. She then goes off suddenly by herself to Paris, with the intention of finding out what has become of them. She visits as many of them as she can and also a few others into the bargain.

This sentimental review gives Giraudoux a pretext for satirical pictures of modern life. Juliette first traces an Assistant in botany at the Ecole Normale Supérieure who is forgetting the world for the sake of minute and completely unknown plants; then she visits an archaeologist who is apparently lost in equally abstruse and useless studies; also a well-known writer who tries to initiate her into the mysteries of the *monologue intérieur*; lastly a frantic and passionate Russian. Finally she returns to Gérard who, by that time, is not too sure of being able to hold for long the affections of such an elusive person as his fiancée.

The only important message contained in the book is the famous "Prière sur la Tour Eiffel." In the course of her peregrinations, Juliette is supposed to call on the narrator of the story; he reads to her an essay he has just composed. This essay begins with a delicate invocation to the city of Paris as seen from the top of the Eiffel Tower. Then it proceeds with an outline of Giraudoux's own views on life and art, and particularly his ideas on Original Sin. This piece, of course, has no connection whatever with the rest of the plot. In fact it had been published separately a year before, in 1923. It deserves special mention, however, for its poetical charm and also for its value as a literary document, which has led certain critics to call it the *Art Poétique* of Jean Giraudoux.

All the works that Giraudoux composed up to approximately his fortieth year have a number of traits in common. Amusement and irony clearly predominate in them. At that time, Giraudoux was young, careless, optimistic, and he found it supremely entertaining to juggle with fragments of reality. He loved the two forms of reality that he knew: he retained a deep attachment to Limousin, and he was also drawn to the vast and picturesque world that had been recently revealed to him. He did not take that world too seriously, yet he enjoyed keenly the many possibilities of entertainment that it had to offer.

On the other hand, he remained faithful to definite moral and logical rules, although he often showed toward them the playful disrespect of a schoolboy on a holiday. He was constantly put in mind of classical quotations and anecdotes, but those heroic or sublime recollections were frequently linked with contemporary events that were banal and commonplace. Giraudoux found those contrasts exceedingly diverting.

Then, on a completely different level, from time to time, the glow of an almost mystic conception of the soul of the universe would cast a fleeting reflection on the surface of some of his works. But even the intermittent effulgence of that deep ideal failed to affect markedly at that time his general view of life. For him, on the whole, in the early 1920s, life was still a wonderful and fantastic game.

Although *Siegfried et le Limousin* was published in 1922, it contained many elements that set it apart from most of Giraudoux's other early works. True, neither gaiety nor flippancy were altogether lacking in this book, but they were associated with manifestations of a more serious mood. Furthermore, *Siegfried et le Limousin* contains, besides important autobiographical data, many external facts that could not be found in his other productions. *Siegfried et le Limousin* combines a transposition of some of Giraudoux's personal experiences with a discussion of political problems that were at that time exercising the best minds of the French diplomatic service.

The fundamental experience in Giraudoux's life that forms the human substratum of *Siegfried et le Limousin* is his encounter with Germany in 1905. At that time, the general pattern of his thought was established on the solid basis of French classical culture. He suddenly discovered that the principles of that culture, which he had believed to be of universal value, could not apply to German reality. He found that reality exciting, fascinating, and instinct with a prodigiously rich poetic power, but it also appeared chaotic and amorphous. How marvelous if French logic and German poetic dynamism could somehow be fitted together!

Another of his discoveries was that at least a part of the German soul was in deep communication with nature. Germany derived from that affinity a force that was hardly ever found in France. That force, however, was highly emotional, impulsive and potentially dangerous. How marvelous again if that force could be harnessed with the moral principles that, according to Giraudoux, constituted "the basis of the dignity of men"![10]

We know that, during his sojourn in Germany, he was captivated by those "marvelous" possibilities. For a while, he could grasp intuitively and simultaneously, as if in a dream, the best that both France and Germany had to offer spiritually. In the end, he found that the French and German elements of his beautiful dream could not unite. Himself a Frenchman above all, he returned to France. His French mind could be at ease only in a French environment. Limousin was calling him. A pedestrian explanation of that state of mind could be that his was merely a case of youthful homesickness. For Giraudoux himself, however, the separation from Germany and the return to France was not simply a change of domicile. It was a moving experience that underlies the story of *Siegfried et le Limousin*.

Other considerations greatly complicated this purely personal problem. Immediately after World War I, a new movement began to develop among statesmen, diplomats, and intellectuals in both France and Germany. In the face of the appalling losses inflicted on the two nations by the recent conflict, many persons believed that the disastrous Franco-German feud should be ended at almost any cost. One of the most serious obstacles to the reconciliation between the two nations was the clash between the French and German mentalities.

Yet some people, such as Giraudoux, felt that an association between French and German cultures was both possible and most desirable. Each of those nations is richly gifted in certain respects and evidently deficient in others. The shortcomings and the strong points of the two parties are not coincident but complementary.

Such an association, however, had little chance to materialize in the early 1920s because of the atmosphere of reciprocal distrust and resentment pervading the French and German masses. When Giraudoux wrote *Siegfried et le Limousin,* he simply gave expression to a hope, almost a dream, that was shared by only a few. A little later, Aristide Briand and Gustav Stresemann attempted to turn that dream into a fact; they failed, but the dream outlasted their failure.

One of the causes for that failure was the inability of the French to understand the workings of the German mind. When the French were thoroughly puzzled by the German way of thinking about crucial questions, they were often content to call the form of thought of their neighbors "nebulous" or "cloudy" or even just "typically Teutonic." When they uttered these ungracious epithets, they were frequently aware that they were not disposing of the problem satisfactorily. Many of them sensed at the bottom of the German thought something of great value that completely eluded their Latin mind. When Giraudoux wrote *Siegfried et le Limousin,* he attempted to help the French penetrate at least some of the hidden recesses of German psychology.

The aspect of the German problem that seemed perhaps the most disconcerting to the French was the contrast between old Germany and modern Germany. Old Germany, at least as she had been described to the French by a long series of great writers, from Mme de Staël to Victor Hugo, was a romantic country, elegiac and tender, turned almost exclusively toward dreams. The image offered by new Germany—materialistic, practical, efficient, ruthless—did not fit at all with the picture that the young Frenchmen had been taught to revere and even to love. In *Siegfried et le Limousin,* Giraudoux underlined the difficulty in reconciling those two antithetic forms of the same culture. He did not hide the strong appeal held for him by the Germany of the Holy Roman Empire, and he riddled with sarcasms not only the small comical mannerisms but also the achievements of the Germany of today.

A further difficulty in establishing a Franco-German understanding was the moral and political situation in postwar Germany. German political life was then in a state of bewildering instability. A succession of spasmodic local revolts, violent street fights, plots, assassinations, and a variety of short-lived coups d'état that became internationally known under the name of *Putsch* kept the country in a state of constant tension, effervescence and disorder.

Beneath the surface agitation caused by those events, any observer of the German scene could discern the swelling of deep and powerful emotional waves. We know now how Hitler succeeded in using these collective emotions. In the early 1920s, many Frenchmen were fully aware of their existence and wholeheartedly wished that these latent wild forces could be tamed by "reason." Of course their notion of the "reasonable" corresponded to a set of mental categories that were imperative to them and to the logical principles that they themselves applied—more or less—to their actions. And they were honestly, though perhaps naively, concinced that if the Germans could apply to their own problems the French rules of good sense, it would be much to the advantage of Germany herself—and of Germany's neighbors as well. By what miracle, however, could a French pattern of thought be imprinted on German political life?

In *Siegfried et le Limousin,* Giraudoux performed such a miracle — a miracle of imagination. He imagined a case of amnesia so unique and so spectacular that it swept away all the psychological and practical difficulties existing in the real world. It has been suggested that Giraudoux's idea of having recourse in his novel to such an imaginary case had its origin in the actual case of his brother Alexandre, who had several spells of amnesia after being shell-shocked during the war. Although that hypothesis is not to be summarily dismissed, the book more probably presents the first adumbration of a problem to which Giraudoux reverted insistently in his subsequent works, and particularly at the time of his great moral crisis — the problem of a man's temporary and partial depersonalization.

In *Siegfried et le Limousin,* Giraudoux supposes that a French soldier, the writer Jacques Forestier, has been wounded in the head and has been picked up in no man's land by the Germans. Because his uniform has been torn away from his body, his nationality cannot be discovered. When he recovers consciousness, his memory is completely gone. The Germans, giving him the benefit of the doubt, reeducate him as a German, under the name of Siegfried von Kleist.

Notwithstanding his amnesia, his faculties are intact. His mind has been emptied, but its logical framework and original reasoning power have remained exactly as they were before the shock. He therefore quickly learns all that his instructors have to teach him, and within a few years he becomes a prominent, in fact outstanding, expert in German political circles.

Indeed, Siegfried possesses something no other man ever had before — the clear and lucid mind of an educated Frenchman, plus the insight and intuition he derives from the substance of German culture. He is able to organize a very rich but also very tumultuous reality — the German reality — according to an orderly and logical plan. With unerring precision and because of his rational critical judgment he is able to guide his German compatriots through the confusion of the postwar period.

A former friend of Jacques Forestier — who is called only Jean in the book, and who believes the French writer to be dead — notices a striking similarity between the publications of Siegfried Kleist and those of Forestier. His suspicions thoroughly aroused, he goes to Germany to make enquiries in the company of one Zelten, a German who is intelligent and broad-minded, although also neurotic, unbalanced, and very much demoralized by the up-heaval of the war. The young Frechman, pretending to be a French-Canadian named Chapdelaine, is accepted by Siegfried Kleist as a teacher of French. He immediately recognizes Siegfried as his old friend. Yet how is Siegfried to be made to realize and feel that he is French himself?

Here many other divergent influences come into play. One is Eva von Schwanhofer, who was Siegfried's nurse after he was wounded and who may be considered as the female incarnation of Germany. In contrast is Zelten's divorced wife, the French sculptress Geneviève Prat. She, however, can hardly be con-sidered a flattering embodiment of *La Belle France,* because she has led a most irregular existence. Nevertheless, Siegfried's affections vacillate amusingly between these women. Then a *Putsch* occurs, staged by Zelten, whose dictatorship lasts only four days. Siegfried is among his opponents, and Zelten in a rage reveals that Siegfried — the great German political authority — is in fact a Frenchman.

Siegfried therefore comes to feel that he is really French. The feminine element plays practically no part in his transformation, because Geneviève rather unexpectedly dies in a hospital after an operation. Forestier's dormant memories at last awake essen-tially when he is brought up against the innumerable trivial yet significant facts that compose everyday reality in his native Limousin. Then, quickly, practically without difficulty, the French side of him displaces the German, and the French conception of reality resumes its natural and normal place within his French rational mind.

A brief outline of the main episodes of *Siegfried et le Limousin* fails to give an adequate idea of the complexity of the novel. In the midst of evident allusions to personal experiences that explain the bizarre psychological shuttling of Siegfried from French culture to German culture and back to France, Giraudoux evokes, almost pell-mell, the possibility of a cooperation between Germans and French on the basis of a harmonious blending of their complementary qualities; the necessity for the French to try to understand in depth the German character; the difficulty of bringing together opposite views on old and new Germany; and finally the highly hypothetical eventuality of reaching a solution to the German political problems through the use of French reasonableness and logic.

Giraudoux, however, never approaches these subjects systematically. Because of the multiplicity of the questions raised and the diversity of the angles from which they are considered, the reader is often left with a feeling of confusion and vagueness. Personal reminiscences and objective statements, subtle pleasantries and rather obvious jokes, strikingly shrewd remarks and snap judgments of the most debatable nature, appeals to common sense and startling paradoxes, are juxtaposed generally with great literary skill but sometimes rather bewilderingly.

In spite of those blemishes, *Siegfried et le Limousin* is a highly thought-provoking book. It was appreciated by discerning intellectuals and was awarded a minor literary prize, the Prix Balzac, but it aroused little attention in the general public.

The appearance of *Bella* created a far greater sensation. By then Giraudoux had tightened his rather loose form of composition. The relatively simple and clear-cut structure of his new work already revealed some of the dramatic qualities that were to make of him, a few years later, an outstanding playwright. Those qualities enabled him to reach a much larger audience with *Bella* than he had with his other books. Furthermore, the very subject of the novel, a transparent and passionate account of the Berthelot-Poincaré duel, added to a well-told story the spice of near scandal by exposing the secret jealousies, rivalries, intrigues, and machinations festering behind the official decorum of the French political scene.

The novel *Bella* is built around the conflict of two families, the Rebendarts and the Dubardeaus. The protagonists of the action are the Minister of Justice, Rebendart, a thinly disguised satire of Poincaré, and René Dubardeau, a high-ranking diplomat who has many traits of Philippe Berthelot. The story of their feud is told by Dubardeau's son, Philippe, who very much resembles Giraudoux himself, but whose personality does not offer the essential element of the book.

Giraudoux broadens the enmity of Rebendart and René Dubardeau into an almost epic struggle between two forms of the French spirit. The Rebendarts are generally men of principle, rigid, ambitious, unbending. The Dubardeaus show more flexibility, more culture, more human sensitivity. The connecting link between the two groups are the brothers d'Orgalesse, informers by vocation and occasional peddlers of gossip; the Jewish banker Emmanuel Moïse, a broad-minded man, both loyal and wily; and the Baron de Fontranges, a representative of high French nobility, offering a typical blend of discouraged passiveness and aristocratic dignity.

Fontranges' daughter, Bella, had been married to Georges Rebendart, the son of the Minister of Justice, but she had become a widow. Bella Rebendart and Philippe Dubardeau fall in love with each other, but they have to conceal their romance carefully, because of the feud in which his father and her father-in-law are already engaged. After various moves and maneuvers in which the brothers d'Orgalesse and Moïse take part, the feud comes into the open.

Rebendart has got hold of documents that will enable him, so at least he thinks, to ruin the whole Dubardeau clan. The essential document is a check that René Dubardeau and his brother Charles, who occupies a high position in the Administration of Finances, have endorsed mainly to oblige a friend. Their action was perfectly innocent, but because of unforeseeable circumstances, it could be construed as an evidence that they had accepted a bribe. Rebendart, after intimidating a few cringing subordinates into assisting him in his plans, formally indicts Dubardeau on a charge of grave prevarication and dereliction of duty. But when he wants to produce the proofs of his accusation, it is discovered that the incriminating documents are no longer in the files of the Ministry.

Then, dramatically, almost theatrically, Bella steps in and declares that she has burnt the documents because of her love for Philippe Dubardeau. In the midst of the following commotion and confusion, she tries to reconcile Rebendart and Dubardeau. The latter is ready to shake hands with his old enemy, but Rebendart, still vindictive and resentful, refuses to do so himself. Thereupon Bella collapses and dies soon afterward.

The interest of *Bella* is not in the development of the events connected with the rather thin plot, or in the romance between Bella and Philippe, a romance crossed by the feud between the two families. The character of Bella, however, is presented more clearly and forcefully than that of any of Giraudoux's previous heroines. She is one of the few women in Giraudoux's works who was not modeled on the personality of his wife Suzanne. The girl who served as a model for Bella has not been identified, although several names have been whispered in that connection by persons who claimed to be in the know. In any case, Giraudoux probably greatly idealized the original by infusing into her all the feminine qualities that haunted his own imagination.

Giraudoux describes Bella as being about twenty-five years old, tall, slender, of striking beauty, with regular, refined aristocratic features. She is unselfish, utterly devoted to the man she loves, and capable of sacrificing herself for his sake. She makes him feel that her greatest happiness is simply to be in his company and she shares absolutely all his tastes. Moreover, she is sweet, submissive, and usually silent![11] The image of that paragon of feminity exerts a definite appeal on the reader — particularly on the male reader.

The greatest appeal of the book, however, resides in the description of the groups of people among whom Bella herself moves. Two of those groups, the Rebendarts and the Dubardeaus, are pictured with vivid and sharp contrasting colors. The Fontranges group is painted in more subdued and neutral shades. Giraudoux's preference for the Dubardeaus is obvious, but he makes a commendable effort to be fair and succeeds in presenting a reasonably balanced view of the best points and the shortcomings of the two families.

The Rebendarts are a self-contained, closely knit clan having comparatively little contact with the world at large. The personality of the Minister of Justice is studied in detail, but even though the other members of the family are not identified by name, they are all clearly cut on the same pattern. All belong to the upper class of French society, and most are distinguished men indeed. They have often reached a high rank in the civil service, several having filled important political posts.

By vocation and training they are essentially lawyers. As such, they usually specialize in criminal cases and, as a result, they are apt to see or at least to suspect mostly the fraudulent aspects of life. Thus they display a distrustful, suspicious attitude toward other men, and maintain an affected posture of total integrity and righteousness. In the public eye they have become the embodiment of honesty, decency, and the strictest moral principles. That they believe in those principles is beyond question. But being, after all, only human, they cannot live up to their own lofty standards; a definite streak of hypocrisy appears in their private behavior. Because, moreover, black sheep occur even in the best families, some members of the Rebendart clan have engaged in actions which, if they became known, would spoil the image that the name of Rebendart calls forth in the mind of all the French. The "bad" Rebendarts are therefore shoved into the background or tucked away out of sight.

In politics, they stand officially for pure patriotism; in fact they represent intransigent nationalism. Again their genuine patriotic feelings are beyond doubt. Yet they often harm the cause of their country through their narrow and legalistic approach to international problems. They cannot understand the world at large, because the world does not obey the rules of strict logic. They do not appreciate the beauty of nature or the value of the heart, and they have no conception of the harmony of the universe.

The Rebendarts are deeply rooted in French provincial life. Their family seat is in Ervy, a small town in Champagne, and their existence is regulated by age-old tradition: "The ritual of French family life reigned there with all its minutiae."[12] A stiff formalism solidly established in the relations between parents and children precludes the development of any warm feelings between them, but it creates for all the members of the group a reassuring atmosphere of security, stability, and discipline.

Neither stability nor discipline are found in the Dubardeau group. The Dubardeaus are not rooted anywhere. They live mostly in Paris, and if they gather sometimes at the country place that one of them has recently purchased in Berry, they do so mostly for convenience and fun; they do not feel that they belong there. Like the Rebendarts they are members of the upper class and also like the Rebendarts they have given France a long list of distinguished men, generally in learning and particularly in science.

In the present generation, their aptitudes and talents are extremely diversified. Among the six Dubardeau brothers, Jacques is the Director of a Museum of Natural Sciences, Charles is an expert in finances, Jules is a general, Emile has been Prefect of Police, Antoine is a physicist, and René a diplomat. That variety is the symbol of their mental attitude: they are interested in absolutely all the aspects of the world.

The six brothers meet from time to time to exchange their views. Thanks to the multiplicity of their forms of experience, they can seize the relations between seemingly different and even divergent features of the universe. That conjunction of many sources of knowledge enables them to attain a total vision of the cosmos and to sense both its unity and its essential harmony. When they gathered in Berry, they paid scant attention to the message whispered by the local spirit of the little province because "they understood the richest language of the earth as a whole."[13]

Their breadth of views goes hand in hand with a wide understanding and tolerance of emotions or ideas that are at variance with their own. Their patriotism is genuine but discreet and tends toward conciliation, moderation, and reasonable compromise. In politics their ultimate hope is to see Europe united and free.

Meanwhile, they are blithely enjoying the pleasures that existence has to offer. Their outlook on life may, of course, seem somewhat disorganized. They are accused of lacking self-discipline and they are certainly nonconformists. Their zest for life, however, gives them a generous dynamism and a profound human appeal. Their family life is free and easy. Their homes are crowded with visiting relatives and friends. Oldsters and youngsters mix there cheerfully in an atmosphere exempt from any trace of formalism, and the children's mad frolics do not arouse anyone's anger, but promote general gaiety.

The antithetic presentation of the characteristic traits of the Rebendarts and the Dubardeaus reflects to a large extent the chasm still existing in Giraudoux's own spiritual life. The Rebendarts, men of rigid principles, men rooted in the soil of their province, are not without similarity to that part of Giraudoux's personality which always remained attached to the strict principles of logic and ethics he had absorbed at school and who was also faithful to his native Limousin.

On the other hand, the Dubardeaus' joyful appreciation of the world, their lightheartedness, also their intimate contact with "the earth as a whole," correspond to the side of Giraudoux who scattered his emotions gleefully through the world in his youth and who, at the same time, longed for a deep union with the cosmos.

Giraudoux's fundamental spiritual problem — his effort to conciliate those opposite terms of his moral dilemma — is symbolized by the gesture of Bella, who desperately attempts to bring together the two men who are so close to her and yet deeply divided by their antagonistic experiences and ideologies. Bella fails in her attempt, perhaps because Giraudoux was aware that the divergent elements of his own thought could not be forced into an artificial unity. Bella's death may indicate that the impossibility of bringing together the various split aspects of his experience that Giraudoux cherished simultaneously — a fact that he had taken lightly for many years — was beginning to appear tragic to him.

In the background of that tragedy, the Fontranges family, to which Bella originally belonged, partakes to some extent of the characteristic traits of the other groups. On the one hand, the Fontrangeses possess stability and solidity like the Rebendarts; they adhere to the same general principles; their behavior is ruled by the same formalism; they are profoundly established in a particular province of France. On the other hand, they have the human warmth, the generosity, the sensitivity, and the appreciation of things beautiful that is found in the Dubardeaus.

The Baron de Fontranges is a fairly typical representative of the ancient French nobility. The ancestors of the Fontrangeses were great Lords in the twelfth century, at the time of the Crusades. Today, the Fontrangeses are still enormously wealthy and can afford to live in idleness and luxury, in the midst of their huge inherited family estate. Their main occupation is hunting. Their main skill is raising race horses and hunting dogs. Even though, in alternate generations, they may be sometimes gentle and kind and sometimes brutal and hard, they generally lack stamina, leading a dull existence on the margin of the modern world. Their apathy can be explained by historical causes: the recent rise of the great democratic tide has pushed them irresistibly into the stagnant backwaters of contemporary life. Yet they retain a unique elegance and a captivating aristocratic charm.

For several years, Giraudoux's imagination remained haunted by these three fictitious families. He then composed a series of works in which the characters he had presented in *Bella,* and a few others closely connected with them, reappeared in new sets of various adventures. Many of those new works are short stories that were published separately, as if they were detached chapters of a comprehensive Rebendart-Dubardeau-Fontranges saga. Fairly rapidly, however, the glamor of the Fontranges eclipsed in Giraudoux's mind the more familiar qualities of the Rebendart and Dubardeau clans. The latter are mentioned only occasionally in *Eglantine,* which was published a year after *Bella* and which may be considered as its sequel.

Eglantine is the name of Bella's young foster sister. She is beautiful and attractive, but rather uncomplicated, insecure, and naive. She receives the attentions of two elderly suitors, Emmanuel Moïse and the Baron de Fontranges himself. She falls in love with one and then with the other. The fondness of a girl for two men advanced in years — both Moïse and Fontranges are sexagenarians — is explained by her craving for stability: "Her desire for reality pushed her naturally toward the people who, since her childhood, had remained the same — that is to say, toward old men. They alone seemed to be the solid and unchangeable part of the world."[14]

This unusual situation provides Giraudoux with the opportunity of presenting a subtle and diverting portrayal of love, self-consciousness, and jealousy in the two elderly rivals, but the development of the plot would remain rather puzzling if it were not definitely stated[15] that the characters of Moïse and Fontranges have a symbolical meaning. They represent, respectively, Eastern and Western cultures, and are pictured as no longer young because those cultures are indeed very ancient.

Emmanuel Moïse, the rich and powerful banker, is described as being both sensitive and ruthless, in turn emotional and practical, together crude and refined and above all deeply human. Born in the Middle East, he has become a French citizen and is utterly loyal to his adopted country. Yet he retains the feelings and the moods of the East. Fontranges, of course, stands for the West. Eglantine, after showing partiality for the attractions of Moïse — the East — finally casts her lot with Fontranges — the West.

The novel *Eglantine* is far from having the dramatic power and human appeal of *Bella*. When Giraudoux described the Rebendart and Dubardeau families, he not only transposed in his novel actual events that had moved him deeply; but he also presented forms of mind akin to his own. The portraits of Moïse and Fontranges are, on the other hand, composed of elements foreign to his deeper self.

As a man thoroughly steeped in Western culture, Giraudoux knew men of the East only through external observation, and he never succeeded in penetrating the arcana of their thought. Furthermore, he came himself from a decidedly *petit bourgeois* environment. Even though he rose socially in the course of his career and gained access to certain aristocratic circles, he nevertheless remained somehow a stranger in the high society represented by the Fontrangeses. Their peculiar moral values seem to have eluded him, at least in their most distinctive shades, and he could never evoke their personalities with the same pungency that had made the characters of Rebendart and Dubardeau stand out in strong and bold relief.

La France Sentimentale appeared only in 1932. It is a collection of eleven short stories, six of which had been published separately before. Eight of those stories deal with minor episodes in the life of characters belonging to the Rebendart, Dubardeau, and Fontranges groups, as in "Le Couvent de Bella" and "Je présente Bellita," Bellita being the name of Bella's twin sister. One story, "Sérénade 13," harks back to the romance between Simon and Anne, and another, "Visite chez le Prince," develops in the same atmosphere as *Siegfried et le Limousin*. Only one, "Le Signe," has no connection with any other topic previously treated by Giraudoux. All those stories are told with great skill, but none is really a masterpiece. Two of them, however, "Le Signe" and "Mirage de Bessines," offer a very special psychological interest.

In "Le Signe," the narrator of the story hears that one of his friends named Dumas has died accidentally, drowned while swimming in a river. At once, he is overwhelmed with grief. He tells how, at the outbreak of the war, he had made a list of fifty of his acquaintances and friends. Thirteen of them had been killed. Each time he had to strike one name off the list, he had experienced genuine sorrow. Each time, however, after a while, nature had sent him "a sign" and his pain promptly faded away. This time, however, he is literally obsessed by Dumas' death and soon drifts into despair. Yet he had known Dumas only casually. Nevertheless, for months on end, Dumas' death continues to haunt him: "This time I waited in vain for the sign that the trees and nature had always given me, more or less distinctly, the day when my sorrow had dwindled within me."[16]

Then, more than a year later, one evening, he finds himself in the country, not far from the place where Dumas had drowned. He no longer expects to obtain relief from his macabre obsession. He even accuses "hypocritical Nature"[17] of having deceived him in the past and adds: "She tried to make me falsely believe in a secret link between her and myself."[18] Just then, suddenly the "sign" comes. "It was done. . . . The sign had been given."[19]

Thus ends abruptly, without further explanation, this strange and weird little tale. It would be puzzling to anyone who would not remember that, according to Giraudoux, "illogical threads"[20] link the most remote aspects of the living cosmos with the most insignificant events of our earthly destiny.

"Mirage de Bessines" also deals with a case of mental obsession but of an entirely different kind. The painter Rémy Grand is first presented as busy making a portrait of Bellita. Then, one morning, all of a sudden, he is awakened by a feeling of intense anguish," like a ship striking a rock."[21] Shortly afterward, he has the hallucinatory vision of the small town of Bessines, where he had spent part of his childhood: "The ghost of Bessines was so harmless in appearance that Rémy would never have considered it as the cause of his painful awakening, if the vision of Bessines had not pursued him throughout the morning."[22]

That morning, Rémy goes to Versailles, and the image of Bessines is interposed like a mirage between his eyes and the vista of the Grand Canal. Later, he tries to work at some painting: "Between his canvas and himself, the profile of Bessines was dancing, a greyish and dull silhouette, like an image in negative of the town."[23] He consults specialists in mental troubles, but without result.

In the end, he decides to return to Bessines alone. As soon as he finds himself face to face with the plain little town, the ghost that had been haunting him vanishes instantaneously. The tale

ends disconcertingly with an emotional outburst by Rémy, who shouts at the top of his voice: "*Merde pour la psychologie et la physiologie et la psychophysiologie. Et merde pour Freud Sigmund.... Et merde pour la psychiâtrie.*"[24]
A clue to the probable origin and signification of Rémy's bizarre adventure may be found in two sentences tucked in the middle of the story: "He [Rémy] had to deal with the worst demon, demon neurasthenia, at whom he had so often hurled defiance. He had so often gloried in having reached his fiftieth year without catching the deadly germs that may come from love, from vanity, from poverty or from wealth, also in having known only sound joys, sound women, sound currencies, that the demon had taken up the challenge and, being unable to find any opening for an attack in his adult age, he had led him to believe that the town of his childhood, his childhood itself, contained a poison."[25]
Giraudoux was in his fiftieth year when he wrote this story. He had enjoyed until then a particularly lucky existence, but he was undoubtedly beginning to feel the premonitory symptoms of the great crisis that was to overtake him very soon. If, as the last lines of the text indirectly though very clearly imply, he sought help from psychiatrists, they certainly told him, as they are wont, that his recent troubles had their roots in "complexes" acquired during his childhood.
Such a diagnosis must have brought about in him an obsessive rumination over his early years in Limousin. Bessines was a small town where he had spent some time in his youth. Giraudoux's brooding and misery apparently lasted until, facing squarely the events of his childhood, he realized that they were actually free from any morbid taint. Then, temporarily forgetting his usual politeness, he sent Sigmund Freud and his cohorts to the devil.
Giraudoux's next novel, *Aventures de Jérôme Bardini,* corresponds to the most acute phase of his crisis. Not a great book, it is a highly revealing one, telling of three separate and yet interlocking fugues. Jérôme Bardini abandons his wife, Renée, and his young child; he leaves his best friend, Fontranges; he gives up his job and simply disappears. His reasons for doing so are not clearly stated. He is not unhappy in his marriage; he loves his

son; he is not dissatisfied with his somewhat dull but not unpleasant work as a government official. He is not suffering from
amnesia. The reader is left to infer that he is driven by some
obscure compulsive craving for freedom.

He goes to America. Although he retains all his faculties and
his intelligence, his past life seems to drop away from him as
if it had never been. In New York, he meets in Central Park a
young girl, Stéphanie Moeller, or Stéphy for short. Stéphy is, very
much like Jérôme, drifting away from her family for no definite
cause. Perhaps she seeks to escape the monotony of her surroundings. In any case, she agrees to marry Jérôme, even though she
knows nothing about him. Surprisingly enough she never tries
to find out who he is and she never asks him any question.
Bardini, however, apparently becomes too dull for her after
a while, and she leaves him without quarrel and without explaining her move.

Bardini, now somewhat lonesome, discovers the "Kid," a boy
of about twelve who has strayed from home. The Kid is definitely a victim of amnesia and is roaming the streets, leading
a free though extremely precarious existence. Bardini "adopts"
the Kid and finds again in the child's responsive affection a
measure of the human warmth that he had not known since the
beginning of his fugue.

Just when he seems about to be cured from his abnormal
detachment from reality, a representative of the authorities
threatens to separate the Kid from Jérôme; the Kid runs away in
a snowstorm. He collapses soon afterward and loses consciousness, but is rescued just in time. The shock of that misadventure,
however, has restored his memory and he returns to his parents.

Meanwhile, Fontranges had started a search for his friend
Bardini. Tracing him to America, he discovers him and brings him
back to France. When they are on the ship, lying side by side
on deck chairs, they have a brief conversation together and
some of the views they exchange help the reader to catch a glimpse,
but only a glimpse, of Giraudoux's thought when he imagined
that rather bewildering cascade of fugues. "Don't you believe,"
says Fontranges, "that the fundamental cause for your trouble
is pride?" He explains that pride is "a resistance to everything
that must penetrate our mind and feed it" —in other words,

a revulsion against reality, "a repulsion for our way of living."
Then he asks: "Are you proud to be a man?" To which Bardini
answers: "No, but I do not see any other creature in the body of
which I would be proud to live." Fontranges adds: "There are
other things besides living beings." — "That is even worse. The
emphatic existence of the physical world fills me with disgust."[26]
This amounts to no less than a total rejection of reality in the
name of "pride," that is to say, of a superior attachment to a perfect ideal. *Aventures de Jérôme Bardini* marks a break in Giraudoux's vision of the world. In the past he had accepted reality
as it is, with all its imperfections and impurities. Here, in the
midst of the turmoil corresponding to his years of crisis, he is
not far from coming to the conclusion that the ideal of which alone
man can be proud is the complete antithesis of all that is found
in the real. Carrying this idea to its ultimate consequences, he
expresses his disgust for everything that exists.

The novel is divided into three parts, entitled, respectively,
"Première Disparition de Jérôme Bardini," "Stéphy," and "The
Kid." Bardini, Stéphy, and the Kid are in a way rational persons.
Their thoughts are perfectly coordinated. Yet they feel an abnormal desire to rid their minds of the material that has been provided by life. Their intellects are still in good working order, but
their minds have been partly or completely emptied of their
store of past experiences. They are in a situation somewhat
like that of Siegfried.

In the case of Siegfried, however, the void created in his mind
by the removal of the French contents of his memory was filled
with the rich substance of German reality. In the case of Bardini,
Stéphy, and the Kid, the new reality remains indefinite and vague.
It does not stand in sharp contrast to all that they have discarded.
Although it does not make them happier, it does not create
harrowing problems for them either.

The novel does not suggest any solution for their latent difficulties. It is purely and simply the story of three fugues. The
three main characters fail to achieve distinctive individuality
because of their partial depersonalization. Bardini, Stéphy, and
the Kid seem at times to be merely reflections of one another —
perhaps through the interplay of multiple mirrors in the style
typical of Giraudoux — perhaps because they are simply reflections

of the same mental mood that was present at that time in Giraudoux himself.

Giraudoux's next novel, which was published four years later, also deals primarily with a case of serious mental disturbance. *Combat avec l'Ange* describes two sets of events proceeding along parallel lines: On one side, the record of the last months of the life of Brossard, a prime minister of France; on the other, an attempt to elucidate the pathological obsessions of an Argentine girl, Maléna Paz. The only link between the two is Jacques Blisson, secretary to Brossard and lover of Maléna.

The character of Brossard has many traits of Briand, and in the background, the troubled political atmosphere of Europe in the early 1930s is evoked by a mass of suggestive details. More original and more amusing is the satirical and evidently true inside picture of the everyday existence of a French prime minister, who has no difficulty in disgracing a chief of police or a colonial governor, but who cannot obtain the dismissal of an usher. Giraudoux draws on the whole a kind and sympathetic portrait of Briand. The essentials of Briand's character, however — as seen through those of Brossard — are not etched with the same vigor as those of Poincaré represented by Rebendart.

Although Briand had an extremely complex personality, Giraudoux was content to portray him in a relatively simple sketch. He showed mainly Briand's broad-mindedness, his tolerance, also his cynicism, his toughness, his contempt for mankind, and his hatred for war. Yet, when he was about to die, he had little care for the cause of peace to which he was devoted body and soul; he only thought of a young woman of whom he had caught a glimpse a few days before. That woman was Maléna.

Throughout her life, Maléna has been so far almost miraculously lucky. She has never known misfortune in any form. Consequently, as she explains to her friend Nancy Rollat, who has had herself a trying, even tragic existence: "I am afraid, I am outside life."[27] She feels that she has never been in contact with reality and that the universe is "lying"[28] to her by hiding from her sight the "monsters"[29] that she knows must exist somewhere. To acquire a sense of the real, she begs Nancy to show her actual examples of complete wretchedness. Nothing easier, is Nancy's reply: misery abounds throughout the world.

Yet Maléna is not satisfied. The cases of unhappiness that Nancy has shown her have remained, so to speak, external to herself, and she has not gained a feeling of genuine distress: "Unhappiness was near her, not in her."[30] She wishes to experience unhappiness as a wife wants to be able to tell her husband that she is with child: "But something was missing in her—and that was precisely the child."[31]

Thus, to be really unhappy, to torture herself, she becomes jealous of her lover Jacques, who is actually perfectly faithful. She nevertheless pursues him with extravagant suspicions.

To justify to herself the distrust that she entertains about him and a certain Gladys—whom she believes to be her rival—she locks them together in two adjoining hotel rooms. It goes without saying that Gladys and Jacques are not in the least interested in each other and Maléna's plan fails.

In the meanwhile, however, Maléna, in the depth of despair, decides to give herself without love to a handsome diplomat, Carlos Pio, who has courted her for some time. Then Jacques receives a "sign" from nature through the intermediary of a toad! Thanks to that sign, he knows that Maléna is in great trouble. He rushes to her, and with the aid of three faithful servants he reaches the hotel room occupied by Carlos Pio and Maléna just in time to prevent the irreparable. Then Maléna collapses and falls into a sort of trance.

When she recovers consciousness, she tells an amazing story. For a long time, she has struggled with an "angel." A gigantic angel. "He was taking my head and knocked it against things that were like walls. . . . He struck me against the ground as fishermen strike an octopus against the stones of a quay in order to make it tender. But I couldn't guess the purpose of the struggle."[32] Who was that angel? "I thought sometimes that he was the Angel of Death. . . . But no! He was a being who had received the order to conquer me alive."[33] In other words, he wanted to compel her to cease inflicting on herself torments of her own creation.

Even though the subject of *Combat avec l'Ange* was evidently drawn mainly from a particular personal experience, the lesson of the book goes far beyond the individual case of a certain neurotic woman. It seems that some human beings need the encounter with adversity in order to become fully aware of the solid and therefore reassuring existence of the world surrounding them. If they float in the midst of too much affluence and ease — if they are too happy — they will crave unhappiness. If need be, they will create for themselves, in imagination, causes for misfortune and misery. Often their secret desire is to find a strong, even hostile, opposition to their well-being, an obstacle against which they can assert and define their personality. Because the hostile element that they invent exists only in their minds, the inner strain and tension thus produced may lead to grave and extravagant delusions that can be eliminated only in the midst of violent emotional storms.

Around 1936, Giraudoux composed a novel entitled *La Menteuse,* which was not published during his lifetime. Fragments of that work appeared in 1958, but the rest of the manuscript — which had been believed lost — was discovered only later, and the complete text was not revealed until 1969. The main object of *La Menteuse* seems to have been to illustrate the well-known aptitude that many women possess to model their personality on the pattern that the men whom they love consider attractive and desirable. The heroine of *La Menteuse,* Nelly, carries that aptitude beyond all limits of normal psychological probability.

Nelly is a professional "kept woman" who has for some time had a sedate liaison with a middle-aged businessman, Gaston. Gaston is prosperous and generous, but personally heavy and dull. His manners are somewhat vulgar, although he is basically good-natured and kind. His views and ambitions are strictly limited to the most material and practical aspects of life.

To please him, Nelly poses as a thoroughly ordinary and commonplace woman. She even invents for his benefit the existence of a child she is supposed to have had in the past and on whom she bestows all the attention and the time she cannot give to her lover. In the end, Gaston proposes marriage to her and because, according to Giraudoux, matrimony is one of the most powerful magnets that can influence the decisions of young women, it is easily understood why Nelly is strongly attracted by the promises of material security that are thus offered to her.

In the interval, while Gaston was away on a business trip, Nelly has become acquainted by chance with a supremely fas-

cinating man, Reginald. Reginald is the very antithesis of everything that Gaston represents. He is a diplomat, still very young-
looking in spite of his forty years, elegant, reserved, refined, and
displaying on all occasions the most tactful manners. Above all,
he has a soul, a preternaturally lofty, idealistic soul. He wants
to find in the woman he loves the incarnation of the most ethereal
virtues.

For his sake Nelly turns into a paragon of perfect purity. Just
as she had invented a child to gratify Gaston's homely tastes,
she tells Reginald about her—imaginary—immense wealth, and
also about a likewise imaginary previous marriage with a man of
very high rank. Then she adds, for good measure, that she had
been so much repelled by his person that, after the wedding, she
"fought" with him for two weeks before, to her "horror," their
actual union was consummated. So she remained (morally)
"pure" even after that marriage. Reginald accepts without difficulty all these fantastic stories, because they correspond to his
own sublime aspirations and ideal daydreams about love.

The return of Gaston brings about inevitable complications
in Nelly's double life. All her schemes and hopes collapse suddenly when her accumulated falsehoods come to light and she
is left alone. Who is then to come to her rescue? No other than
the old Baron de Fontranges! In *Bella*, Fontranges represented
a blend of some of the antithetic aspects of the two families of
the Rebendarts and the Dubardeaus. In *La Menteuse*, he resumes,
of course under completely different circumstances, a similar
intermediate position between Gaston and Reginald. Thus he
will offer Nelly a perfect solution for her problems: he will marry
her, as Gaston would have done, thus giving her the solid security
that she craves, and it is broadly hinted that he will treat her like
a "father" after the wedding, thus making retrospectively come
true—or at least partly true—the romantic tale of purity she had
told to Reginald.

That solution may seem satisfactory to Nelly, who is a very
unusual person in any case, and perhaps also to Fontranges,
who is very far from young. For the reader, however, the sharp
contrast between the opposite characters of Reginald and Gaston,
the too perfect symmetry of their moral and psychological situations, and also the too neatly contrived conciliation of their

differences in the person of Fontranges, will appear artificial and bizarre if it is not understood that Giraudoux simply developed in his novel one of his favorite themes: the encounter between the ideal and reality.

Reginald is obviously the personification of an extreme poetic ideal. Gaston stands no less evidently for gross earthly reality. Fontranges is a convenient, though perhaps not very convincing, means to bring those antagonistic elements of life together. The rigidity of the dualistic structure of the plot, however, and the lack of shading in the presentation of the principal masculine characters — with Reginald lost in the clouds of an impossibly pure ideal, and Gaston irremediably sunk in the swamp of crass materiality — detract a great deal from the interest of the novel.

Giraudoux disposed finally of the obnoxious "reality" through one of his customary literary sleights of hand: Gaston is soon involved in a plane accident and, as could be expected, becomes a victim of amnesia — to the point of being unable to recognize Nelly when she comes to visit him in the hospital. The book suggests, however, that Nelly will not be so easily rid of her "true" love, the ideal Reginald. At the very end of the novel, Reginald is shown lurking behind a pillar in the church where her wedding with Fontranges is taking place.

When *La Menteuse* was published, it was whispered that an actual person had served as a model for the character of Nelly. Yet the personality of Nelly as it appears in the book is both sketchy and confusing. Virtually all the manifestations of her character are lies and lies. Those lies, however, have not all the same psychological source. Some are deliberate deceptions prompted by self-interest and calculated scheming. Others seem determined by a deep feminine protean propensity to conform instinctively to whatever image her man has conceived of her.

On the other hand, some of Nelly's lies appear to be imaginary projections of certain normal, and perhaps even fine, longings that are latent in her and have not received their fulfillment in her actual life. Thus a subconscious craving for motherhood and a nostalgic aspiration toward purity may be at least partly responsible for the patent falsehoods she told to Gaston and Reginald. Sometimes also her lies clearly belong to the domain of neurotic mythomania.

Nelly's personality, however, is not clearly analyzed and does not emerge forcefully from that somewhat monotonous medley of deceptions and delusions. The accumulated lies narrated in the story never coalesce to provide a revealing, unified inner insight into the mentality of the obsessive liar that Nelly is supposed to be, and the statement made several times in the book that women lie as they breathe seems hardly to be an adequate justification for the long string of sometimes puzzling falsehoods that constitute the essence of the story. Giraudoux was probably aware of the flaws in this book and therefore refrained from publishing it.

Choix des Elues is the last novel written by Giraudoux. It is the most complex, perhaps the deepest, certainly the saddest of them all. Giraudoux composed it in his late fifties, and the light gaiety that had characterized many of his earlier works was replaced by a definitely more somber view of life. Giraudoux did not use many direct autobiographical data in *Choix des Elues*, but he certainly drew on past personal experiences for the elaboration of certain episodes. The meandering course of the plot is not too difficult to follow, although it is frequently broken by cascades of logical or psychological impossibilities.

The novel deals with the moral tribulations of a French family permanently established in New York. The father, Pierre, is a brilliant oil engineer. The mother, Edmée, is a housewife apparently content with her lot; she particularly enjoys the love of her two children, Jacques and Claudie. Then one day, inexplicably, Edmée is seized with a feeling of deep anguish, and shortly afterward her behavior becomes very strange. Although she is a perfectly faithful wife, she allows a painter, Frank Warrin, to put his head on her lap. Then she literally falls in love with a garden. Finally she makes a brief fugue, taking her little daughter Claudie along with her.

Edmée's husband, a worthy man with a strictly scientific turn of mind, is unable to understand his wife's thoughts. Believing that a temporary change of scene might bring her back to her senses, he urges her to accept an invitation she has received to visit with Claudie a wealthy American couple, the Seeds, who have befriended them some time before. Once away from home, however, she feels a compulsive craving for freedom, and she does not return to Pierre.

Taking Claudie with her, she goes to Hollywood and there becomes a successful technical and artistic adviser in a motion-picture studio. Her fugue in Los Angeles lasts several years. During that period she does not seem very much occupied by her supposedly demanding profession. She is completely engrossed in her love for Claudie, who in turn adores her mother: "They lived together, pressed one against the other, the life that an animal mother and her young would have."[34]

Later Edmée once again experiences an intense feeling of anguish. This time the pain is so atrocious that at first she believes she is the victim of an attack of angina pectoris. She is not at all physically ill, however, and she understands that her suffering is just "a sign." She realizes soon that Claudie has become an independent being. "For the first time, she felt separated from Claudie. . . . Never before had Edmée imagined that her daughter did not live inside herself. The birth, the first birth, of Claudie had merely caused her to pass from a womb where her mother could not see her into a broader maternity where Edmée could see her. She was still carrying her daughter, but outside herself. . . . But now that link was cut."[35]

New fugue. Edmée and Claudie leave Hollywood without warning. They go to San Francisco. After a while, the delightful, whimsical little elf that Claudie had been in her early childhood turns into a banal adolescent girl with acne, tooth decay, and sties. Claudie has become a conventional schoolgirl who studies her lessons and wins the approval of her teachers: "Your daughter cannot fly in the air any longer! . . . That is fine. . . . You have a daughter of flesh and bone who is interested in embroidery. . . . You may rejoice. Your daughter does not feed on dew any more. She is no longer as slender as a pine. She does not shine like the sun. She cannot be distinguished from the other girls. Congratulations."[36] The magic of early childhood is gone and only an average human being remains, with all its average, pitiful mediocrity.

Another pitiful mediocrity: Edmée takes a lover. The painter Frank Warrin comes to San Francisco. Claudie sees him, and he renews his acquaintance with Edmée, who, although she had remained preternaturally pure in Hollywood, now gives herself to a man she does not love. Claudie seems at first to encourage her mother's liaison with the painter. Then, perhaps because she has a change of mood, perhaps because she undergoes the normal evolution of attitude that affects most young people in regard to their parents at that age, she becomes sullen, restive, and then openly hostile. In vain does Edmée break with Frank. The rift widens between Claudie and her distraught mother, and when Claudie is struck with appendicitis, Edmée leaves her in the hospital before the operation is performed and goes to live in a hotel room.

She is soon joined there by her son Jacques, now a grown-up young man who tries to persuade her to return to New York. She is aghast when she realizes the abyss of misunderstanding existing between them: in his imagination he has cast her in the role of a *grande amoureuse*. He believes that she has left her husband for the sake of a sublime love.

New fugue. She goes to Santa Barbara and remains there for some time as a housekeeper. Eventually, she returns to New York. Pierre receives her without asking any question after an absence of twelve years. Jacques is now married to an ordinary but "very nice" girl, Marie-Rose. Claudie is married to Harold, a "very nice" and thoroughly ordinary young man.

The book ends with a dismal picture of a solemn family dinner. Pierre, Edmée, Claudie, Jacques, Harold, and Marie-Rose are all present, all pleasant and all mortally bored. Although they are all sitting, side by side, apparently in perfect harmony, they are evidently beset with feelings of utter lassitude and loneliness. The glum, heavy atmosphere that weighs on the family dinner party is a symptom of the irremediable and disheartening inability of human beings to communicate and to understand deeply their mutual feelings.

Four different themes run through *Choix des Elues*. The first to appear is the opposition between two types of mind clearly illustrated by Pierre and Edmée, respectively, with Jacques and Claudie repeating in a minor key, as it were, their parents' particular modes of thinking. Those two types — the man of rigid principles and the more flexible person endowed with a rich zest for life — are found in many of Giraudoux's works and correspond essentially to two aspects of his views on human life and character.

Pierre is presented as a typical alumnus of the Ecole Polytechnique, a school where young men, selected through grueling competitive examinations, specialize in the study of higher mathematics, physics, and engineering. Its prestige, in the eyes of the French, is equal to that of the Ecole Normale Supérieure. The *Polytechniciens* are, almost without exception, men of brilliant intellect, but they are frequently accused, rightly or wrongly, of having minds very much like blueprints: clear, sharp, precise, but better prepared for the control of machinery than for the handling of the warm, palpitating, unpredictable substance of life.

Pierre's son, Jacques, having been brought up in America, has not entered the Ecole Polytechnique, but he has exactly the same type of mind as his father. When he is engaged to Marie-Rose, Giraudoux puts in Edmée's mouth—perhaps with a grain of malice—this caustic remark: "Jacques was as much qualified for love as a dog is qualified to become a bishop. Here was Jacques, who was made for Polytechnique, and who now planned to make love."[37]

Edmée, on the other hand, is one of the "elect." She is one of those exceptional beings who are created for the superior spiritual things of life. She cannot be satisfied with the humdrum of an average existence. She is capable of intense emotion, enthusiasm, impetuosity, passion, and poetic rapture. An "elect" like Edmée craves to reach the unknown, the unattainable, and she is ready to flout the best established conventions and rules to pursue her lofty dream. Claudie, like her mother, is an *élue,* and like her she will soon be impatient with the stale diet provided by everyday reality.

The theme of motherly love—or more specifically the love that binds a mother to her daughter, in this particular instance Edmée to Claudie—is next to be presented in full force. Naturally Giraudoux could not find anything startlingly new to say on that very old subject. Furthermore, his description of the relations between parent and child is absolutely free from any hint of Freudianism. Yet, remaining as he does within the limits of common observation and good sense, he has succeeded in producing a small masterpiece of intuitive perceptiveness.

Through a series of subtle notations and remarks, he makes the reader actually feel the union—one might even say the communion—existing between mother and daughter when the child is still very young. Then comes the normal, sometimes sudden, detachment of the growing offspring from her bewildered, uncomprehending mother. Soon, the mother's lack of comprehension is reflected by the developing girl's inability to understand her mother's wounded feelings. She in turn feels misunderstood and in her distress tends to react with hostility to her mother's undeserved reproofs as well as to her awkward advances.

In the midst of those reciprocal and compounded disagreements, the girl is pulled by life toward more personal aims, and eventually she leaves the older woman half resentful, half resigned to her solitude and chagrin. Such is the drama that unfolds between Edmée and Claudie. It is a very petty everyday family drama, to be sure, but a drama that, without being universal, is repeated in a large number of homes everywhere and that is fraught, for all concerned, with intense suffering.

Even more agonizing is the tragedy of "growing up," which forms the third theme of the book. Giraudoux first evokes with infinite delicacy, sensitivity, and tact the captivating and winsome charm of early childhood. At this stage, the young girl appears, at least in the eyes of her mother, truly a little "archangel." Then, disconcertingly, the enchanting archangel turns into a gawky teenager. She is subject to unpredictable whims and caprices; she is boisterous and rebellious when she is not morose and moody.

Further damage sets in when she is not far from her twenties. She may seem all sweetness, kindness, and generosity, but at heart she has become self-centered, both foolish and coldly calculating. Already she moves, driven by powerful instincts, toward her ultimate destiny as a female. Giraudoux, who in the past had drawn so many poetic pictures of mischievous yet alluring *jeunes filles,* here presents the evolution of Claudie in a realistic and almost cruel manner. Yet Claudie is certainly not an exceptional or wicked person. Her case is simply a particular instance of the harm caused by the mere passing of years, which transforms the miraculous promises of early youth into the ineluctable disappointment of adulthood.

When Giraudoux expressed those dismal views, he probably drew on recent personal experiences. Suzanne Giraudoux said that when their son Jean-Pierre was very small, her husband's love for him was deep and touching. Then she adds discreetly: "Later on, of course, it was no longer the same thing."[38] Whatever the origin of Giraudoux's ideas about mother-daughter relationships and the deterioration in a growing young person, the development of those two themes, constantly and skillfully intertwined, confers on *Choix des Elues* a poignant quality not found in his previous novels.

The fourth theme of *Choix des Elues* could be called the Abalstitiel theme. The behavior of Edmée remains for a long time enigmatic. In *Aventures de Jérôme Bardini* the fugues of the various characters take place in an atmosphere of clearly abnormal mental derangement, which allows the reader to accept easily the most disconcerting happenings and actions. Edmée, on the other hand, may be somewhat neurotic but, on the whole, she is perfectly sane. Her successive fugues are baffling until Jacques comes to San Francisco to induce his mother to go back to her husband. She understands then that Jacques is a "messenger"[39] — the bearer of a "sign" — and suddenly she also understands the cause of her obscure impulses.

She remembers seeing in her grandfather's living room an old etching representing a bizarre Russian scene. It showed a Countess entering, riding crop in hand, the main room of an inn where her daughter-in-law was drinking tea with a music teacher, in whose company she had obviously run away from home. No less obviously, the Countess was compelling the wayward young woman to give up her lover and to return to her duty. The caption under the picture said that the music teacher was the Abalstitiel.

Edmée identified Jacques with the Countess and the force that had impelled her to leave her husband with the Abalstitiel. From that point on, until the end of the novel, the Abalstitiel is repeatedly shown as being responsible for Edmée's élan toward the unknown. When Jacques practically succeeds in convincing her that she should go back to Pierre, she feels that "Jacques had conquered the Abalstitiel."[40]

Who is that Abalstitiel who had assumed the appearance of a music teacher and who entered Edmée's life? Abalstitiel is the approximate French transliteration of a Russian word meaning "seducer." In fact the Russian word has overtones almost equivalent to those of the English word "charmer."

That word could doubtless be applied literally to the music teacher with whom the Russian noble lady had eloped. Giraudoux, perhaps intrigued by its vaguely Biblical consonance, obviously attributes to it a completely different and symbolical meaning.

Is the Abalstitiel the symbol of a search for the Ideal? Is he actually an Angel? Or perhaps the personification of the Eternal? Or simply the spirit of withdrawal from reality? He may represent any of these possibilities, and he may even represent them all at the same time. Neither Edmée — nor Giraudoux — ever gave any precise information about his nature, and the mystery surrounding his personality enhances its poetic appeal.

Although Giraudoux, in the first part of his life, loved reality in spite of its incoherences and blemishes, he later came to think that "existence is a terrible degradation"[41] and experienced a feeling of "nausea"[42] at the very idea of creation. More and more, as he advanced in age, he came to identify the ideal with a recoil from reality. These views received their full expression in *Pour Lucrèce,* but already in *Choix des Elues,* the "choice" of Edmée, the elect, is essentially to withdraw from the part of the real in which the circumstances have established her life. Furthermore, it is clearly apparent that her fugue was not prompted by a desire for thrill and adventures. Edmée, it is true, goes to Hollywood, but her life there is completely filled with her love for Claudie. Her fugue is not a flight from an unbearable situation; it is "an excursion into Paradise lost."[43]

Even an elect, however, cannot remain in that wonderful, ideal never-never land. Sooner or later, reality asserts itself. Because every choice implies an alternative, Edmée, after choosing to leave home, decides to return to New York. When she makes that new choice, "a hard choice,"[44] the Abalstitiel, that is to say, the essential, the eternal, the nonreality abandons her: "The Abalstitiel was no longer there. He was betraying her."[45] She was alone, face to face with the swarming of reality: "The universe was growing in profusion in the absence of the Abalstitiel. It was now possible to see what the universe actually is — a false appearance and a lie. But that the Eternal should be fickle, that is incomprehensible."[46]

Yet, the decision of the elect to return to the real is, in the long run, inevitable. Just as Suzanne, after spending five years in her unreal, blissful Pacific Paradise, had to go back to France and be welcomed there by the Controller of Weights and Measures, similarly, Edmée, after twelve years of fugue, returns to a solid, satisfying American turkey dinner.

The Abalstitiel, however, has not disappeared altogether. Claudie is also an elect. Edmée notices with dismay the "signs"[47] in her that she had perceived herself in the past. Claudie is safely and sensibly married. Claudie is a mother, a very happy mother. Yet she is often far away from the place where she is supposed to be: "'You must not be absent so long, Claudie.'—'Ah, yes?' She sat down. She turned her eyes toward her mother, not really to turn them toward her mother, but to turn them away from her husband, from her father, from her daughter.... Truly, the Abalstitiel was not wasting any time.... He was beginning with Claudie."[48]

The novels that Giraudoux composed after 1925 present characteristic traits that differ markedly from those of the preceding period. After the long phase of his youth, he had entered a more sedate and also more difficult age. The necessity of pursuing a career, with all the troubles and tribulations that it entailed for him, the obligations and cares he had assumed as head of a family, closed on him and made him increasingly conscious of reality. Thus many of his new works are based on a strong and consistent presentation of facts that were known to him at first hand.

At the same time, for reasons obviously connected with personal experiences, studies of abnormal mental cases occupy an increasingly large part of his novels. Among them, the problem of the fugue recurs more and more insistently. Both concrete facts and explorations of troubled states of mind offer a dramatic interest and engross the interest of the reader whenever they are introduced. They are not, however, presented in continuous, uninterrupted succession, but divided into separate episodes.

Intermingled with these episodes, runs a more or less imaginary story, often a love story. The incidents of that story are often told without much preamble and indeed justification. The reader is frequently confronted with actions and ideas for which no explanation is given. Here the typical free and fanciful imagination of Giraudoux finds a rich and fertile field. Yet his imagination, although still infinitely subtle and delicate, no longer possesses the airy lightness that made some of his early works resemble beautiful, poetic dreams. Although remaining essentially poetic, Giraudoux's vision was turning more and more toward the deeper dramatic aspects of human existence.

*The essence of the theater is to bring reality
into the realm of the unreal.[1]*
Jean Giraudoux

✣IV✣
Giraudoux's Theater

Giraudoux became a dramatist by chance, almost by accident.
In 1927, the actor-producer Louis Jouvet, whom he knew only
slightly, asked him if he could give him a short play based on
Siegfried et le Limousin. He offered to present it at the Comédie des
Champs-Elysées, of which he had recently become the director.
As Suzanne Giraudoux said: "What a surprise for both of us
his success at the theater! He had been asked to compose one
short act. He wrote three and that was *Siegfried.*"[2]

Jouvet was to play an extremely important part in the development of Giraudoux's career as a dramatist. Giraudoux found in
him not only a perfect interpreter for his leading masculine roles,
but also and above all a man who, artistically, was in complete
harmony with him. There was in Jouvet a mixture of incisive
subtlety, pointed irony, poetic intuition, dreaminess, and strong
evocative power that corresponded almost miraculously to the
complex blend of characteristic traits in Giraudoux himself.

Jouvet had started his career as stage manager and assistant
to Jacques Copeau who, before World War I, had begun a thorough renovation of French theatrical art in his experimental
Théâtre du Vieux Colombier. After the war, in 1921, Jouvet had

left the Vieux Colombier and had struck out for himself in the teeming theatrical world of Paris. Soon he was counted among the outstanding actor-producers of the capital.

As an actor, Jouvet possessed an amazing interpretative flexibility, a remarkable understanding of the parts he took, and perhaps most important, an inner fire that sometimes exploded into vehemence but that, usually kept under control, imparted a vibrant, lyrical quality to his acting. As a producer-director, he was utterly indifferent to the financial returns of the plays he staged. His only goal was to attain the highest degree of perfection in an art that was the very raison d'être of his whole life.

His enthusiasm for the theater was an inspiration for all the actors and actresses who worked with him. Among the actresses who were his partners in the interpretation of Giraudoux's plays, first Valentine Tessier and later Madeleine Ozeray long remained for the Parisian public the incarnations of Giraudoux's poetic heroines. They also strongly influenced Giraudoux's conception of these heroines, because he constantly bore in mind the essential traits of their personalities when he created the characters that they would represent.

Jouvet had an unusual flair for discovering new dramatic authors of high quality and for guessing the type of subject that would appeal to a sophisticated Parisian audience. In 1927, he sensed that a play dealing with Franco-German relations would call forth a vivid, perhaps passionate response in the general public. By that time, the policy of reconciliation between Germany and France initiated by Briand had forcibly drawn the French people's attention to certain crucial aspects of the multiple problems facing the two nations. Although in 1922, when *Siegfried et le Limousin* was published, the question of the similarities and differences between the Germans and the French seemed to have hardly more than an academic interest, the same question had become a subject of burning actuality in 1927.

Giraudoux himself had already toyed with the idea of putting *Siegfried et le Limousin* on the stage. In 1924, when he was asked to contribute to a volume of articles to be published in honor of Charles Andler, he dramatized a scene taken from his old novel, under the title "Première Scène d'une adaptation théâtrale de Siegfried et le Limousin."[3] Later, he undertook to recast the whole of *Siegfried et le Limousin* as a play. For that purpose, he composed a series of successive and tentative versions, the last of which was published after his death under the title *Siegfried von Kleist*.

After Jouvet's request, he set himself again to work and shortly afterward submitted his new manuscript to Jouvet himself and also to the well-known critic Benjamin Crémieux. He probably communicated to them as well at least parts of his earlier versions. Both Jouvet and Crémieux advised him to revise his text drastically. The play he had submitted was overloaded with long, rambling talks that no audience could possibly have followed. A dramatization and a condensation of the whole work was imperative.

Giraudoux was wise enough to abide by the suggestions made by Crémieux and Jouvet. The extent of Jouvet's contribution to the final text is not known, but it must have been a considerable one. Jouvet himself said: "I met Jean Giraudoux and it was a great joy for me to be the first to put his plays on the stage, but he alone could have told you how much the work we did together has helped him."[4]

Jouvet and Giraudoux never actually "discussed" any part of that play or, for that matter, any other play that Giraudoux subsequently composed. Jouvet tended to be very frank in the expression of his views. Giraudoux always remained elusive, evasive, and withdrawn. No real confrontation of their opinions ever took place under any circumstance. Giraudoux, however, would always lend an ear to Jouvet's comments: "Giraudoux was very secretive and silent. But he knew admirably how to listen."[5]

Giraudoux never openly questioned the validity of the objections or suggestions made by a man like Jouvet, who had a thorough knowledge of theatrical technique. He did not accept them uncritically either. He would turn them over in his mind and then, more often than not, he would take in full account the remarks that had been made to him.

The first result of that peculiar form of collaboration was a play, *Siegfried,* which was quite unlike the novel that had been published six years earlier and which was also completely unlike the other plays that he was to write subsequently. *Siegfried* corresponds almost exactly to what the French call "a well-made play." It has a clear, logical structure, a consistent and well-developed plot, an interesting general theme, a few strongly characterized dramatis personae, a crucial climactic scene, and, to cap it all, a satisfying ending that rounds off a not too complicated situation or problem. Those qualities, which are all present in *Siegfried,* contributed greatly to its instantaneous success with the French public.

Siegfried was presented for the first time at the Comédie des Champs-Elysées on May 3, 1928. The general subject of the play closely follows the pattern set by the novel, but important cuts have been made in the development of the plot and even more important changes have been made in the nature of the characters. Limousin, which had played a decisive part in Siegfried's moral reversion to France, disappeared altogether. The emotional attraction that that little province had exerted on Giraudoux himself justified its place in a semiautobiographical tale, but Limousin itself presented no special interest for the general public.

Further, the question raised in the novel about the possibility of a combination of the complementary forms of thought of the Germans and the French became the object of only cursory remarks in the play. Finally the wistful, nostalgic admiration that Giraudoux had repeatedly expressed in *Siegfried et le Limousin* for the old Germany of the Holy Roman Empire was reduced in the play to a rather short tirade by Zelten.

Three new secondary characters were introduced, apparently for comic relief when the situation threatens to become too serious or tense. Hippolyte Amable Robineau is a likable and slightly ridiculous French professor who is engaged in writing a doctoral thesis on the dental consonants in the various German dialects. He replaces to a certain extent the narrator of the story in the novel, and he has a few traits of Giraudoux, being called Hippolyte like Giraudoux himself. He resembles a gentle caricature of Giraudoux as he humorously believed he would have become if he had decided to pursue a university career.

General Jacques de Fontgeloy is the descendant of one of those Protestant noblemen who were driven out of France by Louis XIV and established themselves in Germany. He is thoroughly German but retains intense feelings toward his country of origin.

Thus Giraudoux, after showing a university man comically engrossed in the useless minutiae of erudition, suggests that the military man has an extremely limited mental horizon.

The portrait of the Corsican customs officer Pietri is similarly drawn in an amusing vein. With petty meticulousness he applies the petty regulations that give a sense of power to the petty officialdom of France. He is totally harmless and good-natured, however, and he dreams only of the time when he will be able to retire with a government pension.

The three main protagonists of the novel have undergone radical transformations. Zelten has become to a large extent Giraudoux's own mouthpiece. He believes that the deep and true vocation of Germany is to be a great poetic country and that every attempt to drive her toward an industrial, materialistic expansion is contrary to her nature and will only warp, damage, and perhaps destroy her soul. With that ideal in mind, he has entered active politics. As he puts it himself: "I have made the last effort to prevent Germany from becoming Big Business Co., Inc."[6]

He opposes Siegfried, and particularly Siegfried's influence on the German Constitution, because Siegfried has succeeded, at least temporarily, in making the Germans think logically instead of poetically. He explains to Eva: "To impose on Germany a Constitution elaborated by your pupil is like compelling the dragon of Siegfried—the real Siegfried—to swallow an alarm clock in order to teach him how to tell the time."[7]

Geneviève Prat had played only a small part in *Siegfried et le Limousin*. In the novel she had arrived in Germany for no definite reason. Her death had not had any particular effect on the plot. She was Zelten's divorced wife and it was hinted that she had a most questionable past. In the play, she becomes a deeply sensitive and faithful young woman. She has had no connection of any kind with Zelten, but she and Forestier have been lovers for two years. They were separated by the war, but seven years after their separation, Geneviève is still hankering after her fiancé. She rushes to Germany at the mere hint that he might still be alive. The emotions that she goes through when she discovers that Siegfried is indeed Jacques Forestier are among the most potent interests of the drama.

The Siegfried of the novel was to a large extent an abstraction in which French and German traits of character mingled harmoniously. In the play, Siegfried is a tormented man, mainly because he feels a huge empty gap in his past life. His recollections do not run farther back than seven years, and he does not possess memories of childhood or youth upon which his personality can lean. Later, when he realizes that he is French, he also realizes that he cannot expel from his mind overnight the seven years of his association with the tremendously rich German culture. Although he returns to France, he carries with him a heavy burden of uncertainty and anguish.

When the play begins, Zelten is one of the main leaders of a revolutionary party that plans to take power to rehabilitate the true soul of Germany. Siegfried is one of his most dangerous opponents. Zelten, suspecting that Siegfried is really French, sends a telegram to Geneviève, who has known Forestier in the past and will presumably be able to bring him back to France, thus ridding Zelten of one of his most embarrassing political adversaries.

Geneviève arrives accompanied by Robineau and recognizes Siegfried at once. Posing as a French-Canadian, she is accepted as a teacher of French by Siegfried. Siegfried discovers the hoax, however, and begins to have doubts about her and about himself as well. While he is growing slowly and painfully aware of his real identity, the attempted political coup of Zelten and his friends fails. That failure is not so much due to the influence of Siegfried as to the intervention of Big Business groups from America and from England, which secretly exert strong pressure on Berlin in order to eliminate the idealist Zelten and keep Germany a great economic power in Europe.

Siegfried's personal problem remains. It is solved in a dramatic scene between Geneviève and Eva. Eva had been an essential character in the novel. In the play, she is reduced to a subordinate and almost symbolic role. She embodies with dignity everything that is noble and fine in Germany, and she also embodies duty. Geneviève, on the other hand, embodies France —and truth. Siegfried must not leave Germany, says Eva, because Germany is a great country; but he must also stay because it is his duty to respond to the expectations of sixty million people who have placed in him their trust and their hope.

Geneviève declines to follow Eva in her first argument: "The greatness of Germany, the greatness of France, that is undoubtedly a beautiful subject for antitheses and contrasts."[8] The truth is that Forestier is French and belongs to France. Geneviève chooses as a humble symbol of the ties that bind him indissolubly to his native soil his dog, a pathetic, ridiculous poodle that is still waiting for his master's return.

The last act takes place in a railroad station at the Franco-German border. The station is divided into two sections. The German part is clean, hygienic, modern, and equipped with central heating. The French section is untidy, dusty, stuffy, with a ramshackle stove at the side of which Pietri reads his newspaper. Soon Siegfried-Forestier arrives. He has made up his mind. He is on his way to France. The French reality, however, does not purely and simply displace the German reality in his mind: "Siegfried and Forestier," he himself says, "will live side by side. I shall try to carry honorably the two names and the two destinies that were given me by chance. . . . Perhaps, before long, that memory which still eludes me, those two countries that I have found and lost, that lack of consciousness and that consciousness which give me now both pain and joy will form a logical whole and provide me with a simple existence."[9]

Soon afterward, Geneviève joins him. She also has been torn asunder between a past she had believed dead and a present situation she had never anticipated: "A past? Ah, Jacques, do not try to find one for us. Haven't we a brand-new one? It is only three days old, but lucky are those who possess a past that is quite new. . . . It is in that past that all my thoughts will find now their joy and their sadness."[10]

The moral trials of Siegfried and Geneviève form the main human interest of Giraudoux's play. Siegfried has been bereft of his original past. When he first discovers faint traces of his real old self, he realizes that he has already been transformed into another completely different man. The recuperation of his previous personality and its integration into his new forms of being will eventually entail painful and protracted travail. At the end, however, the play suggests that eventually a blend of the various components of Siegfried's shattered experience may be affected harmoniously.

The case of Geneviève Prat follows an almost parallel pattern.

Geneviève is a deeply loving woman who has lost long ago the object of her love. Since that time she has led an empty, meaningless existence. When Zelten's telegrams bring her a faint ray of hope that Jacques may be found again, she goes to Germany and finds Jacques indeed, but a Jacques who is a stranger. She will have to travel a long and strenuous road before she can re-create a warm and intimate human relationship between them.

The contrapuntal development of those two related, unusual cases is accompanied throughout the play by a number of remarks and aphorisms about the German character. These remarks, made by Zelten, Siegfried, or Robineau, are sometimes debatable, but they are always challenging and often profoundly significant. They contributed in no small measure to the success of the play in 1928, and they remain to this day an element of rich interest and value.

The element that any admirer of Giraudoux's art will miss in that play is a certain magic atmosphere of extravaganza and fun. He will miss also the mist of dreamy and poetic fantasy that wraps itself in light and graceful volutes around most of Giraudoux's other works. Where, too, are the iridescent bubbles of paradox and wit that so often rise from Giraudoux's whimsical pen? Evidently they were all pricked down by the sober critic Crémieux and by the only too judicious Jouvet. Thanks to their advice, Giraudoux constructed a solid and successful play, following the tried and true rules of the stage — but lacking the glittering, imaginative effulgence that constitutes perhaps the essential of Giraudoux's unique enchantment and charm.

After the spectacular success of *Siegfried,* Giraudoux made use of some parts of the earlier versions of the play that he had temporarily discarded. In 1928 he published under the title *Divertissement de Siegfried* the beginning of the third act of *Siegfried von Kleist.* In 1930 he revised that *Divertissement* and reissued it as *Fugues sur Siegfried.* In the first part of *Fugues sur Siegfried,* Zelten is seen attempting to make a rather ludicrous *Putsch* and being proclaimed Regent. But he receives only the support of the actors of the Passion Play of Oberammergau. In the second part, called *Lamento,* Siegfried bemoans the fate of a man without past. In 1935, Giraudoux published the fourth act of *Siegfried von Kleist* with the title *Fin de Siegfried.*

In this work Siegfried-Forestier, having found out that he is not German, takes refuge in the castle of the Prince of Saxe-Altdorf at Nymphenburg near Munich. There he is the victim of a patriotic German secret society that is presumably anxious to spare the Fatherland the shock of discovering that the man long considered the savior of Germany was actually French. He is shot and the bullet hits him precisely in the old war wound that had been the cause of his amnesia. The new traumatism liberates, as it were, all the memories of France that come crowding back during his last moments. None of those publications adds much to the glory of Giraudoux as a dramatist.

The qualities of humor, light satire, paradox, and parody lacking in *Siegfried* abound in Giraudoux's next play, *Amphitryon 38*. This time, Giraudoux drew his inspiration from a well-known Greek legend. Jupiter, having fallen in love with Alcmena, the chaste and beautiful wife of the Theban general Amphitryon, and despairing of overcoming her virtue with the ordinary wiles of a seducer, took on the semblance of Amphitryon and visited her while her husband was campaigning against the enemy. Some time afterward, the infant Hercules was born.

Many French dramatists, including Molière, have been attracted by that curious legend, and numerous plays — thirty-seven at least — have been written on the same theme, so much so that any new and original treatment of the subject seemed well nigh impossible. By composing a "thirty-eighth" *Amphitryon,* Giraudoux had to depart radically from the hackneyed versions of the legend if he was to achieve a work of any interest at all. As a matter of fact, Giraudoux modified only slightly the traditional framework of the story, but he succeeded in infusing into it a rich and warm modern substance.

In *Amphitryon 38,* Jupiter arrives in Thebes accompanied by the god Mercury and assumes Amphitryon's appearance at once. In this form he is welcomed by the general's unsuspecting wife, and he enjoys all the privileges and pleasures of a husband. Jupiter, however, would like to be loved for himself. The following morning, he tries to give Alcmena hints about his divine nature. The thoroughly human Alcmena disappointingly leads the conversation back into purely human channels. Complications set in when Mercury spreads the news of Jupiter's tryst with

Alcmena, as he always does whenever the supreme god favors a mortal woman with his company. The Thebans are naturally very proud of the honor thus bestowed on their city in the person of Alcmena. Rumors of that strange turn of events soon reach Alcmena herself, who is thoroughly puzzled and worried.

She is even more puzzled and worried when Mercury tries to persuade her to welcome Jupiter the next night with full knowledge of his divinity. A virtuous woman may easily reject the improper propositions of a human suitor, but to spurn a god openly might prove very dangerous. Just then, Alcmena is visited by the Queen of Sparta, Leda, who, as everyone knows, had once become very closely acquainted with Jupiter when the god had taken on, for the occasion, the elegant shape of a swan. Leda had evidently retained a not at all unpleasant memory of that encounter. Alcmena now asks her if she would take her place — secretly of course — just for one night in her darkened bedroom: "Put on my veils, spray yourself with my perfume. Jupiter will be taken in and he will lose nothing thereby."[11]

Thereupon Amphitryon, the true Amphitryon, returns unexpectedly from war, after a rapid and brilliant victory. He is radiant with pride and glowing with joy — with joy at the prospect of being soon alone with Alcmena again. He is so radiant, however, and he glows so much that Alcmena is persuaded that he is Jupiter in disguise. When Amphitryon wants to show his wife the depth of his love, she manages quietly and cunningly to direct him to the dark bedroom where Leda is waiting — for Jupiter.

The following day, Alcmena and Jupiter have a long talk together. Jupiter renews his suit; but Alcmena tells him that she would rather die than deceive her husband, and she offers Jupiter — her friendship. Jupiter is moved by this extraordinary case of feminine constancy and conjugal fidelity. Jupiter not only gives her up freely, but also grants her a last wish. Alcmena says to him: "I am ready to believe that everything that took place today was correct and fair; still I sense something shady that oppresses me, and I am not a woman who can stand to have even one ambiguous day in her life. . . . Please give my husband and myself the power to forget what happened today."[12] Jupiter gives her the desired oblivion with a kiss and hands her back "intact"[13] to Amphitryon.

Amphitryon 38 may be considered as being in part a bedroom farce, in part a comedy of errors, and also a game of mistaken identities. It is also and mainly the presentation of a captivating character. Alcmena is the center, almost the pivot of the play. Giraudoux, by making her a modern, living woman instead of a conventional stale legendary figure, succeeded in instilling into the statuesque, rigid lines of the antique the intensity and richness of actual life. Anachronisms of expression, allusions to contemporary events or facts, references to modern ideas and feelings are freely used to create an atmosphere of actuality that constitutes the most striking feature of the play. These elements, however, are presented so discreetly that they never seem incongruous. Still less do they degenerate into offensive realism.

With marvelous virtuosity and ingenuity, Giraudoux hovers between the stately ideal of classical antiquity, with its regular beauty, its poetic charm, its mythical remoteness, and the reality of human experience packed with emotion, humor, and laughter. He passes easily from one to the other, hinting at affinities, alluding to resemblances, sometimes almost playfully letting his imagination soar for a while and then, without effort, coming back to earth again. Thus modern reality becomes animated and poetic under the influence of the old ideal, and abstract classical forms are filled with a new and throbbing life.

Alcmena may be considered the embodiment of the perfect harmonious conjunction of the ideal and reality. On the one hand, she is deeply attached to the high principles that Giraudoux described as constituting "the dignity of mankind."[14] She is unconditionally faithful to her marital vows, and Jupiter believes her when she says that she would sooner be dead than fail in her duties toward her husband: "There is something in her that is immune to attack and that must be the infinite for human beings."[15]

This superior moral element, however, is not for her a theoretical and external imperative. Alcmena's unique spiritual achievement resides precisely in her ability to blend the sublime with the real. She transmutes without effort the supreme laws of ethics into plain, practical human qualities: "Her life is a prism where the moral heritage common to gods and men—courage, love, passion—is changed into qualities that are purely human, constancy, sweetness, devotion."[16]

Alcmena can simultaneously remain at a high level of feminine virtue and also move with pleasure and ease in the familiar domain of everyday reality. She gleefully accepts the totality of the human experience on earth. She says herself: "I am living in an atmosphere as earthly as can be."[17] This intimate contact with all that is human constitutes her main charm. Leda says to her: "What he [Jupiter] loves in you ... is your humanity; what is interesting with you is to know you as a human being."[18] When she is offered immortality by Jupiter as a bribe for her acquiescence to his desires, she refuses and replies: "To become immortal is to become a traitor for a human."[19]

Even though Alcmena represents the exceptional solution to a problem that has been present in Giraudoux's mind throughout his life — the blending of the ideal and reality — she appears in no way an artificial stage creation. Her genuine, lofty sense of duty imparts to her a delicate poetic aura, while her close contact with the real lends her the most convincing accents of truth. Thus she possesses at the same time an almost airy transparence and a reassuring human density. She is much more mellow and self-assured than the tremulous and unsettled *jeunes filles* found in Giraudoux's works.

Always cheerful, resourceful and quick-witted, when she is placed in a situation that seems to offer no honorable issue, she quickly resorts, in all honesty, to the usual womanly weapons of guile and trickery. Furthermore, at the end of the play, when she has every reason to believe that she has succeeded in freeing herself from the entanglements in which she had found herself against her will, she suddenly uncovers in herself the baffling mixture of a sincere desire to follow the right path and of the illogical, ambiguous feelings that are not among the least delightful allurements of the eternal feminine. She says then to Jupiter: "Jupiter, now that you are my friend, speak to me frankly. Are you quite sure that you have never been my lover? ... You have given me up.... My knowledge of men tends to make me believe that it was because you already had what you wanted.... Are you quite sure ... that you have never taken the form of Amphitryon?" — "Quite sure." — "Well then it shows that you had not a very great love for me. Of course, I would never have done it again; but to sleep once with Jupiter, that would have been quite a memory for a little woman like me to have."[20]

The theme of the strange tension created in a woman's heart by the coexistence of an innate urge to deceive her husband and of a sincere resolve to remain a model of conjugal fidelity appears here for the first time in Giraudoux's work. The idea that a wife can find release from that tension by deceiving her husband—with himself—is rejected by Alcmena but only with mild disapproval: "It is the mark of a poor education to deceive one's own husband, even with himself."[21]

Alcmena, being a well-brought-up young woman, would not deliberately be guilty of such a breach of good manners. Yet, thanks to a strange twist of mythological lore, she committed that very faux pas in the arms of Amphitryon-Jupiter. In subsequent works, Giraudoux came back repeatedly to that purely imaginary form of conjugal infidelity. Eventually, it became quite an important element in his general views on marriage and love.

Amphitryon 38 was presented for the first time at the Comédie des Champs-Elysées on November 8, 1929, and proved to be at once a great success. The next play that Giraudoux wrote, *Judith,* was performed two years later on November 4, 1931, and was, according to a colloquial French expression, *un four noir,* a total failure. The two plays hardly seem to have come from the same pen. *Amphitryon 38* had been composed during one of the happiest periods of Giraudoux's life; *Judith* appeared at the beginning of his great moral crisis. Giraudoux, moreover, steeped in Greco-Roman culture, felt at ease in a subject drawn from ancient mythology.

The reasons for his choice of a biblical theme are not altogether clear. He certainly was not a devout Christian. As noted, however, in 1931 he was a member of the Committee on Evaluation of the Allied War Damages in Turkey, and he was constantly in contact there with persons from the Middle East. In *Eglantine* he had taken a Jewish banker, Emmanuel Moïse, as a typical representative of the mentality of the people living in that region. He may have felt challenged by the idea of putting on the stage members of the human group in which he was evidently taking a personal interest.

Although treating a biblical subject, he made no attempt in his play to re-create a biblical atmosphere. Faithful to his custom of revitalizing ancient myths and legends by injecting in them elements of the modern world, he filled his play, not with old Hebrews, at least as we can imagine them, but with Jewish people, as we can see them around us. He even insisted on having the leading parts of the play given to Jewish actors and actresses; and the walk-on parts were similarly taken mostly by Jewish performers. Jouvet assumed the direction of the play, but neither he nor any of the regular members of his troupe acted in *Judith*, which was presented at the Théâtre Pigalle and not at Jouvet's own Comédie des Champs-Elysées.

The Book of Judith is considered apocryphal by the Jews and the Protestants, but it is accepted as deuterocanonical by the Roman Catholic and Orthodox churches.[22] In this book Judith is devoutly religious, profoundly virtuous, unquestioningly chaste, and utterly modest in her behavior. She is the symbol of the figure that, in the eyes of the ancient Hebrews, a Jewish woman should be. In fact, her name, Judith—in Hebrew Jehudith—means "the Jewess" par excellence.

Judith lived in the city of Bethulia, which is not mentioned anywhere else in the Bible. After the death of her husband, Manasses, she spent three and a half years in prayer, seclusion, and mourning, although she was still very young, extremely beautiful and wealthy. At that time, the Assyrian King Nebuchadnezzar sent a powerful army under the command of his best general Holofernes to conquer the land of the Syrians and the Jews. Although Bethulia offered strong resistance to the invaders, Holofernes managed to cut an aqueduct bringing water to the beleaguered city, and the inhabitants of Bethulia, nearly perishing from thirst, were about to surrender.

Then Judith, discarding her drab garments, dressed as richly and seductively as she could and went stealthily to the Assyrian camp, accompanied only by a maidservant who carried food prepared according to Jewish ritual. Judith told the Assyrian sentries that she had important information to give to Holofernes. The latter, struck at once by her beauty, received her courteously.

To win his confidence, Judith told him that the Bethulians were so hungry that they were ready to eat the food consecrated to Jehovah. This would undoubtedly bring Jehovah's wrath upon them, and the city would inevitably fall very soon. Holofernes, delighted to hear such news, treated her very kindly. He allowed her to remain unmolested in the Assyrian camp, and even gave her permission to leave the camp every morning so that she could perform her ablutions in a spring at a certain distance in the direction of the city.

At the same time, however, he lusted after her, and four days later gave a great banquet in her honor, hoping to find an opportunity to gratify his impure desires. The guests at the banquet became grossly inebriated, and Holofernes drank "more than in any other day of his life." After the banquet was over, when Judith was taken by a eunuch to Holofernes' room, she found him lying prostrate in a drunken stupor.

Taking the general's own sword, she cut off his head, put it in the bag that had contained her food and, after crossing the Assyrian lines, as she did every morning, she returned to Bethulia. The Jews then made a sortie and easily routed the Assyrian soldiers who had been utterly demoralized by the news of their general's death. Judith lived afterward in great dignity to a very old age, surrounded by universal gratitude, admiration, and respect.

Giraudoux completely transformed Judith's character and action. He turned her from a pious and respectable widow into a pert damsel of twenty, with extremely modern and broadminded ideas. Giraudoux's Judith has gone to college[23] and led the gay, irresponsible life of a rich, pretty, and popular girl. She is still technically a virgin—although perhaps a little shopworn: "She is a virgin. No other virginity has been more desired and more closely brushed against. Still, it is a virginity. She even has a certificate of the High Priest about it."[24]

No mention is made of her parents, who are presumably dead. Her nearest relative is her uncle Joseph, a rich and cynical banker who has very little influence on his niece. Independent of mind, self-centered, and self-willed, Judith is neither very patriotic nor very religious. One can sense in her, however, the vague feeling of dissatisfaction that is not uncommon among modern youngsters who have been brought up in the midst of too much affluence and comfort.

At the beginning of the first act, the besieged city is buzzing with strange rumors: Judith must go and see Holofernes; Judith alone can save Bethulia; Judith can save Bethulia by killing Holofernes. Who or what is the source of these rumors? Have they been planted deliberately by scheming rabbis? Or are they the expression of Jehovah's superior will? Or are they merely, as Joseph dares suggest, the symptoms of a case of "collective hysteria"?[25]

At any rate, Judith is certainly not keen on undertaking that sort of mission, but when one of her boy friends, Jean, reveals to her that the military situation of the Jews is desperate, she decides to go. The prostitute Suzanne, who strikingly resembles Judith and admires her devotedly, offers to go to the Assyrian camp in her stead. Judith refuses and explains at least in part the reason for her sacrifice: "In the solitude of my nights and in the agitation of my days, I have given myself that mission for a long time already."[26] Does she mean that, tired of her futile existence, she wanted to give it a worthwhile purpose? Perhaps.

The next act takes place in Holofernes' camp. In Giraudoux's play Holofernes is a king and not simply a general. We are told that the camp is overrun with Jewish prostitutes who come there from Bethulia to ply their trade. They are received with crude friendliness by the Assyrian soldiers because soldiers are always in need of women. Among them is the procuress Sarah, who knows that Judith is going to arrive soon.

Sarah hates Judith, because the girl had once had her thrown out of Judith's house. She induces a few Assyrian officers to play a coarse joke on Judith. When Judith asks to speak to Holofernes, she is presented to an invert, Egon, clad in the royal robes. A grotesque scene ensues. Judith submits to Egon's unappetizing kiss. Then she is told of her ridiculous mistake and further cruelly taunted and harried by the Assyrian officers. In her distress, Judith cries for help — from Holofernes.

Holofernes drives Judith's tormentors away and begins a lofty conversation about — the existence of God. Holofernes reveals himself as not at all a brutal barbarian but a generous, vital, self-reliant, truly magnificent man. The conversation is interrupted by Suzanne, who is evidently bent on replacing Judith in her mission. Judith understands then that Suzanne has a lesbian love for her. Furthermore, she also understands then that the other women who have shown her affection in the past had likewise abnormal desires toward her. Completely overcome with disgust and shame, she gives herself to the thoroughly virile Holofernes.

In the third act, at first Jean and the persistent Suzanne arrive stealthily in Holofernes' tent to kill him. They discover that Judith has already done the deed. Soon a crowd of Jews flocks into the tent, and Judith receives a brief explanation of their presence there: "Holofernes' allies are rebelling. Jean is walking through their camp showing them the head of Holofernes, whom you have killed. The troops that were loyal to him are running away."[27]

All praise to heaven the holy hatred that made Judith destroy the enemy of Israel. Hatred? Not at all! Judith has killed him out of love.[28] General stupefaction and dismay. The Chief Rabbi, Joachim, takes Judith aside and tells her that the Jews absolutely need to believe that she has killed Holofernes under the inspiration of God. Judith denies this obstinately: "Not once since yesterday have I felt His presence or His pressure."[29] Joachim insists: "Can you deny that a miracle has taken place through you?" "The miracle," answers Judith, "has come out of a mass of things that were vile, low, and abominable."[30]

Eventually, however, Judith allows herself to be persuaded to play the part that the Jewish people expect from her. She is expected to affirm that "she killed the enemy of God, as God prescribed it, with hatred."[31] Thus she will provide the Jews with the "truth"[32] they require. Thus also, she will herself be able to spend the rest of her life in the midst of admiration, veneration, and glory.

Strangely enough, the successful advocate of that worldly wisdom is an Assyrian bodyguard of Holofernes who is supposed to be "dead drunk" and whose voice expresses perhaps the will of God, perhaps only the advice of common sense. This drunken bodyguard sometimes lapses into unaccountable statements of the events that have actually taken place. Having seen Judith the prey to a frenzy of passion in Holofernes' bed, he calls her "Judith the whore." Thereupon Judith says to the Chief Rabbi: "Perhaps it would be better to have him killed, Joachim." To which Joachim answers: "We will kill him all right." The play ends abruptly with Judith firmly stating: "Judith the saint is ready."[33]

When the play was performed for the first time, the public

and the critics were nonplussed by Judith's behavior. The true motivation of her acts, however, can be readily understood in the context of the development of Giraudoux's general ideas. Giraudoux wrote *Judith* at the time of his great middle-of-life crisis, that is to say, at a time when he was beginning to consider reality—which he had formerly loved—as repulsive, odious, and incompatible with the ideal.

Judith is an "elect"[34] who had led an artificial life of frivolity and pleasure. Tragic circumstances beyond her control bring her face to face with the most sordid aspects of reality. Giraudoux chose homosexuality as a symbol of those sordid aspects. Although modern generations have adopted an attitude of relative tolerance and even sometimes of broad permissiveness to that idiosyncrasy, the generation to which Giraudoux belonged usually considered it a sort of moral leprosy.

This attitude explains Judith's revulsion and her sense of utter degradation simply because Egon, an invert, has given her a kiss: "Egon has touched me. I am not worthy of you any more. . . . I am nothing but shame. I am burning with shame. The lips of Egon, I feel them imprinted in white on that fire."[35] After Judith has become aware of the special emotion that her person arouses in Suzanne, the latter says to Holofernes: "Do not believe that you have seduced that woman. It is not because she finds you handsome and powerful that she gives herself to you. It is out of disgust toward life."[36] It is indeed disgust toward life—a disgust caused by the revelation, through homosexuality, that reality is abject—which throws Judith in Holofernes' arms.

Then, to her amazement and delight, she finds in Holofernes' love the supreme ideal bliss that she had sought in vain in all her years of futile amusement and social vanity. After reaching a summit of felicity and perfect rapture, however, after soaring into the sublime ethereal world that was opened to her by the total fulfillment of love, she finds herself just a woman in bed, with a man, just a man, asleep by her side. The very sight of his body—an all too human, average masculine body—makes her realize with a sickening shock that the ideal realm that has just been revealed to her will turn into the real world, with everything it entails that is low and dirty: "Yes, for the first time I awoke at dawn near another human being. . . . What an abominable thing it was. . . . A dubious and suspicious future was ready to attack the memory of moments that had been sheer wonder. I would have to get up and start living standing, after experiencing a feeling of eternity lying down."[37] Inevitably the real would destroy the ideal. Thus to save the ideal, she destroys the real. To keep her perfect love intact, she stabs Holofernes. She kills for love.

She learns very rapidly, however, that she could not remain indefinitely in that empyrean loftiness of absolute ideal perfection. Insistently, imperiously, the real world around her requests her to use good judgment, to speak and act in a sensible and practical manner—that is to say, she will have to conform, she will have to pretend, she will have to lie, she will have to accept the common lot of common humanity. Just as Suzanne left the Pacific and returned to the Controller of Weights and Measures, just as Edmée had to give up the Abalstitiel and return to the boredom of a middle-class New York home, so Judith had to deny and repudiate her ideal love in order to be comfortably enshrined in the mock legend that is part of the fraudulent reality in the midst of which all human beings live.

The variations of mood found in the character of Judith are perfectly intelligible for anyone conversant with Giraudoux's theories about reality and ideal, but they were not readily followed by the uninitiated general public. Moreover, the two great questions of the influence of God on human actions and of the characteristic traits of the Jewish people—which might have provided a background of high interest to the development of Judith's individual case—are treated only in a superficial manner.

Allusions to the power of God abound in the play, but they remain often ambiguous and vague. The remarks about the Jewish people are likewise numerous. As a rule they are neither derogatory nor laudatory but merely banal and commonplace. The dialogues also lack the brilliance, the sparkle, and the humor generally found in Giraudoux's works. On the whole, *Judith* was considered disappointing and boring. After a few performances before a yawning and dwindling public, the play had to be withdrawn. Exactly thirty years later, in November, 1961, it was revived by the talented actor-producer Jean-Louis Barrault at the Théâtre de France. Once more it failed.

The failure of *Judith* was soon compensated by the unqualified success of Giraudoux's next play, *Intermezzo*. That word was originally used in the sixteenth century in Italy to describe madrigals and other musical entertainments performed between the acts of a play. Later on, these entertainments themselves developed into short plays of a light nature, characterized by a fanciful plot, a great quickness of tempo and an elegance of tone that did not exclude a certain element of farce. Giraudoux first received his inspiration to write a similar sort of comedy from an old, unsigned picture that he owned, representing a group of Italian actors, with their typical picturesque costumes, who specialized in that type of play.

In *Intermezzo*, Isabelle, a young schoolteacher in a small town of Limousin, applies most unorthodox methods of pedagogy to the little girls entrusted to her care. Instead of stuffing them with the dry, conventional notions of the official program, she tries to awaken them to an ideal, optimistic, genuine appreciation of life, and she obtains an enthusiastic response.

She longs to educate the inhabitants of the little town in the same way. She wants to destroy some of their prejudices and create among them the harmonious order that, according to her idealistic views, ought to reign everywhere. Prompted by that noble intention, though forced to act secretly, she would send anonymous letters to various persons, not of course to disturb the peace of happy families but, for instance, to draw the attention of a husband to the virtues of his wife that otherwise he would certainly have overlooked.

Soon the atmosphere of the whole district is completely transformed by her mysterious influence. A supernatural power seems to exert a beneficial though most unusual action on all the happenings, small or great, of the region. When a lottery is drawn, the first prize is not won, as could be expected in this absurd world of ours, by a millionaire, but by a poor man who needs the money badly. Similarly, a motorcycle is won, not as usually before, by a person who could never use it, such as the Mother Superior of the Convent, but by a boy who coveted the thing eagerly. Further, even the persons who die in the town are not the youngest and the kindest, as a blind or stupid fate so often decreed in the past. Death seems to choose discerningly, selecting the oldest and wickedest individuals.

Public opinion is aroused by those occurences. The influence of Isabelle is strongly suspected, and soon a strange rumor spreads about the town. Isabelle, they say, is in communication with a Spirit. Indeed she is, but that Spirit is not frightening or horrible. To Isabelle he manifests himself as a handome, pale young man, draped in a romantic cape, friendly though elusive and remote. He represents all the dead, whom in her youthful, mystic, all-embracing love for the universe Isabelle would associate even with present-day life. He also represents the "ideal," abstract and pure, inaccessible and invisible to the vulgar crowd but revealing itself to an ardent and candid soul. In many respects, he seems to be a shadowy prefiguration of the Abalstitiel who was to appear some time later in *Choix des Elues.*

A pompous Inspector comes to investigate the fantastic rumors that are circulating. He claims to represent "Humanity," which he defines as "a superhuman undertaking ... which has as an object to isolate man and separate him from that ghastly mess that is the Cosmos."[38] Reaching a harmonious union with the Cosmos is precisely what Isabelle had attempted to do. The Inspector, after attending one of Isabelle's classes, suspends her immediately. He replaces her, at least temporarily, by the Controller of Weights and Measures. The Controller stands here, as he did in *Suzanne et le Pacifique,* for clear logic, common sense, and homely reality.

The Ghost, however, continues his manifestations in the neighborhood, and everything goes on in a supernaturally satisfactory manner in the little town. The Inspector then hires "executioners" to dispose of the Ghost. Thus do vulgar and practical-minded people always try to destroy what they cannot understand. The executioners ambush and shoot the Ghost; but the Ghost does not die, and only a "circle of burnt grass"[39] is found where his corpse is supposed to have been.

In the meantime, the Controller of Weights and Measures has fallen in love with Isabelle. He even goes to the length of proposing to her, but he does not wish to share her affection even if only with a Ghost. The Controller can offer the girl the full and warm reality of existence.

Then a sudden transformation, almost a mutation, takes place in Isabelle, as it does in every *jeune fille,* however poetic and dreamy, when she faces the solid prospect of marriage. The

Ghost realizes that he has lost her when she calls the Controller "dear Robert": "Am I wrong to do it?" — "You are right," the Ghost answers, "and I thank you for it. I was about to commit a great stupidity. I was about to commit a betrayal. . . . Fortunately you have committed it before I could do it." — "But what have I betrayed?"[40]

Isabelle has betrayed the Ideal, the world of dreams, in order to become fully human. Then the Ghost abandons her. When he finally vanishes, Isabelle faints away. The Controller calls for help and the Drugstore man — another representative of reality — arrives just in time. He organizes a joyous concert of all the happy noises of the little town, bugles, bells, the whispering of women, the singsong of the schoolgirls reciting their lessons.

Isabelle regains her senses when the words *velours* and *crêpe de Chine* reach her ears. The Ghost has been definitively routed and, as the Inspector puts it, the district is now "in perfect order."[41] Indeed a new lottery has been drawn, and this time the first prize has gone to a millionaire and the motorcycle to a man who has no legs. Naturally Isabelle will marry the Controller.

The fundamental ideas that run through most of Giraudoux's works can be easily followed in this play. Isabelle pursues the generous ideal of life as it should be lived. She combines two distinct forms of idealism as Giraudoux conceived them in the course of his moral evolution. First, she dreams of a life as Giraudoux himself dreamed it when he was at school, when he could not conceive why justice, order, and reason should not be the rule of this world. That ideal of classical logic is strangely commingled in Isabelle with an ideal of an entirely different nature: the ideal of the communion of man with the universe. She rebels against the human civilization represented by the Inspector, which has as an object to isolate man from the Cosmos: "Throughout my youth . . . I have obstinately refused all the appeals that were made to me, except those that were made by the world itself. What our teachers taught to my schoolmates or myself is a civilization of selfishness and politeness made for termites. . . ."

"But," answers the Controller, "you have been granted, the first of your class, your teaching diploma, Mademoiselle Isabelle.

You must have been taught what is human knowledge." —
"What is called human knowledge is at best a religion of man,
and it expresses only a frightful selfishness. Its dogma is to
make impossible or sterile any communication with anything but
the other humans. . . . With that stupid submission to prejudices,
what marvelous appeals have we not rejected at all levels of the
world? . . . I alone have dared to answer those appeals."[42]

The Ghost embodies — if such a word may be used in that
connection — the two different aspects of the Ideal pursued by
Isabelle. On the one hand, his influence introduces order, logic,
reason, and justice into otherwise chaotic human affairs. On
the other hand, he symbolizes the "invisible forces"[43] of the
universe, all the extra human elements of the Cosmos with which
the little schoolteacher has established a mystic union. The Controller represents reality — plain, simple, dense earthly reality,
the thousand small enjoyable trivialities of life.

Isabelle will indeed marry the Controller, but at the cost of
losing contact with the Ideal that had been revealed to her by
the Ghost. Like her sisters Suzanne, Juliette, Edmée, and even
Judith, after an entrancing excursion into "Paradise lost," Isabelle
must return to reality, to banal, flat reality. In *Intermezzo*, Giraudoux draws a not too rejoicing picture of what she has to expect
from her sensible marriage: "The pleasures taken at night and the
habit of taking those pleasures begin. And the craving for good
food begins. And also jealousy . . . and vengeance. And indifference also begins."[44] The Ghost has definitively disappeared from
Isabelle's life, but he is not "dead." He will appear, fifteen years
later,[45] to the daughters that Isabelle will have with the Controller
of Weights and Measures.

Giraudoux's next work was an adaptation of the play *The Constant Nymph* taken from Margaret Kennedy's novel. Giraudoux's
version of the play, called *Tessa, la Nymphe au cœur fidèle*, closely
follows the original. He added considerably to the piquancy of
the dialogue in French through his usual ready wit. Shortly afterward, he planned and even officially announced a new tragedy
on the subject of Brutus; but he abandoned that project without
explanation.

In 1935, the feeling of anguish pervading France in the wake of dramatic international events moved Giraudoux to compose one of his most poignant masterpieces, *La Guerre de Troie n'aura pas lieu*. The setting of the play is the city of Troy on the eve of the famous siege. Helen has just eloped with Paris; if she is not returned to her husband, Menelaus, the Greeks will make war on Troy. Hector, son of King Priam and the most valorous of all Trojan warriors, has returned victorious from another war. In the past, Hector has loved war; but now he has a deep horror of it and he wants to avoid at all cost a conflict with the Greeks, particularly for such a trivial reason as Helen's doubtful love for his brother Paris.

He finds the Trojans in a state of warlike frenzy. The poet Demodokos is fanning the flames of their patriotic fury against the Greeks: the surrender of Helen to her husband would be for Troy a nameless humiliation that the brave Trojans could not endure. Hector then tries to persuade Helen to go back to Greece on her own accord. Helen admits that it is not her love for Paris that keeps her in Troy, but she feels instinctively that she is not fated to go back.

Hector refuses to abandon his desperate fight for peace. He compels an authority on international law, Busiris, who had presented the case for war to reverse his conclusions completely. Nevertheless, the mood of the Trojans is still dangerously threatening and war appears imminent. A new hope of peace dawns when two Greek plenipotentiaries Oiax and Ulysses arrive to discuss the problem of Helen on a diplomatic level. Oiax is a character invented by Giraudoux, and he is not to be confused with two Homeric warriors having somewhat similar names, Great Ajax and Little Ajax, whose heroic deeds during the siege of Troy are recorded in the *Iliad*. Oiax is presented in Giraudoux's play as a brave but coarse soldier, with a limited intellect and always ready to engage in some low and vulgar brawl. Ulysses appears as the traditional legends have described him. He is shrewd, subtle, wily and more than a little cynical.

A long discussion takes place then between Ulysses and Hector, who though honest is prepared to make all the possible concessions and to tell all the lies required by diplomacy in order to avoid a ruinous, useless conflict and to secure peace. Ulysses openly requests that Helen be returned to her husband exactly as she was when she left him — that is to say, "intact." Hector is ready to swear that "Paris has not touched Helen."[46] But would not that mean that Paris, a Trojan, was impotent? When they hear such a slander, the Trojan crowds, goaded into a state of fury, stormily protest against that slur on the honor of their city.

Then the gods, in Homeric fashion, intervene and send their messenger Iris to impart their views on the thorny problem. Their message is, as usual, so completely ambiguous that they seem to leave the final decision to the humans once again.

Ulysses and Hector resume their negotiations alone. It becomes clear that, behind the pretext of the rape of Helen, the true motives of the Greeks in attacking Troy are of an economic nature. "The Greeks," says Ulysses, "think that Troy is rich, her warehouses magnificent, the Trojan countryside fertile. They think that they are cramped for room on their rocky territory. The gold with which your gods are covered, the gold of your harvests . . . have, from your promontories, sent to each of our ships a sign that has not been forgotten. It is not prudent to have gods and crops the color of gold."[47]

Ulysses is gradually made to change his mind. Although certain at heart that Fate wants war, he agrees to take Helen back to Menelaus: "I possess more eloquence than necessary to make a husband believe in the virtue of his wife. I shall even lead Helen to believe it herself."[48] Why is he showing such generosity? — "Do you know, Hector, what is causing me to leave?" — "I do, the nobility of your soul." — "Not exactly. . . . Andromache has the same fluttering of eyelashes as Penelope."[49]

In any case, the peace is secure. The Trojan war will not take place. Then a tumultuous scene occurs when Oiax, completely drunk, makes crude advances to Andromache; however, in spite of the provocation Hector retains his self-control. Demodokos, however, thoroughly enraged, shouts that making peace with the Greeks is sheer cowardice on the part of the Trojans, and he starts calling the Trojans to arms. Hector in a last effort to silence him stabs him to death. Yet, before dying, Demodokos has still enough strength to accuse Oiax and not Hector: "It is Oiax! Kill Oiax!"[50] The Trojans kill Oiax. The Trojan war will take place.

La Guerre de Troie n'aura pas lieu offers a threefold intense dramatic interest. The most obvious is the development of events that will lead to the destruction of Troy. At first the majority of the Trojans apparently do not want war. Apparently also even serious oppositions of interests between nations could be amicably and reasonably arranged if the diplomats, such as Ulysses and Hector, were left alone to settle the differences between the opposing parties. Giraudoux does not fail to show how apparently insignificant details, such as the fluttering of a woman's eyelashes, may play a disproportionate and decisive role in the personal relations of men who have the destiny of whole nations in their hands.

The work of the diplomats can be annulled, however, by the rantings of a handful of fanatics or ideologists. The latter are indeed capable of rousing to a pitch the stupid herd passions of the crowd and of bringing about catastrophic conflagrations at the very moment when the danger appears to have been definitely averted.

These troublemakers also appear as simply the instruments of an inexorable Fate. For the first time, Giraudoux introduced Fate as the hidden cause of all human actions and all world disasters. Although the power of Jehovah, who may—or may not—have inspired Judith's behavior, had remained remote and shadowy, the irresistible sway of Fate dominates all the developments of the Trojan tragedy.

The tragic poets of ancient Greece had already made of the vain struggle of man against destiny the essential element of their dramatic works. In his play Giraudoux succeeded in re-creating the heavy, oppressive atmosphere of unavoidable doom found in the masterpieces of Aeschylus and Sophocles. Fate is not presented in *La Guerre de Troie n'aura pas lieu* as a definite allegorical form. Its invisible presence manifests itself through the obscure prophetic sayings of Hector's sister Cassandra, the somber forebodings of Andromache, the colorful intuitions of Helen, and Ulysses' ironical skepticism. All those repeated warnings of an impending disaster conjure up a general feeling of dread that confers on the whole play an intense tragic power.

The more human aspect of the drama is represented by the fundamental dualism of rational ideal and passionate reality so often encountered in Giraudoux's works. Once more, Giraudoux insists on their irreducibility. He makes Helen say: "It has alway seemed to me that there are two kinds of men: those who are, if you will, the flesh of human life and those who represent its organization and contour. The first have their laughter and their tears. . . . The others have gestures, deportment, command. If you compel those two to form one single race, it will not work at all."[51]

Helen embodies the instinctive and vital element of reality. Andromache personifies pure virtue and high principles. Helen is the more complex and the more seductive of the two. That which is orderly, reasonable, lawful holds no appeal for her. She chooses to submit not to a legitimate husband but to a lover. What are her real feelings toward Paris? Why should she try to analyze them? She has only to follow her instincts. Should she remain in Troy or return to Greece? — "I don't read the future. I see certain scenes that are colorful, others that are colorless. So far, only the colorful scenes have taken place."[52]

Somehow the prospect of returning home — a move that would ensure peace — appears dull to her. If war comes, she will not shrink from hardships, insults, hunger, suffering, any more than her beauty shrinks from the prospect of old age. Are not the unpleasant as well as the pleasant aspects of reality but parts of the prodigiously rich and marvelous life that she loves?

Andromache is much more reasonable. In her eyes, good and evil are separate and distinct. Spontaneously, she chooses the good and rejects the evil. In the light of such a clean-cut conception of right and wrong, every problem becomes simple and its solution obvious. In order to avoid war, let Helen give up her Paris, whom in fact she does not love. So logical is Andromache that, when she realizes that the conflict is inevitable, she beseeches Helen to try to love Paris, so that the war may have at least a legitimate cause.

The split between passion and reason is further expressed when the great question of the return of Helen is submitted to the judgment of the gods. Iris carries these two messages to the Trojans: "Yes, Aphrodite charges me to tell you that love is the law that governs the world. Everything that pertains to love becomes sacred, whether it is falsehood, cupidity or lewdness. She takes care of every lover, from king to shepherd. . . . She forbids you two, Hector and Ulysses, to separate Paris from Helen. Disobey her and there will be war."[53]

When Hector asks if any message has come from Pallas, the

goddess of Reason, Iris replies: "Yes, Pallas charges me to say that Reason is the law that governs the world. Everyone who is in love is out of his mind. . . . She orders you Hector and you Ulysses to separate Helen from this curly-headed Paris. Disobey her, and there will be war."[54]

Clearly, as time went on, Giraudoux could less and less see the possibility of a harmonious solution for the fundamental antinomy that, according to his views, dominates all the emotions and the decisions of mankind.

La Guerre de Troie n'aura pas lieu is a comparatively short play. When it was performed for the first time on November 21, 1935, at the Théâtre de l'Athénée—to which Jouvet had moved— a one-act comedy, *Supplément au Voyage de Cook,* was also given as a curtain raiser. The strange title of that comedy is linked to a small yet not unimportant episode of French literary history. In 1768, Louis-Antoine de Bougainville, in command of the frigate *La Boudeuse,* was making a long and difficult journey around the world. In March of that year he landed in Tahiti, where his crew received the sort of enthusiastic welcome for which that island has become famous.

When Bougainville returned to France, he told the story of his adventures in *Voyage autour du monde.* The part of the book in which he described the Tahitian customs created a great sensation in the intellectual circles of Paris. Just at that time, the ideas of Rousseau about the corruption of society and the goodness of man in the state of nature were the object of passionate discussions among French "philosophers." The myth of the Noble Savage was the center of those discussions. One of the difficulties encountered by the upholders of Rousseau's theories was that all the "savages" hitherto met by civilized Europeans in America or in Central Africa appeared to be neither healthy, handsome, nor happy. The testimony of Bougainville about the wonderful results of a natural life in Tahiti seemed to dispose of that difficulty.

When Bougainville was in Tahiti, moreover, a young Tahitian named Aotourou asked him instantly to take him on a visit to France. Bougainville accepted and brought him to the court of Versailles. Aotourou was an intelligent man and he rapidly picked up enough French to be able to communicate freely with other people in that language. Everyone who came into contact with him was impressed by the elegance and natural dignity of his manners. Soon he became the darling of the ladies of the court. Was he not a perfect example of the happy product of an unspoilt nature? Of course, his presence made even more acrimonious the quarrels among philosophers about the Noble Savage.

Then Diderot wrote his famous *Supplément au Voyage de Bougainville*. While paying full tribute to the personal qualities of the great navigator, he violently attacked Bougainville for bringing to the innocent, free, and happy people of Tahiti the seeds of corruption of the civilized world. The people living in the South Seas had only simple needs, which were easily satisfied by a bountiful nature. Why impose on them cravings for luxuries that could be acquired only at the price of relentless effort? Diderot imagined that an old Tahitian said to Bougainville: "Everything that is necessary and good, we already possess it. Are we contemptible because we have not known how to create for ourselves superfluous needs? When we are hungry, we have enough to eat. When we are cold, we have enough to cover ourselves.... If you persuade us to cross the narrow limits of essential needs, when shall we stop working? When shall we have time to enjoy life?"[55]

Meanwhile, Aotourou, after spending eleven months in Versailles, had become homesick. Bougainville spent one third of his modest fortune to enable him to make the long voyage back to Tahiti. Aotourou went as far as the island of Mauritius, which was then a French possession and was called Ile de France. Before he could reach his native island he contracted smallpox and died on a ship chartered by Bougainville.

In 1935, Giraudoux was Inspector of the Diplomatic and Consular Posts Abroad. He was already preparing himself for a long trip, which he undertook in that capacity some time later to the French establishments in the Pacific and Southeast Asia. He read — as any wise traveler would — the "literature" about the places he was going to visit. He read, or perhaps reread, the work of Diderot, which is a classic for all cultured Frenchmen. There he found ideas that had always been dear to him and that he had already expressed in *Suzanne et le Pacifique*.

He decided to present them again, this time in a short comedy.

He could not use, however, the title of Diderot's work, and he also could not easily use the character of Bougainville, who had always shown the utmost generosity toward the inhabitants of Tahiti. He therefore substituted Captain Cook for Bougainville, because the former had not always been very fortunate in his dealings with Polynesian natives.

As a matter of fact, Captain Cook does not appear in Giraudoux's play. His ship, the *Endeavour*, is anchored at a certain distance from the shore, and he is represented on the island of Tahiti by his Lieutenant, who does not play any important part in the action. The blessings of European civilization are represented by a Mr. Banks, a deacon and the taxidermist of the Cook expedition, and by his wife, a virtuous and withered quadragenarian. Mr. Banks explains to the leading chieftain of the island, Outourou, the basic principles of a civilized society: work, property, morality.

Outourou fails to understand their purport in an island where all the necessities of life grow spontaneously, where everything is held in common, and where everybody is free. He is willing to learn, however, and in any case, he offers Mr. and Mrs. Banks the most generous Tahitian hospitality. Certain features of Tahitian hospitality prove so enticing that Mr. Banks is about to succumb to the charm of a dusky young maid when Mrs. Banks' sudden arrival brings him back to his sense of puritanical restraint and conjugal fidelity. Later, Mrs. Banks herself is about to surrender to the attractions of a husky young man when her husband's arrival prevents her, just in time, from meeting a fate worse than death.

Finally, Captain Cook is ready to let his sailors leave the ship and mingle with the natives. Outourou then explains that he and his fellow Tahitians have at long last fully understood the message conveyed by Mr. and Mrs. Banks. They have received spades. Spades can be used as fans. Property? Mr. Banks had himself acknowledged that one of the most common methods to acquire it in England was theft. In the past, the Tahitian girls had given themselves freely to whomever they pleased. Henceforth they will use their charms to relieve their guests of their valuables. The island is therefore ready to welcome civilized man.

Giraudoux then undertook a tragedy based on the Roman civil

disturbances caused by the plans of reform put forward by the Gracchi. Only undated fragments of that work remain. Some were collected and published after Giraudoux's death.

Giraudoux's next great tragedy was inspired by the legend of Electra. The essential features of that legend as well as the main traits of Electra's character have been so definitely fixed in public awareness by the works of the great Greek poets that Giraudoux could not let his imagination roam as freely as he had done with the much vaguer traditions about Amphitryon or the origins of the Trojan war. In his play *Electre* he therefore followed the main lines of the generally accepted version of the crimes that destroyed the royal family of the Atrides in ancient Argos. He added a few secondary episodes of his invention, and naturally he gave the old story a twist in the direction of his personal ideas.

At the beginning of the play, Princess Electra is about to be married to a plain gardener. Aegisthus had planned that misalliance in order to neutralize the pernicious influence that he detects in Electra, by tying her fate to the fate of a thoroughly commonplace, harmless, and insignificant family. But Orestes, whom Clytemnestra had banished from the city of Argos since his childhood, reappears, posing at first as a "stranger." He drives the gardener away and claims Electra for himself. Soon, however, he tells her his true name, and Electra gloats at the idea of having found in him an instrument that will enable her to wreak her vengeance on Aegisthus and on her mother whom she hates. Orestes asks her the cause for that hatred but he obtains only evasive answers: "Why do you hate her so?" — "I don't know yet. I only know that I have the same hatred for both of them."[56] Eventually, mother and son come face to face, but they remain almost unreal for each other — very much like a "mirage."[57]

In the second act, Electra reveals to the weak and wavering Orestes that their father has been assassinated and that their mother has taken a lover. An atrocious scene follows in which daughter and son try to force their mother to admit that indeed she has a lover. Clytemnestra, thoroughly frightened, takes Electra aside and begs her to protect her from Orestes. She appeals to her as woman to woman and, without telling her the name of the man she loves, she confesses that she does love.

As a result, she says, she is at peace with the world, in complete communion with the Cosmos: "I am in love. . . ." — "So everything is all right with you now?" — "Yes, everything is." — "And are the flowers obeying you? Are the birds speaking to you?" — "Yes, they do. And the linden trees send signs to me."[58] She invites Electra to try and share in that blissful feeling; but the unbending Electra rejects that suggestion with crushing contempt.

Then suddenly the action takes a new turn. The Corinthians have unexpectedly invaded the territory of Argos, plundering and burning everything on their way. They will soon attack the city itself. Should they be victorious, Argos would be utterly destroyed. Aegisthus, who is a brilliant captain, could very probably defeat them, but the army's morale has been seriously impaired. For a long time, Argos has been under the rule of Queen Clytemnestra — a woman. Soldiers and citizens alike want to be under the command of a man. If Aegisthus married Clytemnestra, and thus became legitimate king, the city would be saved.

At that prospect, a complete transformation takes place in Aegisthus' personality. He had shown himself so far to be a despicable cad. With his city in mortal danger, a feeling of intense patriotism sweeps over him and turns him into a hero. After looking at the splendor of Argos early in the morning he says: "Here is what this morning has given to me — to me the sensualist, the parasite, the rascal — a country where I feel pure, strong, perfect . . . a country for which now I swear to live and die, but which I also shall save."[59]

Electra, infuriated at the thought that her mother and Aegisthus will be joint rulers of Argos, calls wildly for Orestes. Aegisthus pleads in vain with her: "You admit that, if I marry Clytemnestra, the city will remain quiet and the family of the Atrides will be safe. Otherwise there will be rioting and arson." — "It is very possible." — "You admit that I alone can defend Argos against the Corinthians who are already at the gates of the city. Otherwise there will be plunder and massacre." — "Yes, you would be victorious." — "And you remain obstinate! You ruin my chances to accomplish my task. You sacrifice your family and your country to I don't know what dream."[60]

The dream to which Electra is ready to sacrifice her country and her family is the dream of perfect justice. Electra stands by her principle of abstract, absolute justice, a justice both superior and indifferent to all human interests and emotions; she remains to the end rigid, inflexible, adamant. The end—that is to say, the murder of Clytemnestra and Aegisthus by Orestes—is not presented on the stage. It is reported in gory detail by a beggar who has been allowed to follow the whole action. As a sort of epilogue, an announcement is made that the Corinthians have stormed the city and are slaughtering people in the streets. Electra repeats monotonously, as if in a trance: "I have justice. I have everything."[61]

A secondary plot, completely invented by Giraudoux, runs throughout the play. Its protagonists are a middle-aged judge called merely "The President"—a courtesy title given to the presiding judge in French law courts—and his young and flighty wife, Agathe. The President is the typical cuckold husband so often found in French popular comedies. The comical troubles of the President, of Agathe, and of one of her young lovers provide a sure laugh when the tension of the tragic events afflicting the family of the Atrides becomes too strong to bear. Their antics, moreover, offer a sort of retrospective parody of the past marital— and extramarital—relations between Agamemnon, Clytemnestra, and Aegisthus, and thus explain indirectly the nature of Clytemnestra's feelings toward her first husband.

Giraudoux has also added to the traditional legend the character of an old beggar who is treated with deference by all, because the Greeks believed that a god sometimes takes the form of a pauper to observe and test the behavior of the mortals. The beggar has a function similar to that of the ancient Greek chorus. He comments ponderously on the actions of the main players and sometimes he summarizes for the public the events that are supposed to take place offstage. Furthermore, three Eumenides appear intermittently when the drama takes a sharp turn. In some respects they are akin to the Furies; but at times they seem to represent the three Fates. Their dismal threats, their shrill cries, their violent curses and insults enhance the feeling of dread and inevitable doom that hangs over the whole tragedy.

The work, however, is dominated by the towering figure of Electra herself. Electra's character can be interpreted at three different levels. On the one hand, she possesses all the moral traits that tradition has attached to her name. She is in love almost sensually, if not with her father himself, at least with the memory she has kept of his person: "I have touched his hands with these fingers. I have touched his lips with these lips. I have touched his skin that you [Clytemnestra] have not touched. . . . With my cheek against his cheek, I have learned to feel the warmth of my father. Sometimes, in the summer, the whole world has the same warmth as my father. And then I am ready to faint away."[62]

She hates her mother with a deep instinctive hatred, and she explains herself: "It is precisely the fact that she gave birth to me that I cannot stand in her. That fact is my shame. . . . I love in my birth everything that I owe to my father. . . . Everything in my birth that comes from my mother, I hate."[63] Any modern psychologist would say that Giraudoux's Electra is a perfect example of — the Electra complex.

On the other hand, Electra represents one of the two aspects of the human character that Giraudoux has set in opposition to each other in many of his works. Electra embodies the strict adherence to abstract ideal principles, high and noble in themselves to be sure, but having little reference to the world of everyday reality. The principle that Electra upholds to the point of fanaticism is the principle of justice. Justice is for her an absolute, above and beyond the gods themselves: "That justice which makes you accept that your city be burned, which makes you condemn your own race, you dare to call it justice of the gods?" — "Far from it. In the realm where I live, the gods are not entrusted with the care of justice. . . . Just repent splendidly after your crime, that is the verdict that the gods have rendered in your case. I don't accept it. When a crime has assailed human dignity . . . there is no possible forgiveness."[64]

On the opposite side, facing Electra and her principles, are Clytemnestra and Aegisthus, who stand for common human reality. They represent the normal human aspirations toward happiness and also the ready, cowardly acceptance of the dubious compromises, the lies, the iniquities, and even the crimes that the pursuit of happiness inevitably implies. To be relatively happy, says Giraudoux in one of his somber moods, man must give up any lofty moral ideal that he may have: "A happy family means a local surrender. A happy epoch means a unanimous capitulation."[65]

For this reason Electra will ruin her family. "What has the family of the Atrides to fear?" asks Orestes in the disguise of a "stranger." Then the President answers: "Nothing as far as I know. But that family is like every happy family. . . . It has to face the most dangerous enemy on earth, which will destroy it utterly . . . the ally of Electra: perfect justice."[66]

Clytemnestra represents the feminine passionate craving for love, regardless of laws and vows. Aegisthus represents the practical care of public good regardless of scruples and ethical considerations. Once more, as often in the works of Giraudoux, principles and practice clash. Ideal and reality confront each other, as they did in the case of Andromache and Helen. This time, however, they stare angrily at each other. Why?

Because Electra is *"une femme à histoires."*[67] That colloquial French expression generally designates a woman endowed with a strong personality, who possesses the gift of arousing the emotions of the people around her, who creates serious complications even in the simplest matters and who stirs up trouble, sometimes in a spirit of mischief, but sometimes also for the accomplishment of truly great things. Without such people, says Giraudoux, mankind would complacently forget its most important difficulties and problems: "If guilty people do not forget the cause of their guilt, if the defeated people do not forget their defeats and the victorious ones their victories, it is not because mankind has a conscience, which in fact tends toward forgetfulness and compromise, but because of the action of ten or twelve *femmes à histoires."* — "I agree with you. Ten or twelve *femmes à histoires* have rescued the world from selfishness." — "They have rescued it also from happiness."[68]

Clytemnestra and Aegisthus would be only too willing to leave well enough alone, and lead a quiet, contented, even though monotonous existence. Electra, however, impelled by the tremendous natural energy within her, pursues them relentlessly, leaves them no peace, and harries them to death.

Giraudoux did not try to harmonize artificially the various heterogenous components of Electra's character. Yet the different elements of her personality — the young neurotic female, the high-principled fanatic, and the rather formidable virago — fall somehow nicely into place to compose a harsh and somewhat repellent but coherent tragic figure. Her virulent hatred for her mother feeds her hunger for abstract, absolute justice, and her pitiless pursuit of justice can be maintained only through the fierce determination of a *femme à histoires.*

Electre was presented with notable success for the first time at the Théâtre de l'Athénée on May 13, 1937. It was followed a little more than six months later, on December 3 of the same year, by a short sketch entitled *L'Impromptu de Paris.* That sketch was obviously inspired by Molière's famous play *L'Impromptu de Versailles.* At the beginning of Giraudoux's sketch, a few actors of Jouvet's troupe are waiting on the stage for the arrival of their director; the other actors are still in the wings, talking among themselves about the problems of the theater or about their own affairs. Then, one of the leading actors on the stage starts rehearsing *L'Impromptu de Versailles.* One by one, the missing players arrive, each reciting some fragment of Molière's comedy.

Jules Robineau, a member of the French Chamber of Deputies, who is in charge of the allotment of government subsidies to the theaters, interrupts the rehearsal: he wants to get in touch with Jouvet at once. Robineau and Jouvet engage in a discussion about various aspects of dramatic art, and the other actors join in their discussion from time to time. This gives Jouvet an opportunity to express some of Giraudoux's ideas on the theater and also to make witty and often sarcastic remarks about the critics, the public, and the actors themselves. The play offers a certain interest for the understanding of Giraudoux's ideas on the theater, but it possesses only little dramatic appeal.

Cantique des Cantiques is the only play by Giraudoux that was presented for the first time at the Comédie Française, on October 12, 1938. The subject has only a very remote connection with the *Song of Solomon* to which the title refers. The play takes place in a *de luxe* Parisian café. An important, wealthy, but middle-aged man, called "Le Président," is waiting for a charming young woman, Florence, who has evidently been his mistress for some time. Florence has decided to get married, and her fiancé, Jèrôme, a candid and callow young man—whose essential merit is to be young—arrives instead of her. Then he leaves hurriedly to buy flowers for her birthday. Florence appears soon afterward.

Florence and the President bid farewell to each other in a sad and tender scene. Their mutual fondness and congeniality are obvious, and their parting fills them both with melancholy. The President understands only too well that an elderly man cannot compete in love with youth. He gives up Florence without struggle when Jérôme comes back bringing his fiancée, instead of flowers, a cheap ring with an imitation zircon as a birthday present. *Cantique des Cantiques* does not add anything new to the worn-out theme of the victory of youth over old age in love. A certain elegiac tone, however, confers on the play a discreet subdued charm, which is kept from sentimentality by a generous adjunction to the most moving scenes of the humor, the banter, and even the spoofing in which Giraudoux always delights.

Giraudoux's next work, *Ondine,* which was performed for the first time at the Théâtre de l'Athénée on April 27, 1939, is one of the very best plays that he ever composed. The subject of *Ondine* is drawn from an old medieval legend that Giraudoux not only dramatized but also reinterpreted in terms of his own ideas. According to an old German myth, the elementary spirits that throng the various aspects of nature are endowed with reason but do not possess souls. Therefore, on the day of the Last Judgment, their whole substance will return to plain matter. A female spirit may acquire a soul if she marries a human. Should her husband show her discourtesy near a body of water, however, she would have to leave him at once and become a spirit again. Furthermore, should the man she has married take another wife, she would be bound to come back and kill him pitilessly.

A German Romantic writer, Friedrich Heinrich Freiherr de La Motte-Fouqué, the descendant of a noble Huguenot family that left France at the time of the persecution of the Protestants by Louis XIV, composed a lovely, poetic *Märchen,* or tale on this subject. He infused into the old myth a human warmth and an enchanting feeling of the mysterious that make this small work a jewel of romantic imaginative creation.

In La Motte-Fouqué's work, called *Undine,* a fisherman and his wife have lost a dearly beloved daughter, mysteriously drowned in a lake nearby. Almost at once, however, on the shore of the same lake—and in exchange, as it were, for their child—they find a marvelously beautiful girl, an ondine, whom they adopt and bring up as well as they can. The ondine, however, having no soul, behaves more like a graceful young animal than a young human, and her unpredictable whims and caprices often fill the fisherman and his wife with sadness and dismay.

When she reaches her eighteenth year, her uncle, a water spirit named Fraistorrent, manages to guide a handsome knight, Huldbrand von Ringstetten, through the forest to the fisherman's hut. The knight is immediately captivated by the ondine's beauty. A good priest who lives in the neighborhood is brought — again through Fraistorrent's wiles — just in time to unite Huldbrand von Ringstetten and the ondine in marriage.

The ondine, formerly insensitive and hardhearted, becomes tender, loving, compassionate. She has a soul. She can enjoy the supreme bliss of shared love, but she can also experience the sorrows and pangs of grief that are part of the human lot. Huldbrand falls under the spell of a scheming, evil woman, Bertalda, whom the ondine did not drive away out of sheer pity, because she believed her to be unhappy.

The ondine, sensing an approaching disaster, causes the opening of the well in the Ringstetten castle to be sealed tight. The well is reopened through a caprice of Bertalda, and the ondine, being the object of a slight near a body of water, has to go away. The imprescriptible laws of the waterfolk, however, have to be obeyed: the ondine has to come back and kill the unfaithful knight. The tears he had caused her to shed well up in his chest, and he falls lifeless in the ondine's beautiful arms.

At the funeral, a lovely blond woman joins the mourners. The old priest who had blessed the ondine's marriage pronounces the ritual prayers for the dead. The mourners kneel. When they rise, the blond stranger has gone. On the spot where she had knelt, there is a spring of clear water — and the water runs until it completely surrounds Huldbrand von Ringstetten's tomb. The people believe the ondine is wreathing in her arms the only man she had ever loved. Many years later, the spring is still shown to the visitors on the castle grounds.

Giraudoux had become acquainted with La Motte-Fouqué's *Märchen* when he was studying for the Agrégation at the Sorbonne after his return from Germany. In 1909, Charles Andler asked him to write a critical essay on *Undine*. Nearly thirty years later, Giraudoux composed his play on the same subject.

In the interval, however, he had elaborated a complex view of the relations between man and the universe. Although he followed La Motte-Fouqué's plot fairly faithfully, he completely transformed—in fact almost reversed—the mystic meaning that the German writer had suggested in his work.

The first act of Giraudoux's play is a masterpiece of subtle humor and poetic charm. A knight errant, Hans von Wittenstein zu Wittenstein, arrives one rainy evening in the hut of an old fisherman, Auguste, and his wife Eugénie. He courteously asks for food and shelter for himself and his horse, and he is received most hospitably by those humble folks. The knight is a very average man, not particularly handsome, not particularly intelligent, rather conceited, somewhat gross, very talkative, and above all very hungry. He says that he is engaged to the king's adopted daughter, Bertha. That lady, however, has put a condition to their marriage: he should cross a forest filled with all the horrible dangers that a true knight ought to be able to overcome. For the time being, he is mainly interested in food and displays a really ravenous appetite.

Ondine, who had been the fisherman's adopted daughter, then arrives and falls in love with Hans at once. The knight is overwhelmed by her passionate utterances and her daring although chaste caresses. In vain the other waterfolk—three ondines and Ondine's own uncle, the king of the water spirits, who appear through the translucent walls of the hut—try to dissuade her from marrying a human. They warn her that if a human husband were to deceive her, as he almost inevitably would, he would no less inevitably die. Ondine, however, refuses to believe that Hans would ever betray her. She binds him to her with her girdle and casts on him a fisherman's net that magically puts him asleep; the curtain falls while she lies down near her fiancé.

The second act is a mixture of the most bizarre events, evidently intended to give a feeling of the utter confusion and disorder that prevail in the human world. Hans von Wittenstein wants to show that world to his young wife. A court entertainment has been planned for the presentation of Ondine to the King. The Royal Chamberlain, the Superintendent of the Royal Theaters, and an Illusionist, who is the king of the water spirits in disguise, prepare a performance that turns out to be a grotesque extravaganza. Magic tricks, funny gags, clever quips, irrelevant literary quotations, sarcastic parodies, and even jokes reminiscent of the *canular normalien* tumble one over the other, leaving the spectator bewildered and uncertain of the purpose of the show. Its purpose is to convey the idea that in the world of man, everything is pretense, makebelieve, and trickery.

When Ondine appears in the King's audience chamber, she makes blunder after blunder. She does not realize that court life is made of a thousand small hypocrisies and deceptions. With disastrous results, she always tells the truth. In vain, the King's wife, good Queen Iseult, taking pity on her innocence, tries to initiate her to the conventions that rule human relationships. Ondine's pitiful efforts to be "human," — that is, to lie — have more catastrophic consequences than her previous frankness.

Meanwhile, Hans has come face to face with his former fiancée Bertha. He soon feels much more at ease with her, who is a rather common and even coarse human being like himself, than with his enchanting sprite wife. The action that follows is easily guessed by the spectators, and Ondine guesses it as well.

When the third act begins, preparations are being made in the knight's castle for Hans' marriage with Bertha. Ondine has vanished for six months without leaving any trace at all. Then suddenly someone announces that a fisherman has caught her in his net. She is brought before a tribunal to be tried for witchcraft. To save Hans from the punishment that awaits him at the hands of the king of the water spirits for his betrayal, Ondine accuses herself falsely of having been the first to break her marriage vows.

Her naive lies are quickly disproved, however, and only then does Hans understand the depth and heroism of her love. It is too late, however, and his inevitable doom overtakes him while Ondine, progressively losing the memory of her human adventure, returns to her original state as a water spirit. Before leaving the human world, she glances at the knight's body, stretched on a long flagstone. "Who is that young man?" she asks. "Why is he not moving? . . . Would it be possible to give him life again?" "Impossible," answers the king of the water spirits. — "How sad! I would have loved him so much."[69]

Giraudoux introduced two main changes in La Motte-Fouqué's *Märchen,* one in Ondine's character, the other in the general significance of the whole tale. La Motte-Fouqué, closely following the tradition of the medieval legend, said that through her union with a man his Undine had acquired a soul. Indeed, in his *Märchen* the ondine's personality undergoes a complete transformation after her marriage to Huldbrand von Ringstetten. She becomes "human"—that is, capable of feeling the joys and also the pains that both enrich and torment the soul of human beings.

Giraudoux's Ondine, on the other hand, states definitely in her conversation with Iseult[70] that, even after her marriage with Hans she possesses no soul. She had been capable of loving him before their union and her capricious character is hardly altered afterward. In fact, her personality, far from improving when she entered the world of humanity, has deteriorated markedly. She has lost all the powers that she had as a birthright. The king of the water spirits says: "She has betrayed them [the water spirits]. She could have retained their power and their knowledge. She was able to perform twenty times a day what you [humans] call miracles. At her call, the River Rhine, the heavens above would always answer and produce prodigies. But no. She has accepted instead the sprained ankle, hay fever, and food prepared with pork fat."[71]

The deterioration that takes place in Ondine when she accepts the fate of mankind gives a key to the idea that Giraudoux wanted to illustrate in his light and fanciful play. Ondine is the personification of one form of the ideal conceived by Giraudoux—the ideal of a perfect communion with Nature and the Cosmos. Ondine both represents and fulfills that communion. She is truly one with Nature. At the beginning of the play, Auguste and Eugénie are talking about her; she has gone out in the midst of a raging thunderstorm. "What can she possibly do outside in that darkness?" asks Auguste. "Why should you worry?" answers Eugénie. "You know that she can see clearly in the dark."—"But that terrible storm!"—"As if you did not know that she does not get wet in the rain."[72]

Later Auguste explains to Hans: "She has never needed a bed, but how often have we caught her asleep on the surface of the lake. Is it because children instinctively guess what nature is? Is it because the nature of Ondine is Nature itself?"[73]

In spite of that warning, Hans declares that he wants to marry Ondine: "I accept with joy all the lakes in the world as fathers-in-law and all the rivers in the world as mothers-in-law. I am on very good terms with Nature."[74]

As soon as he has won Ondine, the stupid and conceited knight wants to take her into the human world: "I want the world to see what is most perfect in the world. Don't you know that you are the greatest perfection?" — "Possibly, but will the world be able to see it?" — "And you will see the world. . . . The world is very beautiful, Ondine."[75]

The world, at least as it is presented in this play by Giraudoux, is not beautiful at all. It is a dismal compound of vulgarity, pettiness, cruelty, and imposture. When Ondine is plunged into that morass of pretense and falsehood, she flounders hopelessly.

Then Hans deceives Ondine. Is he particularly evil? No. He is merely an average man, an ordinary man, a man who belongs to our earthly reality. Here Giraudoux returns to one of his favorite themes: the ideal and reality are incompatible. Any attempt to unite them will first bring about the deterioration of the ideal and ultimately result in their ineluctable separation.

In his *Märchen* La Motte-Fouqué had developed a touching romantic symbol. A girl gains access through love to a superior sense of life. In other words, she acquires a soul. Then she cannot be parted from the man to whom she owes that sublime initiation, and she remains faithful to him beyond infidelity and death. In Giraudoux's play, Ondine has nothing to gain from her marriage with the dull and oafish Hans. Yet, like many ethereal *jeunes filles*, at least in Giraudoux's works, she craves to be united with a representative, however mediocre, of the materially real.

She thus obtains a few moments of joy, but she also undergoes a painful personal debasement and finds herself in contact with the least appetizing aspects of life. In the particular case of Ondine, this common human comedy ends tragically. As a spirit, she can disengage herself from the mire of the real only through the death of her husband and thus return to pure spirituality.

L'Apollon de Bellac appears at first sight one of the most disconcerting of Giraudoux's plays. The comedy develops in an atmosphere that is half realistic and half fantastic. The heroine is a charming young girl, Agnès, who is in search of an office job, although she lacks the most elementary qualifications for that type of employment. Moreover, she is overcome with shyness, to the point of being ready to faint, whenever she finds herself face to face with a man, whether that man be a plain old usher or the President of a big company.

In the waiting room of the "Office of the Great and Small Inventors," she meets a certain Monsieur de Bellac, to whom she explains her predicament. This Gentleman from Bellac then gives her some advice that, he says, will not only secure the job she desires but will also enable her to become "the queen of the world." Thus when she has to face men, or any of the multifarious aspects of the world, she has to tell them boldly that they are beautiful. She does not need to use circumlocutions or to make indirect allusions. She should just say: "You are beautiful." She starts practicing on a butterfly, and then on simple objects such as a chandelier and a telephone. At once, all of them "glow." Her results with an old usher are less spectacular. Yet he gives her a chance to see the the General Secretary of the firm. Her technique becomes perfect. Not only the General Secretary but four members of the board of administrators succumb in turn to her magic spell.

She is ready to tackle the President himself. A most unprepossessing individual, he is very sure of himself and above all tough and shrewd. Yet, when Agnès tells him that he is beautiful he dismisses his private secretary, a disagreeable but very efficient old maid, to give the inexperienced girl the job she wants. Soon Agnès carries her success still farther: the President breaks his engagement to a sensible and practical young woman, Thérèse, and proposes to Agnès, who thus becomes that very important man's fiancée.

Agnès is far from happy with her victory, however. The General Secretary, the members of the Board, the President himself were in fact anything but beautiful. Her triumph was a triumph of imagination, an abstract triumph, which was not resting on anything solid and concrete. She longs to say "You are beautiful" to a man whose appearance would not be in flagrant contradiction with her magic formula. What about the Gentleman from Bellac himself? Le Monsieur de Bellac is not an extremely handsome man. He is an average, wholesome, young, and acceptable sample of the masculine sex. Agnès embraces him and tells him that he is beautiful. When she opens her eyes, the Gentleman from Bellac has disappeared. A member of the Board arrives and asks if Apollon is there—and Agnès answers disconsolately that he is gone.

The various symbols presented in L'Apollon de Bellac can be understood in the light of the circumstances under which Giraudoux composed that small play. L'Apollon de Marsac, for such was its original title, was performed for the first time in June 1942 in Rio de Janeiro by Jouvet, who was then touring the South American continent. Giraudoux had sent him his manuscript from Switzerland, where he had gone to give a few public lectures. The play was thus composed during the darkest moments of the war.

At that time Giraudoux passed through a phase of deep pessimism and gloom. The reality that he had loved so much in his youth appeared repellent and ugly. A hidden inner spring of moral buoyancy still existed in Giraudoux, however. The play corresponds to a temporary resurgence of that irrepressible gaiety and courage that had been the hallmark of his personality for many years. In spite of all evidence that the world is hideous and vile, we must proclaim that it is beautiful. Of course, this does not mean that, in Giraudoux's opinion, the deep—ugly— nature of the real world has changed in any way. Giraudoux hopefully thinks that, through a sort of mirror effect, man will generally obtain a beautiful response by saying that the world is beautiful.

The Gentleman from Bellac, thanks to whose inspiration Agnès was moved to transmute a chandelier, a telephone, and even the President of a stock company into things of beauty through her will to declare them beautiful, is hardly a man of flesh and bone. He is rather a new avatar of the Ghost and the Abalstitiel, who had guided Isabelle and Edmée, respectively, into the superior realm that the elect craves to attain. Just as Edmée and Isabelle had been unable to remain long in the pure, exalted atmosphere of the sublime and had wanted to go back to the common concrete reality of daily life, similarly Agnès longs to find a man, a plain, ordinary man, to whom her practical feelings could genuinely apply.

She turns mistakenly to the Gentleman from Bellac, but the latter is not a plain, ordinary man. He is not another Controller of Weights and Measures. He does not embody reality. He represents the ideal. He therefore deserts her as the Abalstitiel had deserted Edmée and as the Ghost had deserted Isabelle when these women followed their deep feminine instinct that binds them ultimately to the firm and solid trivialities of existence.

The main idea of the play—the refusal to accept as a fact the actual ugliness of life, the determination to declare that human beings and even things around us are beautiful, the belief that it is thus possible to transfigure the world and to inject beauty into the stalest forms of the real—were well understood and well received by the public. The presentation on the stage, however, is usually marred by technical flaws. When the chandelier, praised by Agnès, starts to "glow" with pride, that clever trick always draws a genuinely amused smile from the audience. Of course no similar radiance can be observed on the Usher's or the President's face, and Agnès' emphatic declaration that they are beautiful falls flat. As a result, the surprising success of the girl's stratagem can easily be assigned to masculine vanity alone.

Although a woman—however ill favored by nature—can be expected to purr contentedly if lauded openly for her looks, most people feel that a normal male would, under such circumstances, be merely embarrassed and made uncomfortably self-conscious. When six men in succession are seen falling into the same trap, the credibility gap widens to such a point that the power of illusion, so necessary on the stage, vanishes almost altogether. Furthermore, young Agnès' shift from the realm of the ideal to the world of practicality is so unexpected and so rapid that the motivation of her act is likely to escape the notice of anyone who is not thoroughly acquainted with Giraudoux's ideas.

Despite these flaws, the general tonic effect of the play— which affirms that man's best attitude in life is to declare that the world, with all its blemishes, is indeed beautiful—has been sufficient to make of L'Apollon de Bellac a perennial favorite of repertory theaters and college departments of dramatic art.

Sodome et Gomorrhe is the last of Giraudoux's plays performed during his life. Not directed by Jouvet, who was then absent from Paris on his tour in South America, it was first presented on October 11, 1943, at the Théâtre Hébertot. It is a somber tragedy containing obvious and almost embarrassingly clear allusions to the matrimonial discords that were then disrupting the Giraudoux household.

The subject of the play has nothing to do with the problem of homosexuality that is usually associated with the names of Sodom and Gomorrah. Its general theme is drawn from the passage in Genesis (Chapters 18–19) in which the Lord is said to have destroyed by fire the two evil cities in which men and women failed to be united according to God's will and law. Giraudoux added to this theme a myth apparently inspired by a famous passage in Plato's *Symposium*.

God, says Giraudoux, had at first created not separate men and women but human beings who were joined together to form a series of couples. Then He cut them apart, trusting that "tenderness" would bring them together again: "There have never been [independent] creatures, but only couples. God has not created man and woman one after another or one from another. He has created two bodies united by strips of flesh, which He severed afterward when He fell in a trusting mood the day He created tenderness."[76]

When a true couple has been restored through human tenderness, it shines in the eyes of God as the stars do in the eyes of men. The sight of such human "constellations" is for God a supreme joy—His Paradise. If men and women destroy these perfect couples through their own fault, they deprive God of His happiness, of His Paradise, and thus commit an unforgivable sin: "That He should have to give up, because of your disunion, His true Heaven, that is what He cannot forgive."[77]

The cities of Sodom and Gomorrah have been guilty of that sin, and God has sent a large number of Angels to find out if there are not at least a few genuine couples for whose sake he will spare even the unworthy ones. If such couples cannot be discovered, He will destroy them all with fire.

The Angels' attention is soon concentrated on a woman called Lia and her husband Jean. Lia and Jean are obviously not satisfied with each other. Their mutual grievances are neither very tragic nor very uncommon. Lia complains that Jean is not the perfect man she had dreamed of marrying. He is not the unique being whose presence alone would give a meaning to her life. Jean, on the other hand, has long realized that Lia is not the ideal woman who could be for him the sublime inspiration that he craves.

Another mismatched couple, Ruth and Jacques, also appear. They form, as often happens in Giraudoux's works, a sort of mirror image of the difficulties that beset Lia and Jean. Jean and Lia, Jacques and Ruth hit upon the ultramodern and now fashionable idea of swapping wives — and husbands. That friendly exchange of bed partners does not produce, however, particularly happy results.

Throughout the matrimonial discussions that constitute the largest part of the play, Lia is constantly kept in the foreground. She does not seem very likable, being hard, selfish, insensitive to other people's feelings, and devoid of scruples. Yet she possesses an undeniably forceful personality, and her nimbleness of mind allows her to get the better of Jean in practically every argument they have together, even though she often has recourse, to win her point, either to unconvincing half-truths or even to glaring sophistry. In comparison, Jean seems passive and pallid. He is motivated mainly by weak pretense and superficial vanity.

In the end, Lia, equally disappointed with Jacques and Jean, tries coquettishly to flirt with an Angel. The Angel explains the seriousness of the situation, which, because of her natural levity, she had practically overlooked. He shows her that only a prompt and total reconciliation with Jean can save her and the city as well from God's justified wrath. She makes a half-hearted attempt to form a true couple with Jean. Jean, however, apparently resigned to his inevitable doom, is interested only in showing a brave front at the time of his death: he wants to make the other men believe that Lia and he are completely united in their last moments on earth.

When he formulates that ultimate lie, the destruction of Sodom has begun. All the men move to one side, all the women move to the other; they die separated for all eternity. A supreme touch of black humor concludes the play: when everything is over and everyone is dead, one can still hear a masculine voice and a feminine voice quarreling—apparently also for all eternity.

That gruesome story is almost unrelieved by the comical incidents that usually enliven the most somber of Giraudoux's plays. The play does not carry any other message than the sinister despair that grips man and woman alike before the inevitable bankruptcy of what should be the highest form of love. At the end of a long life that seemed to have been graced by so many charming feminine figures, Giraudoux came to the dismal, hopeless conclusion that men and women will never attain a complete union but will forever remain alien and hostile to one another.

La Folle de Chaillot represents, somewhat like L'Apollon de Bellac, although with a completely different setting, a reaction of willful optimism against a world that Giraudoux sees as corrupt and abject. The subject of the play is an almost melodramatic struggle between villains of the deepest dye and "good" men and women who triumph most satisfactorily in the end. The villains are despicable speculators, venal promoters, and shady financiers who talk among themselves in a Parisian café of the Chaillot district about the most effective ways of fleecing the public.

They are in the act of organizing a bogus corporation for that purpose when a prospector brings them the news that the water of Paris has a faint taste of oil. There must be oil somewhere beneath the surface of the French capital. Of course, placing derricks and pumps throughout the streets and squares of that city would utterly destroy its beauty and charm, but the profits would be enormous. The "villains" decide to investigate the possibilities of carrying out this scheme.

The group of "good" people consists of a nondescript collection of bizarre and down-at-the-heels individuals, such as a ragpicker, a flower girl, a sewerman, a shoelace peddler. They are led by Aurelia, the "Madwoman of Chaillot," a crazy, eccentric, ridiculous old dame, dressed in preposterously old-fashioned gaudy garments, who may not have an absolutely irreproachable past, but who possesses a heart of gold. They all will get together to thwart the plot of the wicked speculators.

A sentimental element is introduced in the play by an idyll between a sweet and innocent dishwasher, Irma, and a no less innocent and sweet young man, Pierre. Pierre having committed a peccadillo—he had issued a check without having corresponding adequate funds in the bank—is blackmailed by the "villains," who want to force him to take part in their dishonest dealings. The upright young man would sooner die than do such a thing, and he tries to commit suicide. He is rescued in time, however, and is given a new will to live by the Madwoman, who simply assures him that life is a good thing.

In the second act, Aurelia has asked for the help of three other Madwomen, who respond eagerly to her call. They also display fantastic, extravagant dresses and discuss plans to rid the world of evil men. Aurelia lives in a shabby lodging in the basement of a building in the Chaillot district. The lodging communicates through a trapdoor with the sewers of Paris. Aurelia, the three other Madwomen, and their humble friends meet there in secret. They have managed to induce the speculators to come and see for themselves the huge quantities of oil concealed under the soil of Paris.

At Aurelia's urging, the wicked men go, one by one, into the sewers; when they are all there, the Madwoman of Chaillot closes the trapdoor on them. Thus evil is eliminated. When Irma asks where "all those men are" now, Aurelia answers: "They have evaporated, Irma. They were wicked men. They say they are eternal . . . and they do everything to achieve that goal. . . . But it is not at all so. Pride, greed, selfishness heats them up to such a point that when they pass over a spot that hides kindness and pity, they simply evaporate. . . . All those bandits have brushed against you on their way out. You will never see them again."[78]

When the play was performed for the first time on December 18, 1945, by Jouvet at the Théâtre de l'Athénée, after his return from South America, France was just emerging from one of the deepest disasters of her history. During the occupation of the country by the Germans, the French had gone through a phase of profound demoralization. Unscrupulous profiteering, fraudulent financial practices, illicit black-market activities were rampant everywhere. When the nightmare ended, a violent reaction set in, prompted mainly by a feeling of disgust and anger toward those who had taken advantage of the public distress to enrich themselves shamelessly.

This movement corresponded to an emotional craving to cleanse the country of all the moral mire in which the French had had to wallow for several years. The public had no time then and little inclination to indulge in the niceties of regular justice. That the country had been besmirched through the dealings of corrupt and vile men seemed only too evident to all. Men felt an almost universal desire to throw all that human filth into the sewers where they belonged.

La Folle de Chaillot, which expressed in a rather elementary manner these rather elementary sentiments, had for that very reason an unprecedented, almost unbelievable success. It ran for nearly three hundred successive performances and carried Giraudoux posthumously to the pinnacle of his fame as a dramatist. *La Folle de Chaillot,* however, is not one of Giraudoux's best plays. The dualistic structure so often found in Giraudoux's works, but usually veiled by subtle and delicate shadings, is reduced here to an almost aggressive schematism, with sharp, almost brutal oppositions of black and white.

Once the element of actuality that had originally conferred on the play its essential appeal had disappeared with the mere passing of time, it became obvious that the Manichean split between Good and Evil on which the story is built implies an oversimplification of facts that even the special perspective of the stage could not make a sophisticated audience accept very easily. The amusing presentation of the colorful little folks crowding a Parisian café, and above all the fantastic figure of the Madwoman herself, do provide an entertaining show, particularly if the main parts are taken by competent actors, but these purely picturesque features are not enough to make of *La Folle de Chaillot* a dramatic masterpiece.

Pour Lucrèce was presented only in 1953 by Jean-Louis Barrault at the Théâtre Marigny. The play is a remote, very remote transposition of the famous story told by Livy, explaining the dramatic events that brought about the downfall of royalty in Rome in 509 B.C. and the establishment of the Roman Republic.[79]

According to Livy, Lucretia was a Roman lady of high rank, the wife of Lucius Tarquinius Collatinus, who himself was related to Lucius Tarquinius Superbus, the seventh king of Rome. While the Roman army was besieging the city of Ardea, the king's son, Tarquinius Sextus, suggested to a few of his companions that they ride one evening back to Rome and find out what their wives were doing in their absence. Those young men discovered that their spouses were busily engaged in — temporarily forgetting their husbands. One exception occurred: Lucretia had remained in her home, virtuously attending to her household duties.

After all the young husbands had returned, somewhat crestfallen, to the army camp, Tarquinius Sextus rode back secretly to Rome and asked Lucretia, his kinswoman, to give him hospitality. Such a request could not be denied in ancient Rome, and Lucretia received him courteously, without suspicion of his evil plans. During the night, Tarquinius managed to sneak into her bedroom. He threatened to murder her if she did not give herself to him, adding that he would declare that he had found her in bed with another man and had killed her in order to vindicate the honor of his friend Collatinus. Rather than to have her reputation sullied forever by such slander, Lucretia submitted to his lust.

The following day she went to her father, Lucretius Spurius, and she also sent an urgent message to her husband, who soon arrived accompanied by Lucius Junius Brutus. Lucretia told them how she had been raped and, unable to live henceforth with her shame, she stabbed herself under their horrified eyes. Brutus then ran to the Forum, flourishing the gory knife with which Lucretia had performed her heroic sacrifice. He called upon the Romans to overthrow the proud, overbearing Tarquinius Superbus and to drive his wicked family away.

The Lucrèce imagined by Giraudoux lived in Aix-en-Provence in the reign of Napoléon III. Her name is Lucile Blanchard and she is the wife of Lionel Blanchard, Procureur Impérial — a function corresponding approximately to our district attorney. He is a conceited, conservative, narrow-minded man filled with all the prejudices of the Victorian era. Lucile, always dressed in immaculate white, is the living incarnation of the principle of absolute purity. She is by nature distant, reserved, somewhat cold. Furthermore, she possesses a weird, disturbing, and mysterious power: when she looks at the persons around her, her glances at once detect and denounce anything in them that is low and impure.

She has among her acquaintances a young woman called Paola,

who is the very antithesis of Lucile. Paola is a luscious, sensuous, impetuous girl, competely devoid of scruples but brimming over with vitality and bent on enjoying life to the full. Her husband, Armand, is an upright and decent man, but evidently not a match for that bundle of nerves, caprices, and passions. Although she deceives him almost openly, he does not at first suspect his conjugal misfortune. He cannot help noticing Lucile's particular coldness toward Paola and wants to know its cause. Lucile does not speak, but her eyes speak for her—and Armand understands their silent message.

Paola, infuriated by Lucile's unwilling betrayal, hits upon a truly hideous scheme. There is in the city of Aix a well-known provincial Don Juan, an inveterate ladykiller, Count Marcellus. He has been one of Paola's many lovers. Paola contrives to give Lucile a narcotic and to carry her into the bedroom of a house occupied by an old procuress, Barbette. Here, one of Count Marcellus' handkerchiefs is tucked into Lucile's hands and her own dress is perfidiously put in such a state of disarray that, when she wakes up she will believe she has been raped by Marcellus.

Naturally enough, Lucile is overcome with shame and Paola gloats over her humiliation and despair. Lucile, however, induces Armand to challenge Marcellus to a duel and Marcellus is killed. Lucile, however, still broods over her disgrace. She confesses what she believes to be her degradation to her husband, but he behaves toward her with an almost unbearable supercilious boorishness. Then Lucile poisons herself. Paola then reveals that she has never been raped by Marcellus. But Lucile is glad to die, being morally nauseated by the foulness of the world that she had found around her. It is indeed only in death that she can preserve her cherished purity.

The development of this unusual and intricate plot rests on a series of ideas found frequently in Giraudoux's works. Most obvious is the opposition between two types of human beings, one embodying abstract principles, the other embodying vital, passionate reality. In many ways, the clash between Lucile and Paola is reminiscent of the contrast between Andromache and Helen, between Electra and her mother. Andromache, of course, was essentially attached to sound logic and clear reason, and Electra wanted justice above all, while Lucile is exclusively dedicated to purity. In every case, however, these characters are the personification of an ideal.

As Giraudoux advanced in age, his characters seemed to acquire more and more the value of pure symbols. Andromache was still in many respects warmly human, but the savage thirst for total justice often appeared inhuman in Electra. Then the preternaturally pure Lucile hardly seems to belong to our world. Simultaneously, a definite deterioration takes place in the characters representing the real. Helen of Troy, although guilty of unleashing a catastrophic war, retains in Giraudoux's play a certain innocence and a winning personal charm. Clytemnestra herself, in spite of her crimes, appears as pitifully pathetic and even at times truly loving and moving. Paola, on the other hand, is almost constantly vicious and odious.

This progressive degradation of the characters representing passionate reality seems to parallel the change for the worse that took place in Giraudoux's personal views of the real itself. In the last years of his life Giraudoux was evidently overwhelmed by a feeling of disgust for the world in which we live. Although he fought as best as he could against that feeling in such works as *L'Apollon de Bellac* and *La Folle de Chaillot,* his final outlook remained grim. A few of the "elect" — of whom Lucile is the last example in his plays — may be personally exempt from the taint of almost universal corruption, but they can escape defilement at the contact of the world and retain their essence of purity only by moving out of this world altogether.

During his youth, a happy Giraudoux had fondly believed that the ideal and reality could meet. In his mature age, he had toyed with the hundred possibilities of interplay between them. When he grew old, he reached the disconsolate conclusion that they are incompatible. Rather than debase the ideal, rather than submit to the loathsome claims of reality, he chose to retain the ideal intact — in death. This is the fundamental meaning of *Pour Lucrèce* and the last message of Giraudoux himself before his own end.

In the last years of his life, Giraudoux became interested in the cinema and wrote the scenario for two films. *La Duchesse de Langeais* is merely the dramatization of one of Balzac's short novels. Giraudoux closely followed the plot of the original story, eliminating only a number of rather heavily realistic details and adding to the dialogues a light, subtle irony not found in Balzac. Giraudoux's scenario of *La Duchesse de Langeais* was used, after several transformations, by Jacques de Baroncelli for the production of a film in 1941.

Somewhat later, in collaboration with Reverend P. Raymond Bruckberger, a Dominican well-known for his liberal ideas, Giraudoux composed a scenario originally called *Les Anges du Péché*. The text elaborated by Giraudoux and Bruckberger was adapted for the screen by the director Robert Bresson and presented to the public in 1943 under the title *Le Film de Béthanie*.

Béthanie[80] is the name of a Dominican community established in 1867 by Reverend P. Lataste to give assistance and hope to women, especially to "fallen" women, who were in particularly distressing circumstances. The general idea of the film was Giraudoux's own, and Bruckberger's part in the work consisted essentially in checking the accuracy of the technical details and of the particular atmosphere to be found in an ecclesiastical environment.

The heroine of the scenario is a young girl, Anne-Marie, who very much like Lucile Blanchard is thirsting after total purity. She leaves her honest but commonplace family and enters the convent of Béthanie as a novice. Even in that highly proper environment she is shocked by the petty hypocrisies and mediocre compromises that are inevitably part of the daily life of the convent. Her craving for absolute purity, mistakenly called pride by the other nuns, isolates her almost completely from the other novices.

Through one of the "fallen" girls who have been "saved" by the Order of Béthanie, she hears of a certain young woman, Thérèse, who is to be released from jail after serving a term for petty theft. Anne-Marie obtains permission to try and induce Thérèse to come to the convent immediately after her liberation. She does not succeed in her attempt, although her personality makes evidently a strong impression on Thérèse. When Thérèse leaves jail, she purchases a gun and shoots her lover who has deserted her. Then she seeks shelter in the Béthanie convent, where Anne-Marie takes her under her special protection and care.

Soon Anne-Marie makes herself thoroughly obnoxious to the

other nuns through her intransigent, inflexible insistence on absolutely faultless behavior in all those around her. She is evidently not made for conventual life, which must imply a certain amount of tolerance of the normal minor weaknesses of average human nature. Simultaneously the police, searching for the murderess and following several clues, have the Béthanie convent under constant observation.

Anne-Marie eventually leaves the convent. Instead of returning to her family, however, which would have meant a complete surrender of her sublime ideal, she wanders aimlessly and goes to pray every night on the tomb of Father Lataste, the founder of Béthanie. She is found there one evening utterly exhausted, in a dead faint, by the nuns who take her back to the convent. Thérèse is called on to take care of her. She dies soon afterward, however, but only when, under her purifying influence, Thérèse has decided to give herself up, on her own will, to the police inspectors. The film ends with all the nuns singing a hymn to the Virgin Mary — a symbol of perfect, immaculate purity.

The fundamental idea running through *Le Film de Béthanie* is strikingly similar to the theme of *Pour Lucrèce*. The two were composed by Giraudoux at about the same time and they illustrate the same aspect of his thought. Anne-Marie is, like Lucile, dedicated to the ideal of absolute purity. Like Lucile, she finds it impossible to accommodate herself to the contemptible practices prevailing among ordinary human beings. Even in the supposedly fine ambiance of a religious community, she finds the same moral confusion that affects the outside world. She refuses, however, to sacrifice her moral ideal, and she obtains its final fulfillment only in death.

I do not need to interpret life in order to judge it.
My opinion on people, on plays, on fashions takes shape
spontaneously after a few days, clear and definitive.[1]
Jean Giraudoux

⚗ V ⚗
Literary Essays
and
Political Polemics

Although Giraudoux was an extremely prolific writer of essays, his work in this genre is far from having the same value as his novels and plays. As a rule, his essays are not the result of serious and objective research. In most cases, they simply mirror, like many of his other works, some facets of his personality. He seldom delves deeply in any given subject, and he often passes judgments on people and on facts after a minimum of investigation and study. Yet owing to the originality of his mind, his opinions— often paradoxical—are usually arresting and challenging; on occasion, they are truly illuminating. The most important of his essays are devoted to literary criticism and to political questions. But a number of his articles and short essays can be grouped only under the general title of miscellanies.

Twenty-one essays on literary subjects, written between 1927 and 1940, were collected by Giraudoux and published in 1941 under the title of *Littérature*. They are of unequal length and value. Only those of genuine interest will be briefly examined here.

The first and perhaps the most paradoxical is a study of Racine. Although the life of Racine is imperfectly known, critics have assumed that the essential traits of his theater are the reflection of definite traits of his personality and character. They believe that he had a deep religious faith instilled in him by the Jansenist environment in which he spent most of his youth. They also surmise that he had an agitated private life, filled with intense and stormy love affairs. The conflict in Racine between piety and passion is a favorite theme for innumerable academic dissertations in French high schools and universities.

Giraudoux claims in his essay that Racine, as a professional playwright, apparently lived in close contact with the broadminded world of the stage, and consequently must have had a few liaisons with actresses, although these affairs must have been very banal. In any case he made a perfectly sensible and bourgeois marriage, ending his life as a model husband and father. Giraudoux, moreover, finds no evidence in Racine of a religious faith markedly different from the unquestioning, conventional devotion then widespread among his contemporaries.

According to Giraudoux, the main source of Racine's inspiration is not to be sought in personal feelings or experiences, but in the spirit of the century in which he lived, and particularly in the preexisting literary forms that he used, which were the product of a long social and cultural evolution. Further, the ideas and principles that governed his life were simply those that he had absorbed during his long and studious years at school.

The next essay, on Choderlos de Laclos, the author of *Les Liaisons Dangereuses,* follows a more orthodox pattern. Laclos appears strangely "modern" in certain respects, particularly in his "substituting eroticism"[2] for love. Giraudoux explains the appearance of naked eroticism in Laclos' novel by the influence of the society in which Laclos himself lived. In that society, which was soon to be destroyed by the French Revolution, all moral values were already disintegrating, thus allowing the crudest elements of human nature to appear on the surface.

Gérard de Nerval, the remote forerunner of the surrealist movement, is the object of a brief but shrewd study. Giraudoux shows that, although Nerval never produced a true literary masterpiece, he exerted a deep and durable influence on French thought. The tragic circumstances of his life and death made him a model and almost a symbol of a certain form of French sensibility.

The essay "Dieu et la Littérature" was originally destined to serve as a preface to a de luxe edition of *Suzanne et le Pacifique* for which the painter Gabriel Daragnès had composed a series of illustrations. The essay is presented as a letter addressed by Suzanne to Daragnès. Its title is very deceptive. It does not deal with the portentous question of the presence of God in literature in general, but merely with the limited problem of his near absence from the works of Giraudoux and particularly from *Suzanne et le Pacifique*.

A brief sketch on *L'Esprit Normalien* offers a penetrating analysis of the spirit prevailing at the Ecole Normale Supérieure. Among the multifarious facets of that spirit, Giraudoux naturally chose to emphasize two aspects corresponding to the two principal traits of his own character: the cult of idealism and a very special conception of reality. As noted, these traits, which were essential parts of his personality, found a fertile ground for further development at the Ecole Normale.

The essay "De Siècle à Siècle" is the printed version of a talk that Giraudoux gave at the Université des Annales in 1930 to commemorate the hundredth anniversary of Victor Hugo's play *Hernani,* which marked the triumph of French Romanticism on the stage. Far from praising Victor Hugo and his cohorts, Giraudoux excoriated them pitilessly. For him, true Romanticism is the German form of Romanticism. It is a movement of deep emotional revolt against "all human institutions" and a mystic search for a superior union with "all the rest of Nature."[3] Because Giraudoux can find scarcely a trace of these transcendent yearnings in the French poets of the 1830 group, he accuses them of fraud and flings at them the supreme insult of "bourgeois."[4] He further asserts that the only revolution that the French Romanticists effected in literature was a purely verbal revolution.

Littérature also includes five essays on theatrical technique particularly in France, but also in Germany and Spain. Giraudoux considers in some detail the nature of the relations between the dramatic author on the one hand and the actors, the producers, and the political authorities on the other. These essays provide a good insight into the difficulties encountered by any playwright and suggest several solutions.

Giraudoux's most notable achievement in literary criticism is undoubtedly *Les Cinq Tentations de La Fontaine.* Giraudoux and

La Fontaine have many striking similarities. Like Giraudoux, La Fontaine received an extremely solid foundation of Greco-Latin culture. On the other hand, almost alone among the great writers of the classical age in France, La Fontaine felt a deep personal love for nature, creating a close intimate bond between his sensibility and all the forms of life on earth. His approach to reality also recalls Giraudoux's attitude. La Fontaine had a deep appreciation for the world around him and thoroughly enjoyed its variegated and poetic aspects, but he also perceived the fundamental cruelty and ruthlessness inherent in many forms of the real. Finally, La Fontaine's general detachment from gross material interests and his carelessness in everyday life are in many ways akin to Giraudoux's "indifference."

Giraudoux chose that very carelessness, which was so much in evidence in La Fontaine's private life, as the focal point of his study of the man and his work. In five connected essays — corresponding to five lectures he gave at the Université des Annales — he explained how, thanks to that "carelessness," La Fontaine had eluded five "temptations" that might have caused him to fail in his vocation as an artist.

His first temptation was for him to accept a tame, well-regulated existence. He escaped that deadening fate through his "absent-mindedness." Although he married, he promptly forgot all his most elementary duties toward his wife and family. His second temptation was the lure of women. He was uncommonly susceptible to their charm and seems to have been endowed with an uncommon power to charm them. Fortunately he was rescued from the dangers of a great love by his laziness. A great love necessarily implies great effort and strain. La Fontaine preferred to that toil and travail the easy indulgence of a series of casual amours.

Then La Fontaine was tempted by the attractions of a brilliant and refined society life. He took his first steps as a society man at the Château de Vaux, in the entourage of his protector, Fouquet, the fabulously wealthy Superintendent of Finances. A successful society life calls for a constant careful attention to minutiae of etiquette and subtle niceties of behavior. La Fontaine was unable to concentrate his attention too long on anything, let alone on such meaningless trifles.

Giraudoux says that La Fontaine must have been tempted to become a fashionable author. He could have easily mastered the literary tricks used by the writers of his time and he might have tried to gain a reputation in the genres that were considered elevated and noble, such as the tragedy, the epic poem, or the ode. He was saved from that temptation by his love for animals, by his feeling for nature, and by his modesty. Writing unpretentious Fables, he found that he could give a full measure of his genius in them.

Finally, La Fontaine was tempted to become a philosopher. Had he succumbed to that temptation, he would very probably have adopted the sterile doctrines of the Skeptics. He resisted that temptation merely because it would have required great exertion to reject the principles instilled in him by this first teachers. It was so much easier for him to remain faithful to the reassuring ideas that he had received painlessly at school!

The parallelism between the alternatives that La Fontaine had to face and some of the choices that Giraudoux had to make in the course of his career is obvious. That essential similarity of their reaction to the challenge of the world enabled Giraudoux to grasp intuitively and to explain coherently many disconcerting features of La Fontaine's character and art. The erudite commentaries laboriously put together by scholars who have studied La Fontaine's works more often than not obscure his true personality. Because the most confusing and contradictory elements of his actions and his thoughts had a curious counterpart in Giraudoux's own experience, Giraudoux was frequently able, through a flash of personal insight, to illuminate them brilliantly.

In 1942 Giraudoux gave a series of lectures in Lausanne. The text was published after his death in 1947 as *Visitations*. Here he expressed once more his views about the theater and described his literary plans for the future, quoting large extracts from plays on which he was then working, notably *L'Apollon de Bellac* and *Sodome et Gomorrhe*.

In 1943, for the two hundred and fifty-fifth anniversary of Marivaux's birth, Giraudoux composed a tribute that was read on the stage of the Comédie Française. Giraudoux and Marivaux resemble one another in many ways, notably in an extreme subtlety of expression, a delicate sense of the most elusive shades of feeling, particularly in love, a suave, discreet, and sometimes almost tender irony, and a tendency to draw around characters and events presented on the stage graceful, dreamlike arabesques of pure imagination.

As a result, Marivaux and Giraudoux have both been accused of affectation and artificiality. Undoubtedly, the world in which they move is not the world of everybody's commonplace, trivial experience, but the poetic, fantastic world found in their works is truly their own natural milieu. Giraudoux could therefore assert, without feeling that he was developing a paradox, that Marivaux's theater contains no trace of artifice but is completely true to reality. One may perhaps add: his reality.

Giraudoux's political writings are concentrated in the prewar and war periods. The most important is *Pleins Pouvoirs*. When it was composed, in 1939, many French people perceived that France was passing through a phase of extremely dangerous weakness. Giraudoux gave five lectures at the Université des Annales, explaining almost brutally to his audience the main causes of the French decline.

In his first lecture, he stated that the enfeeblement of France might well mark a crucial turning point in the destiny of the country. Until then, in spite of a number of temporary setbacks, France had remained a first-rank power and an independent nation. Now France was threatened with the possibility of becoming a vassal nation: "The condition offered to us today is low and final: it is a condition that France has never known even in what was called her worst hours. . . . It is vassalage."[5]

He went on to show that in the past the role of France has been to constitute a spiritual stimulation and a perennial challenge to the other people of the world. If France became a second-rate country, it would no longer be able to play that role which, according to Giraudoux, is her essential raison d'être: "Such is the destiny of France: if she remains a first-rank nation, she is a symbol. . . . Should she become a nation of second order, she would be a sort of deserter. . . . The day France becomes a second-rate nation, France will be lost."[6] Thus the problem of the continued power of France is not for the French a question of prestige. It is a matter of survival: "We are back to the stone age of the subject: the preservation of life for our country and ourselves."[7]

According to Giraudoux, the greatest threat to the survival of France lies in the failure on the part of the French to keep up with the population explosion taking place all over the world. The shrinking influence of France in the world is in direct relation to the shrinking of the number of Frenchmen compared to the total number of inhabitants of our planet. Giraudoux denounces the causes of that catastrophe: a pitifully low birth rate, an appalling neglect of the elementary rules of hygiene, and a lamentably inadequate medical service.

The second French calamity studied by Giraudoux is the rapid deterioration of the French urban environment. At a time when the population is flocking in masses to the cities, the cities are allowed to rot and nothing is really being done to prevent the spreading of the decay. The third serious problem plaguing the French is caused by their failure to provide their country with the technical equipment that would allow them to remain at the fore of the modern industrial nations. Their obsolete methods of production and their woefully insufficient investments in public works constitute a constant handicap in the economic race that is the dominant feature of our modern competitive civilization.

Giraudoux frankly admits that the main factor of the French decline is the recent erosion of French civic morality. He gives a disheartening and only too convincing picture of the corruption, inefficiency, and slackness prevailing at all levels of the French social order. Yet he refuses to believe that the French people at large are responsible for that state of affairs. He thinks that a small clique of speculators, swindlers, and gangsters — a regular mafia[8] — is the real cause of the trouble.

"It is an understanding between those for whom fraud is more rewarding than honesty; it is the disappearance of every trace of moral conscience that causes man to lose all sense of collective obligation and makes the citizen oblivious of any duty toward the state. The members of that mafia are not recruited in particular places or according to a particular ritual. They meet by chance in reception rooms, in railroad compartments, in the lobbies of administrative buildings, of newspapers, or of banks. They have no special signs by which they recognize one another — except that their appearance shows that no sense of citizenship exists in them. . . . All that takes place between persons having different religions, different political beliefs, but whose guiding principle is the same: making money."[9]

If the members of that mafia could be removed, the morale of France would undoubtedly be sound again. Giraudoux performed that miraculous removal in *La Folle de Chaillot*.

Giraudoux's picture of the demoralization of France certainly contains much truth. Whether it covers the whole truth is of course debatable. Notably, however, among the conditions necessary for the restoration of the general health of France Giraudoux considered that one of the most important was a revival of the element that he himself called "national honesty."[10]

These severe judgments and stern warnings made an extremely strong impression on the general public when they were published. Even today, they have lost only little of their appropriateness. The style of the book, moreover, is direct, plain, and completely free from the frills and verbal curlicues that so often decorate and sometimes mar Giraudoux's most serious productions.

The other political writings of Giraudoux are of lesser interest. The radio speeches that he made during the so-called "Phony War" were never fully published. After the capitulation of France in 1940, he composed an essay, "Armistice à Bordeaux," which appeared only in 1945. Giraudoux then asserted that signing an armistice with the victorious Germans was the only wise step that any French government could take to avoid the utter destruction of France.

During the last part of the war, Giraudoux outlined a program of rehabilitation of the country after the end of the hostilities. This study remained unfinished, and the fragments of several chapters that could be fitted together were published after his death under the title *Sans Pouvoirs*, which contains very little that is original and new.

The "miscellaneous" essays written by Giraudoux in his literary career are, as a rule, of secondary importance. Four of them, however, offer a certain interest. In 1927 Giraudoux contributed "L'Orgueil" to a book of essays on the seven deadly sins in which each sin was treated by a different author. The other authors were Paul Morand, André Salmon, Pierre Mac Orlan, Max Jacob, Jacques de Lacretelle and Joseph Kessel.

The French word *orgueil* has a connotation markedly different from our word "pride." *Orgueil* refers to an excessive and offensively high opinion that a man may have of his own importance and value in the world. According to Giraudoux it represents essentially a struggle of man against God. Giraudoux did not conceive that struggle as an epic rebellion against the Deity but as the expression of the disproportionately lofty idea that certain men have of their own selves. Women, who have instead a harmless vanity, are practically exempt from it. Furthermore, it is usually absent from really outstanding men, being found more commonly among mediocrities. It manifests itself through a contempt of God-given life as it is. It fosters vain efforts to rise above the normal human condition and generally ends with a longing for self-defeat and death.

In 1928 Giraudoux published a slender book of aphorisms called *Le Sport,* in which he advocated athletics for French youth. Giraudoux was not a real athlete himself, although he had some honorable performances on the track field to his credit in high school. The Frenchmen of his generation often considered any prowess in sports a mark of low intellectuality. Giraudoux was one of the first to react against the prejudice and to show the value of physical exercise for the maintenance of good health.

In 1934 he gave a series of lectures on the French woman, in which he followed with mild approval the development of feminism in the modern world and particularly in France. He did not fail to note, without animus though not without humor, that although modern ladies strive to become self-reliant and strong, they are not altogether anxious to relinquish the privileges conferred on them when they were dependent and weak. The text of those lectures appeared only in 1951 under the title *La Française et la France.*

In the last years of his life, Giraudoux became intensely interested in the problems of urbanism. The notes that he made on that subject were collected in the posthumous volume *Pour une Politique Urbaine.* His ideas on the subject are eminently sound, although not particularly illuminating. He wants man to live in healthy, attractive, modern surroundings, and he denounces the stupid administrative regulations that paralyze intelligent private initiative. Berating the great financial interests that cover huge tracts of land with bleak housing developments or hideous commercial buildings, he accuses the public of being apathetic and lacking aesthetic as well as practical imagination. He offers no effective remedy, however, for these perhaps incurable evils. His appeal for drastic action remains the expression of a generous man who clearly sees the growing misery of modern city dwellers, but who is powerless to solve the inner contradictions and overcome the cruel absurdities of the civilization in which we live.

*A world where one owes no accounts, no smiles,
no tears to any person, where desire is replaced
by continual satisfaction and the religion offered
to the Lord replaced by politeness toward His creation.*[1]
Jean Giraudoux

⚜ VI ⚜
The World
of Giraudoux

The view of the world implied in the works of Giraudoux is in no sense
organic or systematic. No fixed or definite idea of the interrelations
of the various aspects of life can be discerned in these works.
Sometimes contradictory statements appear about the same person or object, presenting in rapid succession opposite views of the
same reality. Widely divergent impressions occur side by side,
and the reason for such association is left to the imagination of the
reader. Nevertheless, an undoubted unity of tone runs throughout
that diversity and uncertainty, so that a few leading trends of
thought may be more or less isolated and studied.

That uncertainty is particularly evident in Giraudoux's conception of the Godhead. Three completely different influences seem to
have modeled his thought in this regard. As a Frenchman partak-
ing of the great spiritual tradition of Western culture, Giraudoux
had been impregnated with the Judeo-Christian religious ideas.
As a scholar steeped in Hellenic lore, he had come to sense the
deep meaning of certain myths familiar to the ancient Greeks. As
an intelligent individual, he naturally pondered over eternal metaphysical problems and probably reached tentative and completely
personal conclusions about God. The views issuing from these

159

three sources of thought never blended in his mind to form a unified whole.

Although Giraudoux belonged to a Catholic family, he never practiced his religion and Suzanne Giraudoux has said that "he was not a pious man."[2] Yet the Judeo-Christian idea of a Creator who is also the fountainhead of all moral values remained deeply imbedded in his consciousness. Virtually all his references to that particular notion of the Divinity are inspired by the Old Testament and owe nothing to the Gospels.

This conception of God lingered at the background of his mind all his life, and he seems to have fought against it. The main reason for his hostility toward the Old Testament God was that he saw in Him and His laws a threat to human happiness on earth. Thus Holofernes says to Judith: "I am the friend of the gardens with beautiful lawns, of the houses that are well kept, of lovely china sparkling on the tablecloth. . . . I am the worst enemy of God. . . . Think how sweet your days would be if you had not to fear and pray. Think of your breakfast in the morning without any prospect of Hell and your five o'clock tea without mortal sin. . . . I am offering you simplicity and calm. . . . I am offering you pleasure, Judith. Before that tender word, you will see Jehovah disappear."[3] Giraudoux, however, was well aware that he could not rid himself so easily of Jehovah's haunting presence; he made Judith reply to Holofernes: "Jehovah comes back frighteningly quickly."[4]

Giraudoux was much more in sympathy with the deities of Hellas. Although Greek religion varied considerably from Homer to Euripides, nevertheless the same general feeling ran through all its manifestations and was in perfect harmony with some of Giraudoux's essential intuitions. The ancient Greeks felt that the universe contains a multiplicity of forces tending in all sorts of different directions. These forces — represented in their mythology by the Gods — determine through their interactions, associations, or antagonisms, a bewildering complexity of forms and almost unlimited possibilities of particular fulfillments.

The polytheism of the Greeks reflected the polyvalence of the hidden energies ruling the world. The proliferation of the Greek gods, their limitations, their imperfections, their contradictions, and their crimes were the mythical expressions of the innumerable variants that are at the origin of all the shapes of the real. Giraudoux's own disconnected view of the multiple aspects of the universe was in perfect agreement with that pluralistic perception of the prodigious variety of dynamic elements existing in the cosmos. He was genuinely attracted by the religious myths embodying the Hellenic particular vision—so similar to his own—of the fragmented essence of the universe.

At the same time Giraudoux turned over in his mind, as any cultured man would, all the problems connected in our modern world with the question of the existence of God. The ultimate results of his meditations on that subject will never be known. Giraudoux has partly explained his reticent attitude in this regard in a fictitious letter written by Suzanne to Daragnès: "You are so kind as to let me know that certain bibliophiles of Lyons, for whom you have made illustrations of my trip and my solitude in the island, are surprised not to have found even once in it the mention of God. . . . Of the visits that God may or may not have paid me in my island, nobody will ever know anything."[5] Yet a few scattered but convergent statements made by Giraudoux in several of his books may give a fair idea of his personal religious thought.

In *Combat avec l'Ange*, Brossard is asked by his secretary Jacques Blisson if he is an atheist. "I an atheist? By no means. It is the word 'to exist' [when applied to God] that shocks me. . . . We [humans] do exist. . . . But to apply that notion of existence to God is just as impious and erroneous as to picture God in our own image."[6] In *Electre*, Aegisthus states: "Between the infinitudes of space and time . . . there are tremendous indifferences that are the Gods. I imagine them not at all as being constantly occupied with that supreme and mobile mildew of the earth which is called mankind, but as having reached such a degree of serenity and ubiquity that it can only be called beatitude, that is to say, absence of consciousness."[7] In the same play, although in a different vein, the gardener explains his views of the Gods: "It is not fitting for a gardener to ask God to send a storm, even a storm of tenderness. And such a request is so useless. . . . One can feel so well that now, and yesterday and tomorrow and always, all of them, as many as they are, and even if there is only One, and even if that One is absent, they are quite ready to proclaim joy and love. . . . But I have always found silence more convincing. I beseech you God, as a proof of your affection . . . to be silent."[8] And Suzanne writes to Daragnès:

"Is God so really anxious to have us speak of him? Is it not his preference to be a secret rather than a revelation? I shall never say to anyone that I am sure that God exists, except to God himself. The belief in God is the beginning of a love, that is to say, a silence."[9]

The use of the word "silence," which frequently occurs when Giraudoux refers to the relations between God and man, and also his refusal to apply to God the notion of "existence" with the meaning that we attach to that word on earth, seem to provide clues to Giraudoux's personal conception of the Divinity. Those clues point to a belief of a "divine" element in the Cosmos. That element, however, is not an existing personal God, as that expression is commonly understood, but essentially "a silence" to whom man can offer homage only through his own silence.

This last "metaphysical" and utterly personal view of the Deity did not exclude in Giraudoux's mind the biblical God against whom he struggled or the Hellenic mythic forces that he favored. Like many other men of our troubled epoch of religious uncertainty and doubt, he probably often passed from one opinion to another. He certainly felt no deep anguish in the face of the contradictions and incompatibilities that those variations implied. Giraudoux was neither a theologian nor a philosopher. He never attempted to elaborate a coherent system reconciling the various forms of his religious experience: the Jehovah of the Bible, the Hellenic symbols of the Powers at the core of the Cosmos and the Eternal Silence of his own meditations. He was quite content to let them float poetically in his indifferent and untormented mind.

Three subsidiary notions are related to Giraudoux's views of the Godhead: the influence of Fate, the theory of the Signs, and the privileges of the Elect. Giraudoux's ideas on Fate varied considerably throughout his career. Until around 1932 the world appeared to him as a nexus of multiple forces acting irregularly and capriciously on human life, but not unfriendly to man. Men could find their place in the universe and adapt themselves to the complex but not incomprehensible interplay of the great laws of nature. If men failed to adjust to the vagaries of their environment, they did so simply for lack of insight on their part and were responsible for their failure. During that first part of his life, Giraudoux used the word *destin* in a light, even sometimes irreverent manner. It was a convenient formula for explaining the unexplainable, but not much objective substance lay behind it.

After the great moral crisis that marked the middle of his life, Giraudoux's view of Fate took on a much deeper and darker hue. He then saw Fate as a superior entity, foreign and hostile to man. It was the expression of the limitations imposed on man's autonomous behavior in the midst of the universe. Giraudoux's conception of Fate at that time recalled in many respects the conception that the Greeks had of ἀνάγκη—from which it was idle to expect consideration or mercy. Giraudoux, who was thoroughly versed in Greek culture, probably drew from the Greek tragic poets the feeling that the major tragedy in human experience is the hopeless, desperate struggle of a human against overwhelming, crushing destiny.

The Greeks, however, had fairly definite ideas about the nature of ἀνάγκη: it was a supreme impersonal law to which even the Gods were subjected. Giraudoux's ideas on Fate are much more indefinite. In many passages of *La Guerre de Troie n'aura pas lieu*, the disastrous inevitability of certain events does not seem determined by a superior law or power; they are simply the natural consequences of causes over which man has no control.

Hector and Ulysses may argue about Helen's return to Sparta, but the real reasons for the Trojan war were the desire of the Greeks to plunder the riches of Troy and the collective madness created in Troy by a fanatical rabble-rouser. Neither diplomacy nor intelligence can prevail against greed and folly, and the Trojan war will take place.

Similarly, in *Choix des Elues*, Giraudoux evokes the complicated and compelling political, economic, and emotional factors at the origin of most wars and refers to "that mixture of gods, men, metals, and trade currents that bring the young men to the battlefields."[10]

On the other hand, in *Judith* and *Electre*, the human will, apparently motivated by human passions, may be, after all, only the blind instrument of a hidden divine will. Furthermore, in *La Guerre de Troie n'aura pas lieu*, destiny is sometimes viewed as a cosmic element that is jealous of the happiness and prosperity of human beings. Ulysses says to Hector: "The universe knows that we are going to fight." Hector answers that the universe may be mistaken, and Ulysses replies: "Let us hope so. But when destiny has raised two nations for many years and has opened for them the same future of inventiveness and omnipotence... the universe knows very well that destiny does not mean to prepare for them two paths of colorful fulfillment and expansion. Destiny wants to have its own festival, that is to say, to unleash that brutality and that human folly which alone seem reassuring to the gods. That sounds rather like petty politics. I admit it. But we may just as well say it between us: that is the policy usually followed by destiny."[11]

To those various interpretations of the action of Fate, a remark made at the beginning of *La Guerre de Troie n'aura pas lieu* adds a different and distinctive note. Andromache declares: "I don't know what destiny is." And Cassandra replies: "I am going to tell you what it is: it is simply an accelerated form of time."[12] That statement seems to be a variant of the old and well-known philosophical theory according to which the events that we can observe in slow succession in our world are only the development in time of events that are present in all eternity.

Giraudoux probably did not favor one particular interpretation of destiny above the others. Destiny might assume the form of the concatenation of intricate and uncontrollable causes, or of a secret and irreversible decision taken by the Divinity, or of the influence of a superior, abstract yet malignant force, or of a metaphysical necessity deriving from the nature of the Eternal — in any case, the result is the same: man discovers that he is not the master of the events that are shaping and ruling his life. Mysterious and multifarious powers surround him, oppress him, and drive him more often than not to his doom. The word *destin* conveniently summarizes those powers, and it is not easy, or indeed important, to determine exactly who bears the responsibility for their action. The supremely tragic aspect of human life is that man finds himself powerless to direct his existence in a universe that he senses to be hostile to him.

Giraudoux's belief in "Signs" certainly corresponds to a series of unusual personal psychic experiences that he must have had. It was probably reinforced in his mind by a similar belief that was accepted unquestioningly in ancient classical civilizations. Throughout the historical and dramatic works of the Greek and

Latin authors who contributed so much to the formation of Giraudoux's ideas references are repeatedly made to presages, omens, and signs—ranging from the flight of birds to the roll of thunder—which, if correctly interpreted, could serve as guides for human behavior. Such signs may warn men of imminent dangers or on the contrary encourage them to persevere in a certain course of action; they sometimes portend the anger of the gods or again they may come as reassuring evidence of their favor.

As noted, Giraudoux felt, very much as the ancients did, that the universe was crowded with unseen forces. He was convinced that, under certain circumstances, these forces lying at the core of the cosmos attempt to contact man. He has given striking examples of this curious phenomenon in the short story "Signes" and in a well-known passage of *Combat avec l'Ange,* where Jacques Blisson, alone one evening in a hotel room, suddenly experiences a combined feeling of tenderness and anguish. At first he cannot guess the cause of that unexpected emotion. Then he discovers that it is linked somehow with—the song of a toad. "The toad's song was knocking against the night as a finger might knock against a windowpane.... Tirelessly though without haste, it was challenging me obstinately, rhythmically, and that rhythm was now the rhythm of my anxiety. I was sure of it now. It was a sign that the night was sending me. I had just to interpret it. Gladys? Was it about Gladys? I tried the name of Gladys against the toad's song, but the thought of Gladys did not become sweeter or harsher while the toad was singing.... Then I submitted the name of Maléna. And there it was. Suddenly everything became clear to me...."[13] In a flash, Jacques had the overwhelming intuition that Maléna was in serious danger and needed his help.

A few weeks later, a long time after he has rescued Maléna from her predicament, he finds himself again one evening in the garden of the same hotel and hears the toad once more. "With my flashlight I discovered him, almost right under my window, between two plants of geranium. The stem of one of the flowers was before his mouth, practically barring it. He did not care; he was still singing.... Very much like a signal that goes on ringing once it has been started, he was going on calling for help for Maléna."[14]

Numerous other, though generally shorter, allusions to that theory of "Signs" are found in Giraudoux's works from the beginning to the end of his career. Thus, already in *Suzanne et le Pacifique,* Suzanne says: "The first quail was calling; the signals given by the birds already had a meaning for us."[15] In Giraudoux's last play, *Pour Lucrèce,* Lucile states: "I would have obeyed a stone if a stone had told me to die. But the stones told me to live. I would have fallen down if a dog had snarled at me. But the dogs licked my hand. And that permission to live that every human, even if not guilty, asks every morning from the objects and animals, they gave it to me with all possible sweetness."[16]

The persistence in his works of references to signs sent to human beings by the cosmos shows that Giraudoux attached a definite meaning to manifestations generally overlooked by most modern men, but his scattered mentions of these phenomena never coalesce to form the body of a doctrine and for that reason remain somewhat enigmatic and perplexing for the ordinary reader.

Hardly less enigmatic and perplexing is Giraudoux's idea of the privileges of the elect. The huge majority of men concentrate their attention on more or less definite practical goals. Their ambitions and their efforts are directed toward the fulfillment of some material desires or the acquisition of actual and tangible profits. In other words, they live entirely in the world of everyday reality. But since that world is generally low and mean, those who partake of it exclusively are at best simply mediocre and at worst utterly degraded.

According to Giraudoux, however, a privileged group of human beings seem to have been called on to reach a "Paradise lost" beyond vulgar reality. These elect have a longing for the ideal, for a higher, purer realm altogether inaccessible to common humanity. Most of the elect who appear in Giraudoux's works — Suzanne, Isabelle, Edmée, Claudie, Judith, Lucile — are young women who have somehow received the gift — one could almost say the grace — of entering somehow into direct contact with the soul of the cosmos.

That gift, or that grace, is bestowed on them for reasons unknown and for a limited time only. The elect may suddenly leave the world in which ordinary men abide — sometimes through a fantastic journey like Suzanne, sometimes through a visionary flight of imagination like Isabelle, sometimes through a fugue like Edmée, sometimes in a sublime rapture like Judith—but sooner or later thay have to return chastened to the normal, banal, humdrum human condition. Lucile alone, who has chosen death as a means of escape from a degrading existence, evidently has no return.

Thus, even though the elect are a small élite of the spirit, their lot is not particularly enviable. In fact, it seems to become harder and harder as Giraudoux himself becomes older and more somber in mood. The escapade of Suzanne in the Pacific has all the joyful appearances of a game, and her possible marriage with the Controller of Weights and Measures can be viewed without alarm. Isabelle's association with the Ghost, however, plunges her in many difficulties. She emerges from them, of course, with the love of another Controller, but the play suggests that their union will not make her happy ever after. Judith, having enjoyed the briefest spell of bliss, is condemned to sacred solitude for the rest of her life. Edmée, after countless tribulations, faces the dismal prospect of everlasting boredom. Finally, at the end of his life, Giraudoux offered Lucile, the purest of all the elect, the only solace of a tragic death.

The idea of death plays an important part in Giraudoux's works. That idea never conjures up in his mind feelings of terror and horror, as it usually does in the average man: "The prospect of my own death, of the death of my friends did not arouse in me any care, any anguish."[17] For Giraudoux, death is above all the release from the mediocrities of existence: "When I think of the great rest that death will give to our lassitudes, to all our petty worries, I am grateful for its fullness and its abundance."[18]

Death ought to be accepted calmly and without struggle. A perfect death—the death of Eglantine—is pictured in Moïse's imagination: "She was simply becoming less and less pink and lively every day. She reached the state of supreme immobility by self-restraint, by a politeness toward nothingness that increased hour by hour."[19]

Giraudoux does not refer to the dead with sorrowful regret. They provide him with a ductile and supple material on which his fancy will work. Whereas living characters are usually a source of disappointment, the dead are consistently flexible and can give to life the complement of perfection that it naturally lacks. "The dead? I go into mourning a thousand times — mourning that is not really my own. Young men, young women whom I have met once or twice and of whose death I have suddenly heard appear to me and become familiar acquaintances. I dream about them continually. . . . Thus can insignificant shadows bring me all that is missing in life, in friendship, in love."[20]

Giraudoux pictures the existence beyond the grave somewhat as the Greeks of the Homeric period conceived it — as an existence without torture or bliss, similar to life on earth and yet attenuated, phantasmagoric, simplified, and evolving without material obstacle in a vague, grayish, shadowy atmosphere: "'Is everything different where you are, Edith?' — 'Everyting is the same. Except that we have sovereign command over all things that with you are hostile. We can catch birds and sunbeams. Our shadows do not revolve around us like a compass measuring out life. They are always the same length as our bodies and never go before us. What has been said about the asphodels is true; the meadows are covered with them and with cowslips as well.' — 'Do you gather them?' — 'We never stoop. We always walk erect.' — 'Edith, Edith, so it is true. Your ankles, your knees are all in one?' She leans against my shoulder, sobbing, and I comfort her passionately. Tearing herself away from me, she plunges, still erect, into the wall; now only her hand is extended from the tapestry. I kiss it, but it is like imprinting a caress on one engulfed in a quicksand."[21]

Being dead is not a torment. It implies a sort of immaterial laziness: "What pleases me in the prospect of death is the laziness of death, that rather heavy, numb fluidity whereby people in fact do not die but are only drowned."[22] Nevertheless, the dead are not eternal: "There comes a time when they are seized with fatigue. A plague of the dead blows on them; a tumor of annihilation gnaws at them. The beautiful grey of their shadows becomes silvery and oily. Then the end is near. The end of everything."[23]

To that subdued image of death corresponds an equally subdued picture of life. Its more permanent and established aspects, such as the fundamental elements of human nature, are deliberately overlooked. On the other hand, its most external and fleeting manifestations — the changing of moods or of seasons, the elusive shades of thought, the racing of clouds across an autumn sky — are recorded with subtlety and precision. Giraudoux did not attempt to set forth eternal laws or to determine unalterable verities, but simply to present, as they occur, the multitudes of trifles that constitute daily life. This deliberate superficiality is closely related to a very delicate sense of morality. Giraudoux is perfectly aware that, in the depths of every human being, hideous uncontrollable thoughts are stirring. Modern psychologists seem to have made it their business to bring these thoughts to the surface and to expose them to view, thus permitting them to infest and spoil everything around them. Giraudoux believes that the best plan is to keep them buried out of sight: "All the evil in the world comes from the fact that supposedly pure persons wanted to dig up secrets and spread them under the sun."[24]

It is sometimes said that those unlovely things constitute the essence of man's nature. Giraudoux denies this, believing that they are only minute elements of a rich and complicated whole. They exert an undue influence only if they are artificially developed beyond their normal size and importance. Thus, in the name of clear thinking and wholesome moral living, in the name of idealism, Giraudoux would banish from conscious attention and consideration the monsters that constantly threaten to emerge from the depths where they belong. The true art of life consists in keeping in check, by exercise of strict self-control, all the repulsive thoughts, the impure cravings, the unlovely desires that might besmirch our moral nature. The best way to achieve that aim is to ignore them resolutely and systematically.

Juliette, having caught a glimpse of all the unpleasant tendencies latent in her comes to a definite conclusion: "Juliette suddenly perceived, lying motionless in the depths of her being, all the monsters that are unleashed when the mind becomes confused, all of them contrary to what she thought she knew and loved, monsters lying dormant but nevertheless existent—the reverse of her love for Gérard, of her affection for her uncle, of her taste for pancakes, of her modesty. She felt conscious of all the things that a human being guards and protects by keeping silence with himself, and she realized that everyone who does not carry with him an internal replica of himself that is both deaf and dumb constitutes a trapdoor by which evil may flood the world."[25]

The suppression of these evil tendencies within ourselves should not require a great display of energy or call for superhuman effort. Life is obviously not perfect. It is wise not to attach too much value to its gifts—which are often bestowed out of season: "All the good things of life have been granted to me one year or one hour too late."[26] We may even despise life a little, in order to insure our mental freedom. But to grapple with life and to struggle against nature to improve or dominate either is a dangerous process foredoomed to failure.

Giraudoux's attitude is one neither of revolt nor of resignation, but of courteous understanding and politeness. The word "politeness" recurs as a leitmotif whenever he tries to define his attitude toward human existence. Although life may often prove deceptive and disappointing, a man must go on behaving well from a standpoint of pure breeding.

Giraudoux's writings raise no question of prospective punishments or rewards in this world or in another, nor of supreme devotion to an absolute. Yet just as a polite man retains his manners even amid unsatisfactory surroundings, so a self-imposed discipline will enable him to accept all that life has to offer. He will not ask for more, but will associate with his fellow men kindly and unassumingly, acting as if—which unfortunately is rarely the case—life was generous and fair, and other men dependable and friendly.

Such a man, thinks Giraudoux, is really a civilized man: "Civilization ... is a state of personal modesty that leads the civilized man to make the course of his life run parallel to nature (thus incidentally avoiding an encounter with that pitiless person), to attach ... the smallest possible value to life, to pay its opposite death a certain amount of deference ... and on the other hand, by reason of that mild contempt for life, not to complicate it on earth by demands exceeding human needs; to practice—but without making oneself a nuisance to others and through self-discipline—the qualities that would be necessary if life were just, pleasant, eternal, qualities such as courage, activity, some moderation and kindness."[27]

This philosophy, if generally accepted, would result in a world of perfectly free and independent people, conducting themselves with tact and respect toward each other, exercising self-restraint, never incurring obligations or perpetrating intrusions, never cruel though somewhat formal and cold. A sincere contentment would pervade a clear, transparent atmosphere. Then we would have "a humanity in which every man would be distinct from the rest, in soul as well as in body, as a star is distinct from the other stars, in which relations between humans would only consist of inflexions, assents, transparencies . . . in which silence itself would be a common good and pleasure . . . in which the human atmosphere . . . would constantly have the limpidity of the evenings in early spring."[28]

This conception of life resembles a dream, and indeed it is a poetical dream like so many other products of Giraudoux's imagination. Yet it clearly indicates the orientation of his thought. For him, every living creature, when enveloped in a cloak of politeness, is individualized and isolated to such a point that reciprocal influences cease to be markedly perceptible. The world resolves itself into a collection of independent units, all of which are equally interesting. Why prefer one to another?

A man, a plant, an animal are all equal under the law of Giraudoux's all-comprehensive politeness. He loves them all, singly and collectively just as they are. This all-embracing love and spontaneous confusion become a sort of half-indifferent, half-pantheistic acceptance of the universe as it is. Giraudoux, very much like Juliette is affected by "the disease that consists in treating objects like human beings, human beings as if they were Gods and Virgins, the Gods like cats and weasels—a malady caused not by a life spent in libraries, but by personal relations with the seasons and small animals, excessive pantheism and politeness toward all creation."[29]

What then should be man's practical attitude toward nature? Man is part of nature. That man is wise who adapts himself to nature, who follows nature consciously and deliberately. Any attempt to fight nature will only result in disrupting the harmonious relations prevailing between the various elements of the world. Only too often in the past, but more particularly in recent times, man, urged on by his restlessness and greed, has tried by dint of hard work to force his will on nature. He has succeeded only in damaging the environment in which he has to live and in creating utterly artificial conditions of existence, which have largely contributed to his estrangement from the core of

the universe and thus brought about untold moral miseries.
In *Suzanne et le Pacifique,* Giraudoux denounced the stupid
action of Robinson Crusoe, who instead of accepting gracefully
the lavish gifts of a bountiful nature, wore himself out with obstinate, frantic, and unnecessary work. In *Supplément au Voyage
de Cook,* he riddled with sarcasms those who set purposeless
effort as a goal for human life. He showed the preposterous
Mr. Banks attempting to convert nature-wise Outourou to the
religion of hard work. Outourou asks him: "What does the word
'to work' mean, Mr. Banks?" — "It means that you should not lie
softly on the grass but grab your tools and dig the soil until the
evening." — "But that would be our death, Mr. Banks. As soon as
we dig or plow the soil, it becomes sterile. . . . We have had here,
on the island, a man who worked. . . . He was digging wells while
we have spring water running plentifully everywhere. He was
preventing our pigs from eating our grass and he fattened them
with a special sort of mush and made them burst and die. Everything around him was perishing. We had to kill him. There is no
room for work here." — "The grandeur of man is precisely that he
can find a reason for toiling where even an ant would rest."[30]
    Toward the end of his life, logically enough, Giraudoux turned
his attack against the cult of the machine. Clearly, machines are
the most effective means of aggression that man possesses against
nature. Thanks to machines, man has increased a hundredfold
his power to wreck his natural surroundings, to organize for
himself a separate order of existence and thus destroy within
himself the magnificent spiritual gifts that a close contact with the
core of the cosmos can provide. "Every standardization imposed
on any act, every substitute found for a natural product, every
skill withdrawn from a hand and entrusted to an engine, every
voice taken away from vocal cords and given to a sound box is
a blow . . . dealt to the state of marvelous alertness and awareness
which all that is beautiful and noble in the world has enabled
us to reach."[31]
    Giraudoux's personal relations with nature may be compared to
a series of confidential conversations carried on in a subdued
voice. They contain a mixture of intimacy, polite reserve, discreet
appreciation, and distant respect that confers on them a tonality
all their own. In Giraudoux, one finds no spectacular description of

landscapes, no outburst of enthusiasm over shapes and colors, but only a few modest notes that are sufficient to create an atmosphere and to establish a subtle bond of communication between man and things.

For instance, some autumn impressions are presented as follows: "You must not think that dead leaves fall suddenly like ripe fruit, or noiselessly like withered flowers. . . . There are leaves that fall at night, brushing against a branch and pausing anxiously, then starting again and, in fear lest they awaken the tree, making more noise than ever. Only the aspen leaves are shed at once, silvery no longer. . . . From my bed I could see and hear them falling. Autumn was spreading under the lime trees like a silken net, softening the fall of the leaves."[32] Throughout Giraudoux's works, one finds similar delicate descriptions and notes, showing how deeply imbued he had been with the charm of the countryside.

Human characters, however, play by far the most important part in Giraudoux's writings. He is far more interested in the personages themselves than in their adventures. In his novels and plays, the plot is often outlined casually, but the feelings and the reactions of the characters are told in a minute manner. Yet Giraudoux was not an adept in psychology. He does not pretend to any new and personal discovery about the workings of the mind and the heart. He does not probe very deeply in the analysis of human sentiments. Of course, many clever and penetrating observations are met in his works, but as a rule he is content to pass lightly over the well-explored field of normal reactions, occasionally indicating some delicate and elusive shades of thought or perhaps adorning the sober pattern of plain facts with arabesques conceived by his imagination.

Most of Giraudoux's characters are endowed with great sensitivity. As a rule, their emotions are not very deep, but they are liable to assume all sorts of forms. Giraudoux sets down a great variety of impressions; some are lightly touched upon, others are allowed to vibrate with many rich and subtle inflections. These modulations are to be found almost exclusively in the realm of sentiment. Giraudoux's works are practically devoid of sensuality and passion. References to purely intellectual problems are few and far between. Yet the inner life of his characters is far less rich than might be inferred from their capacity to receive impressions. They look mostly outward. They are wide open to the influences of the external world, constantly changing from moment to moment.

They are so receptive that each individual separate element of a total impression exerts on them its own distinct effect; their personality often seems diffused in a multiplicity of fragmentary feelings concerning the most insignificant events. Trifling details occupy an enormous place in their consciousness. In *Juliette au Pays des Hommes,* when Gérard learns while shaving that his fiancée is deserting him and going to Paris, he cannot repress a start that makes him cut himself. "One cannot imagine how much moral anguish it takes to outweigh the hurt from just a clumsy stroke of razor. In such a predicament, the first care in the world that a man will have, even if he hears the whistle of the train that is carrying his fiancée away from him, is not to run to the window but to run to the mirror and stop the bleeding."[33]

What were the soldiers in the Great War thinking about when they were killed? Were they filled with hatred for the enemy? Or with idealistic confidence in the justice of their cause? Not at all! — "If they had been allowed to express a regret, it would have been perhaps that they had not been rid during the month, the week or at least the day preceding their death of their toothache, their colic, and also of that General Antoine who forbade them to wear mufflers."[34]

One of the main reasons for Clytemnestra's hatred of her husband is that Agamemnon had — to her — the infuriating habit of raising his little finger on all occasions. "From the day he came to take me away from my home, with his curly beard and that hand, the little finger of which he raised constantly, I have hated him. He would raise that little finger when he drank, raise it when he drove his chariot . . . raise it when he was holding his scepter. . . . And when he was embracing me, I could feel in my back only the pressure of four fingers. He was driving me insane. . . . The King of Kings has never been anything for me but that little finger and that beard which was forever curly."[35]

Special mention must be made of the way in which Giraudoux has presented young women in his writings. Like most of his other characters, they do not present unified personalities. They are composite figures offering a variety of traits with different origins. Some of their qualities are common to practically all girls, regardless of time and clime; some others are typical features of the period during which Giraudoux spent his youth; some of their reactions to the world correspond closely to Giraudoux's own personal views on life; finally, some of their most attractive attributes seem to be merely the result of the normal idealization that usually transfigures young females in the eyes of an imaginative and ardent young man.

Between adolescence and marriage, most young women everywhere on earth, but particularly in Giraudoux's works, live in a state of expectation combining hope and fear. They are perilously poised on the edge of two worlds, the protected world of childhood and the world of complete adult fulfillment, which they anticipate with throbbing curiosity and wonder. Having not been hurt, as a rule, by life and yet being instinctively aware of their own frailty, they can be by turns venturesome, bold, and also riddled with timidity, uncertainty, and doubt.

Scheming is frequently for them a spontaneous means of defense, but in the midst of their unpredictable changes of feelings and moods, they know that the key to their destiny is Man, and they eagerly tend with all their being toward him. They are ready for love. They dream of perfect ideal romance — and then, disconcertingly, their emotions are likely to crystallize around an unsubstantial Ghost, or an elderly gentleman like Fontranges, or a dull and callow youth like Hans von Wittenstein.

Apart from those very general traits of character, the *jeunes filles* in Giraudoux also bear the mark of the particular transition phase during which Giraudoux had his first love experiences. They have not given up the late Victorian standards of modesty, reserve, and restraint. They still have a good measure of morals and manners. Yet new modern horizons are opening before them.

They are strongly tempted to enter the unknown domains that a more tolerant society allows them to explore, but they waver, in tremulous indecision, between the old values that they do not want to abandon and the lure of thrilling and perhaps exalting adventures. More often than not, being ignorant of the dangers they may encounter on their way, they take steps that lead them farther than was considered wise in Giraudoux's youth. Occasionally they stumble and fall into unsuspected traps; but they pick themselves up, generally without too much damage done, and pursue their quest valiantly.

In Giraudoux's novels and plays, however, this quest ends in a rank prosaic manner. Giraudoux's *jeunes filles* are, very much like Giraudoux himself, pathetically divided between the ideal and reality. These dreamy creatures have an innate sense of the practical. They can hear distinctly the call of everything that is elevated, exciting, noble and pure, but they also have the vocation of being housewives. The contradictions implied by these opposite trends of their nature form a part of their mysterious appeal and of their ambiguous charm. Their constant oscillations between unreal sublimity and sensible domesticity are the very signs of their alluring indefiniteness. In Giraudoux's works, however, the *jeune fille* always reaches the same dreary finale: marriage and humdrum home life.

Before that inevitable acceptance of the fundamental exigencies of the feminine condition, the *jeune fille* is, at least in young Giraudoux's fascinated eyes, the perfect though ephemeral embodiment of all that is lovely and entrancing in creation. He deliberately refuses to see the petty weaknesses, the stains and blemishes that afflict young women as they do the other members of the human race. In his works they appear as creatures seen in a dream. They radiate the same airy charm as the feminine characters in the plays of Marivaux. They have the gift of seeing in the world signs and symbols that are not perceived by the grosser cast of human beings among whom they live. They look so graceful, so immaterial that they scarcely seem to belong to the coarse, average earthly things that we know.

That idealization of the *jeune fille*, which is particularly marked in Giraudoux's early works, did not outlast the clearsighted experience of his morose maturity. The portraits of Judith and Electra are painted in discordant and somber colors. Is it because the self-assured, emancipated, independent "modern" Misses whom he then saw around him, and who were so different from the fluffy young things he had known at the turn of the century, appeared to him as too strident and harsh? Is it because he himself, being no longer very young, could no longer look with the same benign indulgence on certain aspects of feminine assertiveness and guile? In any case, without denying the potent charm of girls, he clearly perceived and exposed almost cruelly its practical meaning and purpose.

The splendid blossoming of young women is a trick used by

nature to bring about the consummation of its own ends. If a girl
finds herself suddenly endowed with all the attributes that can win
a masculine heart — generosity, tenderness, compassion, devotion,
nobility of aims, purity of sentiments, sensitivity to beauty — it is
merely because she has to capture him in order to fulfill her own
function on earth.

"Claudie... was following the trail of her three aunts, of her
four great-grandmothers, of billions and billions of young girls
who had come before her. One could see, creeping in her actions,
those feelings toward others, that attention, that pity, that devotion which are supposed to be the signs of moral blossoming
but which represent in fact the placing into proper position of that
net with which the virgins prepare unconsciously yet ferociously
the fulfillment of their happiness at the expense of the others. . . .
Edmée knew from experience what to think of those spells of emotion before nature... of that dedication to great causes, of those
marks of weakness before things beautiful that carry girls to a
crest of sentiment from which they swoop down on man, with
their jangling nerves, their opinionated certitudes, and their
instinct of domination."[36]

Catching a suitable mate is a normal girl's main goal and essential achievement. As long as she has not been in direct contact with
men, she may have sincere illusions about herself, but when he
appears in her life, she is overwhelmed with desire and dread.
Instinctively she uses her recently acquired charm with telling
effect. As soon as she has succeeded in her assigned role, all the
magic powers that she had temporarily possessed, all the poetic
gifts that had been bestowed on her — being then without purpose — vanish as if by enchantment: "Suddenly Man arrives on the
scene. Then all of them contemplate him. . . . They quiver before
him in hypocritical admiration, beset at the same time by a fear
such as even a tiger could not inspire in them. . . . Then the mischief is done. All the walls of reality through which they could see
a thousand heraldic symbols, a thousand delicate traceries become, as it were, darkened for them and all is over." — "All is over?
If you are alluding to marriage, you mean to say that life is just
beginning."[37] Life is beginning on a different plan. The girl is no
longer a *jeune fille* but a woman, and she forms with the man of her
choice a completely new entity, a couple.

Woman is depicted by Giraudoux as essentially kind and weak. In most cases, she really wants to be good, but circumstances and her inborn coquetry constantly play tricks on her. Half passively, half through curiosity, she often finds herself involved in adventures that she will later contemplate with charming remorse. Woman is of course not perfect, however much men like to imagine her so: "You must have met women who, as far as you could see, seemed to personify intelligence, harmony, and sweetness."— "Yes, I have met some like that."—"What did you do then?"—"I came closer to them, and that was the end."[38] In the case of women, as for the rest of the universe, it is wiser—and more polite—to look on the pleasant surface and not to pry into the secrets underneath.

Guerre de Troie [margin annotation]

Giraudoux's ideas about the human couple followed an evolution strictly parallel to the course of events and emotions that developed in his own matrimonial life. The first complete presentation of a married couple in Giraudoux's works is found in *Amphitryon 38*. When Giraudoux wrote that play his marriage was harmonious and happy. The atmosphere of the play reflects the pleasant and trusting mood in which he was at that time.

The wife is shown there as being the mainstay of domestic felicity and the mainspring of conjugal love. Amphitryon is a decent and satisfactory husband. Alcmena is faithful to him because she loves him with a love meaning for her complete fulfillment and leaving no place for outside temptation. She is an honest woman, essentially practical, but with that grain of poetic feeling and that slight touch of mischievous humor which prevent her from being conventional and dull. Jupiter succeeds, it is true, in having his way with her, but he does so only by behaving like a despicable cad, and his dishonorable action does not impair Alcmena's dignity or her union with her chosen man.

Hector and Andromache are also almost an exemplary couple. Their attachment to each other is solid and secure. Yet, one may already sense that that harmony is, at least in part, the result of conscious reciprocal concessions and the outcome of strenuous efforts. As Andromache says: "The life of two married people who love each other, is a perpetual struggle. . . . Hector is the contrary of what I am. He does not share any of my tastes. We spend our time conquering each other or sacrificing ourselves."[39]

The first important cleavage in the couple appears in *Aventures de Jérôme Bardini*. A similar split is described a little later in *Choix des Elues*. In each case, no open hostility occurs between husband and wife. Outwardly, Jérôme and Renée, Edmée and Pierre could be considered tolerably well united. Their life in common is not tempestuous, and none could express a really serious grievance against the other. Only a deadening monotony and boredom have settled on their daily life. That situation threatens to destroy in the best of them every trace of ideal and spirituality. Thus, the best of them, the man in *Aventures de Jérôme Bardini*, the woman in *Choix des Elues*, resort to the same means of escape from the stale atmosphere of their home life: the fugue. It has been seen that their fugues, like most human actions, had many complex causes. Yet, among other things, the flight of Jérôme and Edmée from their marriage partners is a glaring evidence of the profound rift that had developed in their households.

That rift turns into a complete break in *Sodome et Gomorrhe*. That play was written at a time when Giraudoux and his wife had decided to live practically apart from each other. The bitter diatribes exchanged between Lia and Jean show indirectly how far their estrangement has gone. Lia and Jean vent their reciprocal grievances through recriminations and vituperations that make of their relations a real conjugal hell. Not only has every trace of love between them completely disappeared, but their mutual resentment makes their life in common a virtual impossibility. Thus the couple ends in a final, inevitable dissolution.

According to his custom, Giraudoux does not explore deeply in any of his books the psychological or moral causes of the ultimate debacle of the human couple. He notes, however, small details showing a fissure even in the seemingly most solid unions. For instance, a faithful wife may deceive her husband — with himself, in imagination, of course. In *La Guerre de Troie n'aura pas lieu*, the venerable old King Priam asks his loyal wife Hecuba: "You have deceived me, you?" — "Yes, a hundred times, but with yourself alone."[40]

More serious is the case when a wife deceives her husband with — the universe. This means that she has already become quite detached from him and that she seeks intimate satisfaction and thrill, no longer with him, but with the cosmos. In *Amphi-*

tryon 38 Jupiter explains that strange process of feminine fulfillment in the following manner: "You would not believe, my
dear Mercury, the surprises that a faithful wife holds in reserve. . . .
The faithful wives are those who expect from springtime, from
the books they read, from perfumes, from earthquakes, the reve-
lations that the other women expect from their lovers. In short,
they deceive their husbands with the whole world, except with
men."[41]

Agathe, in *Electre,* gives more definite information about
that singular form of adultery: "We deceive you with everything.
When I wake up and my hand . . . touches the wood of the bed, that
is my first adultery. . . . How often have I caressed that wood. . . .
It is made of olive tree. What a soft grain it has! What a charming
name! When I hear the name of olive tree, I cannot help giving
a start: it is the name of my lover. My second adultery is when
I open my eyes and see the light of day filtering through the
venetian blinds. My third adultery is when my foot touches the
water in my bath."[42]

Almost imperceptibly, the slight separation between spouses
widens and becomes in time a gaping, unbridgeable abyss.
Giraudoux does not put the blame for that tragic evolution on
one party more than on the other. He simply describes the irresistible progress of insidious misunderstandings that eventually pry apart man and wife. When his own marriage was
successful, Giraudoux drew an enticing picture of a happy
conjugal union. As years went by, he showed more and more
how the tediousness of a banal life in common wears down the
strongest marital ties.

At that stage, repeated fugues prefigure in his works—as they
did in his life—the final and fatal issue. Once all links of love
and convention have been severed, the couple as such ceases to
exist, and man and woman are left forever divided, forever
enemies, hurling stinging reproaches at one another eternally.

Naturally that grim view of the destiny of the human couple
should not be considered a faithful picture of the relations between husbands and wives in mankind at large. The gay outlook
found in *Amphitryon 38,* the glum atmosphere pervading *Choix
des Elues,* the gruesome menace weighing on *Sodome et Gomorrhe*
are separate mirror images of certain phases of Giraudoux's

own sensibility and matrimonial life. The very disconnectedness of those pictures precludes the possibility of any generalization about the nature of the human couple. Yet, at each stage of Giraudoux's personal experience, the vividness and the uncanny accuracy of his remarks cast a revealing light on some fragmentary aspect of probably the most crucial element of human happiness and misery on earth.

Human beings appear in Giraudoux's works not only as individuals but also as representative of many different nations. People from France, Germany, North and South America, from the modern Middle East, from ancient Greece and Judea pass before the reader's eye in a long motley cosmopolitan procession. Yet Giraudoux is essentially French and often approaches foreigners from the outside; their characteristic traits are seldom clearly outlined.

Even France is not the object of a full-length systematic description on his part. One finds in his works a large number of remarks on French culture and character, but those remarks never tend toward a unified view of the French nation or French problems. They must be considered a series of scattered observations often extremely shrewd and perspicacious, but bearing on completely different, unrelated aspects of the same complex reality.

The two main aspects of French culture on which he insisted particularly are evidently connected with his personal experience. Giraudoux was born and grew up in a middle-class provincial environment. For him, France was always a country of petits bourgeois, thrifty, honest, conscientious, peaceful, practical, homeloving, unimaginative, slow in changing their ways, frequently unable to understand events taking place beyond their narrow horizon, but deeply attached to their modest and moderate form of quiet existence. For him, Bellac and the Limousin remained the true heart of France.

In the course of his studies, he became imbued with another form of thought that is certainly profoundly French. As Giraudoux repeatedly noted in his works, the French mind works best in the framework of clear, abstract, logical structures. An educated Frenchman spontaneously seeks to discover in the welter of impressions offered to him by the world a definite and coherent pattern. An instinctive, but also deliberate, rationalism dominates most of his intellectual activities. He shuns direct contact with raw, inchoate nature and, for the sake of rational lucidity, is sometimes ready to do violence to the real.

Giraudoux both loved and denounced this trait of the French mind. He was impregnated with it himself and appreciated its value, but he became aware of its shortcomings when he came into contact with German thought. In *Siegfried et le Limousin,* the narrator of the story has a dream. In that dream, Siegfried Kleist is being transmuted from a German into a French character. "Kleist was exclaiming to me that the atmosphere was becoming clearer for him, that his reasonings were provided with proper dialectical hinges and his passions with adequate articulations, that the insects appeared to him smaller and more slender, that the singing of birds, the meaning of which he had understood up to then, was to him nothing more than a mere warbling."[43]

Somewhat later, after a few years of work in the diplomatic service, having had many contacts with foreign points of view, he perceived a completely different image of France. Since the French Revolution, France has been generally considered abroad as a most troublesome nation. At the same time, she is viewed by many as the symbol of justice and liberty in the world. France is a constant thorn in the flesh for the rich, smug, self-satisfied powers. She is also the hope, the inspiriting example for the poor and oppressed people striving after an ideal. "The destiny of France is to be the troublemaker of the world. . . . She has been created . . . to ruin the plot of the establishments and of the eternal systems. She incarnates justice, but only insofar as justice prevents from being any more right those who have been right too long. She represents good sense but only when good sense becomes the righter of wrongs and the avenger. As long as a France exists, the affluent nations will not be able to rest in peace, whether they have reached their opulence through hard work, through the use of force or through blackmail. . . . The mission of France is fulfilled if, in the evening, the solid bourgeois, the prosperous clergyman, the secure tyrant says to himself: 'Things would not be too bad; but there is that damn France.' And you can imagine the counterpart of that monologue in the bed of the exile, of the poet, of the oppressed."[44]

When Giraudoux attempted to give a more or less comprehensive definition of the role of France in the modern world, he simply saw in her the representative of a happy medium between the gigantism of certain national groups and the powerlessness of tiny political entities; also the embodiment of a golden mean between the frantic, exhausting drive toward material achievement and success, and the disheartening renunciation of the good things of life. France, according to Giraudoux, has, like ancient Greece, attained an almost perfect equilibrium between the needs of man and the requirements of nature. "French civilization, like Greek civilization, has found the justification of man in man himself. . . . It is a conception that is both modest and sensitive—yet also full of reserve toward the gigantic or minuscule beings, to which that civilization grants the full right to exist. It is not a metaphysical formula making of man a god and urging him to follow a life of ambition and effort. It is not a material formula turning man into nothingness and forcing him into a life of renunciation. Halfway between those two extremes . . . France has found the exact relationship between man and our planet. . . . Against the civilization of moral defeatism, she has found a doctrine of relativism. Against the civilization of grandeur, in which the effort required to live is out of proportion with the pleasure of being alive—in short against the civilization of pride—she has found the civilization of politeness."[45]

Foreign visitors to France may wonder if the expression "civilization of politeness" may be applied to what they experience and what they see when they remain for some time in that country. Giraudoux must have been aware of the discrepancy between his optimistic judgment of France in this regard and certain facts that he could not fail to notice around him. He therefore qualified his general judgment with the now classical distinction between France and the French.

"The word *France* evokes the notion of courtesy, of perfect relations between individuals. . . . The word *French*, on the contrary, evokes only too often cantankerous individuals, disputes in the streets, impolite travelers, rude busdrivers. The word *France* evokes the idea of justice and union; the word *French* evokes nepotism, squabbles, disunion. . . . The word *France* evokes the idea of conscientious work and of meticulous perfection in a finished product; the word *French* evokes the idea of improvisation and temporary expediency. The word *France* evokes the idea of a man standing above pettiness; the word *French* evokes the idea of a man who is never completely free from any taint of scandal. . . . For the impartial observer, there is no possibility of doubt: there has been a slackening of the moral fiber of the nation."[46]

Apart from France, Germany is the only country about which Giraudoux has made a number of telling remarks, which are concentrated in *Siegfried et le Limousin* and in the play *Siegfried*. Giraudoux did not try to give an exhaustive account of all the harmonious or discordant themes in the infinitely rich and complex German moral symphony. He chose a few striking notes, which were generally consonant with his own experience and with his personal view of life, and he developed around them variations that are sometimes paradoxical and sometimes deeply true.

The fundamental note in German character is, according to him, a deep inborn feeling for poetry. "Germany is a great country — industrious and ardent — a country resounding with poetry, where the singer who sings out of tune reaches the heart of the listener more often than the singer who sings in tune in other climes."[47] Giraudoux also senses the existence in the German psyche of a latent streak of violence that may occasionally explode in outbursts of uncontrollable "paroxysms"[48] beyond all norms and bounds of reason: "It is a brutal and bloodthirsty country, merciless to the weak."[49]

The great tragedy of the German nation is that the Germans, at certain phases of their history, impelled by those obscure "demoniac"[50] forces, have forgotten their true nature, have left the realm of the spirit, and have launched into the materially colossal: "The truth is that, for about a century, Germany has frequently overlooked her fundamental qualities and has overestimated her temporary impulses."[51]

According to Giraudoux, the real vocation of Germany is not to be first in military power or industrial production, but to lead in spirituality and pure thought. "Germany does not need to be strong. Germany has just to be Germany. Or rather she has to be strong in the unreal, she must be great in the invisible. . . . Each time Germany has wanted to build something practical, her works have collapsed within a few decades, but every time she has had faith in the gifts that have been bestowed on her to transform a great thought or a great deed into a symbol or a legend, she has built for eternity."[52]

All the disasters that befell Germany in this century come from her failure to follow her nature: "Instead of following the advice of her soil, or of her past . . . she has built, under the influence of a pedantic science and of megalomaniac rulers, a gigantic and superhuman image of herself and, instead of giving the world, as she had done many times before, a new form to human dignity, she has given this time only a new form to pride and misery."[53]

These statements are possibly one-sided, limited in scope, and sometimes highly debatable, but they undoubtedly stem from Giraudoux's genuine sympathy for a Germany he had learned to understand and love, and also from his profound distress in the face of the catastrophic events that were leading that country to disaster and ruin.

Giraudoux's references to other nations are very disappointing. The United States is very indistinctly sketched in *Amica America, Aventures de Jérôme Bardini,* and *Choix des Elues.* The comparison between East and West, which purports to be the theme of *Eglantine,* offers little beyond the suggestion that the people of the Middle East have introduced a great deal of nervousness and recklessness into modern life. Other casual remarks on England or Russia are often clever but do not convey the impression that a new light has been thrown on an old subject.

In fact, Giraudoux never attempted to offer objective information about the outside world. Objects, persons, nations interest him only insofar as they constitute a medium in which his poetic personality can reflect itself, or as they provide him with material for his imagination and a rich field for his art.

❧ VII ❧
The Honeycombs
of Art

The deep nature of Giraudoux's art is even today an uncertain and controversial subject. The controversy started in earnest in March, 1940, when Jean-Paul Sartre published his article "M. Giraudoux et la philosophie d'Aristote" in *La Nouvelle Revue Francaise.*[2] Analyzing the peculiar turns of expression, the methods of description, and the mannerisms of style in *Choix des Elues,* Sartre concluded that Giraudoux's view of the world closely resembled Aristotle's conception of the universe. He added that this was probably the reason for the strange fascination that Giraudoux's writings exert on the imagination of the modern reader.

Indeed, even though, according to Sartre, Aristotle's philosophy has become obsolete for nearly four centuries, men still long for the orderly and reassuring Aristotelian interpretation of the cosmos: "Nobody believes today in an alleged accord between man and things, and nobody dares to hope that the core of nature will be accessible to us."[3] Yet "we are all of us, at certain moments, disciples of Aristotle."[4] This idea explains the appeal of Giraudoux's universe: "It enthralls us by its indefinable charm and its air of novelty; but if one gets really close to it, one discovers that it is the world of Aristotle, a world that has been buried for four hundred years."[5]

Some time later, in 1945, Claude-Edmonde Magny, a critic who certainly did not have the philosophical stature of Sartre, but who was deservedly respected for her erudition and intellectual acumen, upheld in *Précieux Giraudoux* the thesis that the world of Giraudoux is "much more Platonic than Aristotelian."[6] She used the same method as Sartre to prove her point; she decided to "analyze" Giraudoux's "rhetoric" painstakingly, but she attained results that were diametrically opposed to those of Sartre: "On the decisive point where Aristotle parted with Platonism . . . Giraudoux is on the side of Plato and not of his unfaithful disciple."[7]

Does Giraudoux's art derive its quality and power from an implied Aristotelian conception of the world or from a subtle Platonic ideal perfusing its texture? The arguments marshaled by the two critics to support their respective, and irreconcilable, interpretations of Giraudoux's art seem just as convincing, and frequently just as farfetched, in one case as in the other.

Giraudoux, as a highly cultured man and a remarkable Hellenist, was certainly familiar with the theories of Aristotle and Plato; yet he never acknowledged any direct indebtedness to either. The only philosophy to which he referred as having had any influence on him was the philosophy of the Stoics.[8] Giraudoux never wanted to organize his ideas according to a definite pattern. As noted, he frequently juxtaposed contradictory statements and jumped merrily from one viewpoint to another. In these circumstances a perceptive critic can cull a number of stylistic examples "proving" one theory about his art; another set of examples can also be collected to "prove" the opposite theory.

The art of Giraudoux is extremely elaborate and complicated. The uninitiated and unprepared reader frequently wonders where he is being led, and sometimes even loses sight of the point from which he started. Giraudoux's works contain no trace of any logical, regular, well-constructed plan, such as is usually found in most French novels and plays. He seems to proceed at random, impelled by his tireless and ever-changing fancy.

Giraudoux has offered the following explanation for his apparent incoherence: most of his books were written hurriedly, his professional duties not allowing him to polish and perfect his original conception: *"Siegfried et le Limousin* required twenty-seven days. I take a blank sheet of paper and begin to write. The characters are born as I proceed. After five or six pages, I see the way clear."[9] He also admitted that "as a rule it is a very bad thing to write a book too quickly. But it would be necessary to have time, a great deal of time, and nowadays most writers, beside their literary profession, have another profession that is often entirely different."[10]

It would be too simple to accept the idea that lack of time is a satisfactory explanation for all the difficulties and obscurities found in Giraudoux's writings. He was too much of an artist to express himself inadequately for any reason. If he was continually improvising, he apparently did so to preserve the spontaneity and freshness of his inspiration. After stating that for an author writing is a joy, a real holiday, he added: "If one can spend one's holidays enthusiastically writing, it would perhaps spoil them to be scratching out words, attending to the smallest details, and constantly striving after perfection."[11]

A work of Giraudoux hardly ever presents a continuous logical development of ideas. It is more like a familiar, desultory talk. The bulk of the work consists of factual statements intermingled with allusions, remarks and commentaries, sometimes intended to link the facts, sometimes merely suggested by association.

Although the facts presented are frequently unimportant in themselves, they possess a curious evocative power. If Giraudoux has to describe an individual or a bit of scenery, he does not stress their most striking features. He will mention instead a few minor details, a little mannerism of a man, the slant of a roof, the glittering of leaves in the rain and, as if by magic, the person, the village, or the corner of the countryside in question will take shape in the mind's eye and stand forth vividly.

Giraudoux intentionally omits the seeming essentials, but the reader's imagination is challenged, re-creating the picture with more life and intensity than an exhaustive description could have done. Thus, through this form of art, living things and inanimate objects alike are endowed with a peculiar weird existence. Because they are hardly ever portrayed directly, but are forcibly suggested to the mind, they are almost hallucinatory — tremendously real and yet partly absent. The phases of their presence and their absence alternate according to a rhythm that confers on them a singularly original vibration.

Giraudoux's descriptions usually have a very limited scope. Seldom attempting to characterize the general tone of an ensemble, he considers all the fragments of reality separately and distinctly, and he assigns to each its proper color. He does not like to mix different shades. Although he avoids bright hues and prefers subdued tones, he is moved to give pure and clear expression to each aspect of the universe that he is considering. Giraudoux's vision of the world therefore evokes a multiplicity of colored dots, all in juxtaposition but not blending, full of freshness and luminosity but spread only over the surface of reality and hardly ever revealing the depths.

In his literary style Giraudoux reflects the fundamental tendencies of the man. Because improvisation is one of the sources of his originality, he allows each sentence to take shape spontaneously, almost casually, even playfully. As he himself stated: "There is an element of gambling, of luck, in every sentence of prose as much as in every line of verse. It is that element of improvisation that gives to a work life and, above all, poetry."[12]

Improvisation, of course, does not go hand in hand with perfection of form and clearness. Indeed Giraudoux's style is far from perfect and it is not always clear. Often the logical articulations are deficient. Sometimes the syntax is twisted, and ordinary words are forced to mean something other than their accepted sense. As a result, the general purport of many passages is doubtful and even genuinely puzzling. This is far from the ideal of clarity and precision sometimes considered the most typical characteristic of French prose. Well aware of the possibility of such criticism, Giraudoux retorts: "Simplicity and clarity constitute only one of the characteristics of French style. The French soul is too complex and, fortunately or unfortunately, too much linked with poetical and philosophical considerations for the language viewed by certain critics as the only true French to be sufficient for its needs."[13] Thus Giraudoux will, when necessary, deliberately discard clarity and correctness to express the complexity of his thoughts and feelings more adequately.

One of the most typical features of Giraudoux's style is the abundance of antithetic statements. This is evidently a transposition of the fundamental dualism that dominates his personality. Most of his works rest on the structural opposition of two concepts—France and Germany in *Siegfried*, East and West in *Englantine*—or of the personalities representing them—the Rebendarts and the Dubardeaus in *Bella*, Hector and Ulysses, Andromache and Helen in *La Guerre de Troie n'aura pas lieu*.

Giraudoux seldom makes a choice in the alternatives he considers. In rapid succession he presents antagonistic aspects of the same fact, looking at it from one point of view, and then from the other. The result is sometimes the juxtaposition in the same sentence of contradictory elements—the adjective belying the noun, for instance, or the adverb, the verb. He loves to make joy appear sad, sorrow cheerful, to make things that are strange appear natural and things that are perfectly natural appear very complicated. In *Amphitryon 38*, Alcmene says to Amphitryon, whom she believes to be Jupiter in disguise: "A very good imitation indeed. An ordinary woman would be deceived by it. Everything is there: those two sad wrinkles for smiling and this comical little hollow for tears."[14] Later, Jupiter says to Alcmene: "Since this morning, I have been admiring your courage and your obstinacy, how you devise your stratagems with loyalty and your lies with sincerity."[15]

Another striking trait of Giraudoux's style is its richness in metaphors. Indeed this wealth of imagery is largely responsible for the peculiar and original color of his writing. The images are seldom vivid or powerful; they are instead strange and surprising and not likely at first to appear natural. After due reflection, however, they often reveal to the reader affinities between one subject and another that would not ordinarily be suspected.

One may question, however, whether the images presented by Giraudoux are always as spontaneous as he would apparently have us believe. They are undoubtedly never trite or conventional, but to what extent is Giraudoux's own eye allowed to see things under normal conditions? How alarming is a statement such as this: "It is noon. A light wind stirs the plantain trees. If you press your finger against your eye, everything will appear radiant with fanciful colors."[16]

One often feels that Giraudoux purposely presses his fingers against his eyes in order to see a rainbow that does not exist in reality. His images of the world are not distorted by any intellectual interpretation, but they sometimes seem distorted at the origin of their perception by a deliberate process of self-delusion.

Giraudoux evidently delights in these feats of literary acrobatics. Very much like a musical virtuoso who loves to display his technical skill, Giraudoux will launch fanciful variations on a theme, not so much with the purpose of conveying any definite idea as for the pleasure of combining difficult figures, all for his own enjoyment as a consummate artist. He is so fond of drawing fantastic arabesques of style that one feels tempted to apply to him the remarks that he made about one of his characters: "Bernard endeavored to achieve a complete stylization of each action performed by him during a day, of each landscape, of each emotion. In the same way, certain hives of bees construct honeycombs of superior workmanship. But they never fill them with honey."[17]

Honey is definitely to be found within the light and fragile edifices of Giraudoux's literary art. Nevertheless, their lightness and fragility have led many people to believe that his works are hardly more than a display of artificial virtuosity. Certain critics have denounced that artificiality so intensely that the word *Précieux*—used in a definite derogatory sense—has become almost officially attached to his turn of mind and to his work. That accusation of *Préciosité* is doubtless justified within certain limits, but it has recently been grossly exaggerated.

The *Préciosité* was a complex movement that developed in France in the early part of the seventeenth century. It initially represented a reaction in high aristocratic circles against the prevalent vulgarity and coarseness of manners that followed nearly fifty years of constant civil and religious wars, and also against the widespread licentiousness that was the legacy of the extreme moral liberalism associated with the Renaissance.

Clearly, Giraudoux had nothing to do with that historical situation and with the efforts made around 1610 and afterward by society ladies in Paris to introduce some refinement of language and behavior in their salons, and to restore a measure of decency in the sentiment of love. These society ladies, who called themselves *Précieuses*, were not very much interested in philosophy. France was then passing through a period of intense spiritual and intellectual turmoil, and many different philosophical trends were concurrently developing side by side.

Platonism, then flourishing in Italy, particularly in Florence, had only a small influence in France and was mainly known there through the teachings of the Congregation of the Oratory, which had been founded by the Florentine Filippo Neri. Stoicism had a somewhat larger following. Epicureanism appealed to the fairly numerous disciples of Pierre Gassendi. After the publication of the *Discours de la Méthode* by Descartes in 1637, a large section of the cultivated public rallied to the Cartesian theories, but at no time could any specific philosophical doctrine be identified with the *Préciosité* movement. It is therefore manifestly inaccurate to assert, as has been done,[18] that the inspiration of Giraudoux's art corresponds to philosophical principles implied in *Préciosité*.

The *Précieuses*, largely indifferent to philosophy, were intensely interested in literature. They favored works—particularly novels, but also maxims and "portraits"—dealing with psychology and analyzing with extreme subtlety the emotion of love. On that point again, Giraudoux's personal tendencies were definitely at variance with those of the *Précieux* writers. In his own work, he touched on psychology only lightly. Furthermore no evidence exists that he had any admiration for, say, Benserade, Voiture, or Mlle de Scudéry. His favorite seventeenth-century authors were Racine, Molière, and La Fontaine.

In style alone, it is possible to detect a similarity between certain forms of expression frequently encountered in *Précieux* writers and certain turns of sentence that appear spontaneously in Giraudoux. Like the authentic *Précieux*, Giraudoux has a weakness for all that is delicate and exquisite. Like them, he indulges in subtle effects of verbal elegance. Like them he skillfully juggles curious allusions and images. He shares their taste for startling, pointed remarks, twisted metaphors, and farfetched comparisons and parallelisms.

He alludes, for example, to the heroism of a doctor who had both his hands amputated one after the other because they had been dangerously affected while he was giving radium treatment to cancer sufferers. He then proceeds to compare that doctor to the Athenian soldier who, at the battle of Salamis, in order to prevent a Persian ship from escaping, seized hold of the vessel with his right hand. When his right hand was cut off by the blow of an axe, he caught hold with his left hand. When his left hand was also severed, he held on by his teeth. The similarity between the two situations may not seem too obvious to the reader when Giraudoux refers to a man "who had his fingers, then his hand, then the other hand cut off while holding close to the radium (if you will and if you have grasped that allusion to the battle of Salamis) the vessel of our sufferings."[19]

In spite of such similar blemishes, the style of Giraudoux owes a great part of its appeal to the very defects that may seem irritating, but that are entertaining and amusing if they are accepted in the spirit of fun in which they were usually written. Indeed, a delicate vein of satire and irony runs through most of Giraudoux's works. Occasionally that irony borders on the spoofing typical of the *canular normalien*. More often, one can imagine Giraudoux writing with a slight smile.

Although he knows well that life can be tragic at times, he invites his readers not to take any of the human follies too seriously; he will be the first to laugh at his own weaknesses, failures, and frustrated vanities. Except in *Bella,* his irony is never venomous. It is more like a general, nonchalant amusement toward the whole tragicomedy of existence.

On the whole, Giraudoux was essentially a great spontaneous artist. Many aspects of his work that are sometimes considered artificial do not have their source in any actual artifice but in the very nature of the poet that he was. Speaking under the transparent guise of one of his characters, he said himself: "A poet? I must be a poet."[20] He did not compose, it is true, poems in the current sense of the word, except in his very early youth. He disliked subjecting his inspiration to the rules of traditional prosody: "May God preserve me from writing in verse, from putting what I think on separate lines, from causing my life to be laminated by passing it through their rolling mill."[21]

Indeed the whole material of his work was the material of his life itself, seen through the prism of his poetic vision, which, however, was not a unifying element. The motley world in which he moved was too diversified to be viewed otherwise than in a fragmentary manner. On the other hand, Giraudoux's own mind was too rich in manifold potentialities to be reduced to a singleness of intellectual or spiritual perception. Giraudoux's mental attitude was not that of a philosopher trying to organize the data of his life experience according to a system precluding all others.

His was the attitude of a poet welcoming the totality of the impressions provided by the universe. He did not attempt to impose on their variegated forms a theoretical order that was not their own. He simply let his imagination rove almost at random, glancing at the surface of the world, unhampered by arbitrary rules and guided only by his inexhaustible poetic fancy.

The world of Giraudoux, however, is not one of chaos. It is a composite world in which the multiple facets of the universe are reflected in the multiple facets of his personality, but the quality of his personality imparts to the parcels of the cosmos that it mirrors the poetic glow that we perceive in his writings. In fact, the subject of Giraudoux's works is his life itself as reflected in the multifold mirror of the world. In the interplay of reciprocal mirrors so typical of Giraudoux's art, it is not always easy to say on which side the reflection started. Giraudoux himself said: "The poet is the man who can read his life as one reads handwriting in reverse in a mirror."[22]

Jean-Paul Sartre, after developing his theory that Giraudoux's art was impregnated with Aristotelian influence, sensed that his argument lacked the support of something essential for the understanding of Giraudoux's works, namely a confirmation that only a knowledge of Giraudoux's life could give. In search of that confirmation, he ended his essay by saying: "Perhaps that writer who is so discreet . . . will one day tell us about himself."[23]

He evidently realized, with his usual shrewdness, that the key to Giraudoux's art can be found only in his life. Giraudoux's works do not correspond to an ambitious plan to solve the problems that beset the modern world. He merely considered those few elements of the universe that happened to come within his reach, and with them he created a delicate and poetic harmony.

Notes

Chapter I

1. Frédéric Lefèvre, *Une heure avec... Première Série,* Gallimard, Paris, 1924, "Jean Giraudoux," p. 150.
2. Jean Giraudoux, *Provinciales,* Grasset, Paris, 1955, Œuvre Romanesque, Vol. I, "Allégories"–III, "A l'Amour, A l'Amitié," p. 71.
3. ————, *Suzanne et le Pacifique,* Grasset, Paris, 1955, Œuvre Romanesque, Vol. I, Chap. I, p. 259.
4. *Ibid.,* p. 256.
5. ————, *Adorable Clio,* Grasset, Paris, 1958, Œuvres Littéraires Diverses, "Nuit à Châteauroux," p. 218.
6. ————, *L'Ecole des Indifférents,* Grasset, Paris, 1955, Œuvre Romanesque, Vol. I, "Jacques l'Egoïste," IV, p. 113.
7. ————, *Simon le Pathétique,* Grasset, Paris, 1955, Œuvre Romanesque, Vol. I, Chap. I, p. 632.
8. *Ibid.,* pp. 637–638.
9. ————, *Juliette au Pays des Hommes,* Grasset, Paris, 1955, Œuvre Romanesque, Vol. I, Chap. VI, "Prière sur la Tour Eiffel," p. 600.
10. ————, *Littérature,* Grasset, Paris, 1958, Œuvres Littéraires Diverses, Chap. III, "L'Esprit Normalien," p. 539.
11. ————, *Siegfried et le Limousin,* Grasset, Paris, 1955, Œuvre Romanesque, Vol. I, Chap. II, p. 423.
12. *Simon le Pathétique,* Chap. III, p. 652.
13. Franz Toussaint, *Jean Giraudoux,* Fayard, Paris, 1953, Pégase, pp.

143–144. Cf. Paul Morand, *Monplaisir,* Gallimard, Paris, 1967. Giraudoux, *Souvenirs de notre jeunesse,* p. 153.

14. *Adorable Clio,* "Adieu à la guerre," p. 261.
15. *Ibid.,* "Epigraph," p. 261.
16. André Bourin, "Elle et Lui. Chez Madame Jean Giraudoux," *Nouvelles Littéraires,* Paris, November 16, 1950, No. 1211, p. 1.
17. *Ibid.*
18. Jean-Pierre Giraudoux, *Le Fils,* Grasset, Paris, 1967, "Enfantines," pp. 43–44.
19. "Elle et Lui. Chez Madame Jean Giraudoux," p. 1.
20. *Ibid.*
21. *Ibid.*
22. *Ibid.*
23. *Ibid.*
24. *Le Fils,* "Enfantines," p. 43.
25. *Ibid.,* "Un Reflet du miroir," p. 71.
26. Gilbert Ganne, "Jean-Pierre Giraudoux. Un Fils régent en exil," *Nouvelles Littéraires,* Paris, December 18, 1969, No. 2204, p. 11.
27. "Elle et Lui. Chez Madame Jean Giraudoux," p. 1.
28. *Le Fils,* "Secret de Jean," p. 209.
29. "Elle et Lui. Chez Madame Jean Giraudoux," p. 1.
30. Marthe Hanau was a journalist well known for having close connections with important men at the Quai d'Orsay. Partly thanks to those connections, she was able to publish valuable financial information in the newspaper *La Gazette de France et des Nations.* She used the reputation as a financial expert that she had thus acquired to persuade gullible readers to entrust their savings to her. The transactions she undertook with their money, however, were more to her advantage than to their own. After a sensational trial, in which many prominent men were implicated, she was condemned to two years in jail.
31. The Oustric Bank was closely associated with Raoul Péret, Minister of Finances in a Briand Cabinet. Rumors of fraudulent dealings by the bank spread in Paris, and shortly afterward the bank failed. When legal action was initiated against its directors, it was discovered that Péret, who had become Minister of Justice, had used his influence to block the judicial proceedings. In the course of the public scandal that ensued, many other high-ranking politicians were compromised in the Oustric affair.
32. Alexandre Stavisky was a professional swindler very active in the Parisian criminal underworld. He succeeded in establishing

contact with an amazingly large number of leading politicians and important members of the judiciary. With their connivance, and sometimes with their definite complicity, he organized a large-scale swindle operation based on the Bayonne Municipal Pawnshop, and he fleeced the public of huge sums of money. When the scandal came to light, he tried to flee to Switzerland, but was assassinated, probably by the police, before arriving there. The disclosure of his association with some of the most important statesmen of his time brought about a violent explosion of riots in Paris.

33. "Elle et Lui. Chez Madame Jean Giraudoux," p. 1.
34. Ibid.
35. Le Fils, "Adolescence et même un peu plus tard," p. 84.
36. Ibid., "Après l'Adolescence," p. 98.
37. "Elle et Lui. Chez Madame Jean Giraudoux," p. 1.
38. Le Fils, "Après l'Adolescence," p. 100. Cf. also Maurice Martin du Gard, "Les Mémorables," Revue des Deux Mondes, Paris, December 1, 1968, p. 479.
39. "Jean Giraudoux. Un Fils régent en exil," p. 11.

Chapter II

1. Jean Giraudoux, Juliette au Pays des Hommes, Grasset, Paris, 1955, Œuvre Romanesque, Vol. I, Chap. VI, "Prière sur la Tour Eiffel," p. 601.
2. Frédéric Lefèvre, Une Heure avec... Quatrième Série, Gallimard, Paris, 1927, "Jean Giraudoux," p. 118.
3. Jean Giraudoux, L'Ecole des Indifférents, Grasset, Paris, 1955, Œuvre Romanesque, Vol. I, "Jacques l'Égoïste," II, p. 106.
4. Frédéric Lefèvre, Une Heure avec...Première Série, Gallimard, Paris, 1924, "Jean Giraudoux," p. 150.
5. Jean Giraudoux, Amphitryon 38, Ides et Calendes, Neuchâtel & Paris, 1945–53, Théâtre Complet, "Variantes II," Vol. XIII (1947), Act III, Sc. 4, p. 218.
6. ———, Simon le Pathétique, Grasset, Paris, 1955, Œuvre Romanesque, Vol. I, Chap. I, p. 636.
7. ———, Suzanne et le Pacifique, Grasset, Paris, 1955, Œuvre Romanesque, Vol. I, Chap. I, pp. 249–250.
8. L'Ecole des Indifférents, "Bernard, le faible Bernard," II, p. 164.
9. Ibid., "Jacques l'Égoïste," VI, p. 125.

10. *Ibid.*
11. ———, *Ondine*, Ides et Calendes, Neuchâtel & Paris, 1945–53, *Théâtre Complet*, Vol. IX (1946), Act II, Sc. 11, pp. 106–107.
12. ———, *Littérature*, Grasset, Paris, 1958, *Œuvres Littéraires Diverses*, Chap. III, "De Siècle à Siècle," p. 562.
13. *Juliette au Pays des Hommes*, Chap. VI, "Prière sur la Tour Eiffel," p. 601.
14. *Ibid.*
15. *Ibid.*, pp. 601–602.
16. ———, *Amphitryon 38*, Ides et Calendes, Neuchâtel & Paris, 1945–53, *Théâtre Complet*, Vol. III (1945), Act II, Sc. 2, p. 62.
17. ———, *La France Sentimentale*, Grasset, Paris, 1955, *Œuvre Romanesque*, Vol. II, "Mirage de Bessines," p. 416.
18. ———, *Aventures de Jérôme Bardini*, Grasset, Paris, 1955, *Œuvre Romanesque*, Vol. II, "The Kid," IV, p. 338.
19. ———, *Combat avec l'Ange*, Grasset, Paris, 1955, *Œuvre Romanesque*, Vol. II, Chap. III, p. 499.
20. ———, *Pour Lucrèce*, Ides et Calendes, Neuchâtel & Paris, 1945–53, *Théâtre Complet*, Vol. XVI (1953), Act III, Sc. 6, p. 139.
21. *Ibid.*, Act III, Sc. 8, p. 143.
22. *Ibid.*, Act III, Sc. 6, p. 138.
23. *L'Ecole des Indifférents*, "Don Manuel le Paresseux," III, p. 138.
24. ———, *Choix des Elues*, Grasset, Paris, 1955, *Œuvre Romanesque*, Vol. II, Chap. XI, p. 804.
25. ———, *Suzanne et le Pacifique*, Grasset, Paris, 1955, *Œuvre Romanesque*, Vol. I, Chap. X, p. 381.
26. *L'Ecole des Indifférents*, "Jacques l'Égoïste," VI, p. 125.
27. Jean-Pierre Giraudoux, *Le Fils*, Grasset, Paris, 1967, "Importance de Jean," p. 243.

Chapter III

1. Jean Giraudoux, *Juliette au Pays des Hommes*, Grasset, Paris, 1955, *Œuvre Romanesque*, Vol. I, Chap. VI, "Prière sur la Tour Eiffel," p. 602.
2. Jean-Pierre Giraudoux, *Le Fils*, Grasset, Paris, 1967, "Secret de Jean," p. 210.
3. *Le Dernier rêve d'Edmond About* was first published in the student magazine *Marseille Etudiant* in December 1904. It was later included in *Les Contes d'un matin*.

4. Jean Giraudoux, *L'Ecole des Indifférents*, Grasset, Paris, 1955, *Œuvre Romanesque*, Vol. I, "Jacques l'Égoïste," IV, p. 116.

5. ———, *Suzanne et le Pacifique*, Grasset, Paris, 1955, *Œuvre Romanesque*, Vol. I, Chap. I, p. 260.

6. *Ibid.*, Chap. IX, p. 358.

7. *Ibid.*, Chap. VII, p. 330.

8. *Ibid.*, Chap. X, p. 389.

9. *Ibid.*, Chap. X, p. 379.

10. ———, *Amphitryon 38*, Ides et Calendes, Neuchâtel & Paris, 1945–53, *Théâtre Complet*, "Variantes II," Vol. XIII (1947), Act III, Sc. 4, p. 218.

11. ———, *Bella*, Grasset, Paris, 1955, *Œuvre Romanesque*, Vol. II, Chap. VI, p. 76.

12. *Ibid.*, Chap. III, p. 30.

13. *Ibid.*, Chap. I, p. 12.

14. ———, *Eglantine*, Grasset, Paris, 1955, *Œuvre Romanesque*, Vol. II, Chap. II, p. 147.

15. *Ibid.*, p. 151.

16. ———, *La France Sentimentale*, Grasset, Paris, 1955, *Œuvre Romanesque*, Vol. II, "Le Signe," p. 403.

17. *Ibid.*, p. 409.

18. *Ibid.*

19. *Ibid.*

20. *Ibid.*, p. 404.

21. *La France Sentimentale*, "Mirage de Bessines," p. 411.

22. *Ibid.*, pp. 411–412.

23. *Ibid.*, pp. 412–413.

24. *Ibid.*, p. 425.

25. *Ibid.*, p.422.

26. ———, *Aventures de Jérôme Bardini*, Grasset, Paris, 1955, *Œuvre Romanesque*, Vol. II, "The Kid," IV, pp. 338–339.

27. ———, *Combat avec l'Ange*, Grasset, Paris, 1955, *Œuvre Romanesque*, Vol. II, Chap. IV, p. 512.

28. *Ibid.*

29. *Ibid.*

30. *Ibid.*, p. 526.

31. *Ibid.*

32. *Ibid.*, Chap. IX, p. 614.

33. *Ibid.*, p. 615.

34. *Choix des Elues*, Grasset, Paris, 1955, *Œuvre Romanesque*, Vol. II, Chap. VI, p. 721.

35. *Ibid.*, p. 729.

36. *Ibid.,* Chap. VII, pp. 737-738.
37. *Ibid.,* Chap. IX, p. 769.
38. André Bourin, "Elle et Lui. Chez Madame Jean Giraudoux," *Nouvelles Littéraires,* Paris, November 16, 1950, No. 1211, p. 1.
39. *Choix des Elues,* Chap. IX, p. 771.
40. *Ibid.,* p. 776.
41. *Combat avec l'Ange,* Chap. IX, p. 499.
42. *Aventures de Jérôme Bardini,* "The Kid," IV, p. 338.
43. *Choix des Elues,* Chap. IX, p. 804.
44. *Ibid.,* p. 771.
45. *Ibid.,* Chap. XI, p. 797.
46. *Ibid.,* pp. 798-799.
47. *Ibid.,* p. 809.
48. *Ibid.,* p. 810.

Chapter IV

1. *L'Impromptu de Paris,* Ides et Calendes, Neuchâtel & Paris, 1945–53, *Théâtre Complet,* Vol. VIII (1946), p. 16.
2. André Bourin, "Elle et Lui. Chez Madame Jean Giraudoux," *Nouvelles Littéraires,* Paris, November 16, 1950, No. 1211, p. 1.
3. *Mélanges offerts à M. Charles Andler,* Publications de la Faculté des Lettres de Strasbourg, Strasbourg, 1924.
4. Letter of Louis Jouvet to Marianne Mercier-Campiche quoted in Marianne Mercier-Campiche, *Le Théâtre de Jean Giraudoux et la Condition Humaine,* Domat, Paris, 1954, pp. 8–9.
5. *Ibid.*
6. *Siegfried,* Ides et Calendes, Neuchâtel & Paris, 1945–53, *Théâtre Complet,* Vol. I (1945), Act III, Sc. 2, p. 81.
7. *Ibid.,* Act I, Sc. 2, p. 14.
8. *Ibid.,* Act III, Sc. 5, p. 101.
9. *Ibid.,* Act IV, Sc. 3, pp. 118–119.
10. *Ibid.,* Act IV, Sc. 6, p. 131.
11. *Amphitryon 38,* Ides et Calendes, Neuchâtel & Paris, 1945–53, *Théâtre Complet,* Vol. III (1945), Act III, Sc. 6, p. 96.
12. *Ibid.,* Act III, Sc. 5, p. 140.
13. *Ibid.,* Act III, Sc. 6, p. 144.
14. *Amphitryon 38,* "Variantes II," Act III, Sc. 4, p. 218.
15. *Amphitryon 38,* Act II, Sc. 3, p. 68.
16. *Ibid.*
17. *Ibid.,* Act II, Sc. 5, p. 84.

18. *Ibid.*, Act II, Sc. 6, pp. 98–99.
19. *Ibid.*, Act II, Sc. 2, p. 62.
20. *Ibid.*, Act III, Sc. 5, p. 137.
21. *Ibid.*, Act I, Sc. 6, p. 46.
22. The Book of Judith is not found in the Hebraic Holy Scriptures. It is, however, included in the Septuagint Greek version of the Bible; the Hebrew original has been lost. It is also included in the Vulgate Latin version of the Bible made by St. Jerome; instead of the original Hebrew text, St. Jerome used a somewhat shortened version in Aramaic.
23. *Judith*, Ides et Calendes, Neuchâtel & Paris, 1945–53, *Théâtre Complet*, Vol. II (1945), Act II, Sc. 2, p. 67.
24. *Ibid.*, p. 69.
25. *Ibid.*, Act I, Sc. 2, p. 14.
26. *Ibid.*, Act I, Sc. 8, p. 52.
27. *Ibid.*, Act III, Sc. 5, p. 117.
28. *Ibid.*, Act III, Sc. 4, p. 115.
29. *Ibid.*, Act III, Sc. 6, p. 125.
30. *Ibid.*, p. 126.
31. *Ibid.*, Act III, Sc. 7, p. 131.
32. *Ibid.*, p. 130.
33. *Ibid.*, p. 139.
34. *Ibid.*, p. 130.
35. *Ibid.*, Act II, Sc. 4, pp. 82–83.
36. *Ibid.*, Act II, Sc. 6, p. 92.
37. *Ibid.*, Act III, Sc. 4, p. 113.
38. *Intermezzo*, Ides et Calendes, Neuchâtel & Paris, 1945–53, *Théâtre Complet*, Vol. IV (1946), Act III, Sc. 1, p. 108.
39. *Ibid.*, Act III, Sc. 1, p. 104.
40. *Ibid.*, Act III, Sc. 4, p. 129.
41. *Ibid.*, Act III, Sc. 6, p. 144.
42. *Ibid.*, Act II, Sc. 3, p. 75.
43. *Ibid.*, Act III, Sc. 6, p. 126.
44. *Ibid.*, pp. 130–131.
45. *Ibid.*, p. 131.
46. *La Guerre de Troie n'aura pas lieu*, Ides et Calendes, Neuchâtel & Paris, 1945–53, *Théâtre Complet*, Vol. VI (1946), Act II, Sc. 12, p. 108.
47. *Ibid.*, Act II, Sc. 13, p. 123.
48. *Ibid.*, p. 126.
49. *Ibid.*, p. 127.
50. *Ibid.*, Act II, Sc. 14, p. 131.
51. *Ibid.*, Act II, Sc. 8, pp. 95–96.

52. *Ibid.,* Act I, Sc. 9, p. 55.
53. *Ibid.,* Act II, Sc. 12, p. 116.
54. *Ibid.,* pp. 116–117.
55. Denis Diderot, *Supplément au Voyage de Bougainville,* C. Marpon & E. Flammarion, Paris, 1883, Chefs d'Œuvre, Vol. VII, Chap. II, "Les Adieux du Vieillard," p. 129.
56. *Electre,* Ides et Calendes, Neuchâtel & Paris, 1945–53, *Théâtre Complet,* Vol. VII (1946), Act I, Sc. 8, pp. 67–68.
57. *Ibid.,* Act I, Sc. 11, p. 175.
58. *Ibid.,* Act II, Sc. 5, p. 114.
59. *Ibid.,* Act II, Sc. 7, p. 150.
60. *Ibid.,* Act II, Sc. 8, pp. 140–141.
61. *Ibid.,* Act II, Sc. 10, p. 161.
62. *Ibid.,* Act II, Sc. 8, p. 139.
63. *Ibid.,* Act I, Sc. 8, p. 66.
64. *Ibid.,* Act II, Sc. 8, p. 143.
65. *Ibid.,* Act I, Sc. 2, p. 23.
66. *Ibid.,* p. 26.
67. *Ibid.,* p. 21.
68. *Ibid.,* pp. 22–23.
69. *Ondine,* Ides et Calendes, Neuchâtel & Paris, 1945–53, *Théâtre Complet,* Vol. IX (1946), Act III, Sc. 7, p. 167.
70. *Ibid.,* Act II, Sc. 11; p. 106.
71. *Ibid.,* Act II, Sc. 11, p. 106.
72. *Ibid.,* Act I, Sc. 1, p. 9.
73. *Ibid.,* Act I, Sc. 7, p. 42.
74. *Ibid.,* p. 43.
75. *Ibid.,* Act I, Sc. 9, p. 54.
76. *Sodome et Gomorrhe,* Ides et Calendes, Neuchâtel & Paris, 1945–53, *Théâtre Complet,* Vol. XI (1947), Act II, Sc. 7, p. 90.
77. *Ibid.*
78. *La Folle de Chaillot,* Ides et Calendes, Neuchâtel & Paris, 1945–53, *Théâtre Complet,* Vol. XI (1947) Act II, p. 136.
79. Livy, *Ab Urbe condita libri,* I, 58 ff.
80. Originally Bethany was the name of a village in Judea, the home of Lazarus and his sisters Martha and Mary (John, 11, 1).

Chapter V

1. *L'Ecole des Indifférents,* Grasset, Paris, 1955, *Œuvre Romanesque,* Vol. I, "Jacques l'Égoïste," IV, p. 116.

2. *Littérature*, Grasset, Paris, 1958, *Œuvres Littéraires Diverses*, Chap. I, "Choderlos de Laclos," p. 493.
3. *Ibid.*, Chap. III, "De Siècle à Siècle, p. 562.
4. *Ibid.*, p. 557.
5. *Pleins Pouvoirs*, Gallimard, Paris, 1939, Chap. I, "Le Vrai Problème Français," p. 10.
6. *Ibid.*, p. 26.
7. *Ibid.*, p. 9.
8. *Ibid.*, Chap. V, "Notre Conscience," p. 198.
9. *Ibid.*, pp. 198–199.
10. *Ibid.*, p. 210.

Chapter VI

1. Jean Giraudoux, *Aventures de Jérôme Bardini*, Grasset, Paris, 1955, *Œuvre Romanesque*, Vol. II, "The Kid," III, p. 332.
2. André Bourin, "Elle et Lui. Chez Madame Jean Giraudoux," *Nouvelles Littéraires*, Paris, November 16, 1950, No. 1211, p. 1.
3. *Judith*, Ides et Calendes, Neuchâtel & Paris, 1945–53, *Théâtre Complet*, Vol. II (1945), Act II, Sc. 5, pp. 86–87.
4. *Ibid.*
5. *Littérature*, Grasset, Paris, 1958, *Œuvres Littéraires Diverses*, Chap. III, "Dieu et la Littérature," p. 533.
6. *Combat avec l'Ange*, Grasset, Paris, 1955, *Œuvre Romanesque*, Vol. II, Chap. III, p. 499.
7. *Electre*, Ides et Calendes, Neuchâtel & Paris, 1945–53, *Théâtre Complet*, Vol. VII (1946), Act I, Sc. 3, p. 30.
8. *Electre*, "Entracte, Lamento du Jardinier," pp. 88–89.
9. *Littérature*, Chap. III, "Dieu et la Litérature," p. 533.
10. *Choix des Elues*, Grasset, Paris, 1955, *Œuvre Romanesque*, Vol. II, Chap. XI, p. 803.
11. ———, *La Guerre de Troie n'aura pas lieu*, Ides et Calendes, Neuchâtel & Paris, 1945–53, *Théâtre Complet*, Vol. VI (1946), Act II, Sc. 13, pp. 121–122.
12. *Ibid.*, Act I, Sc. 1, p. 12.
13. *Combat avec l'Ange*, Chap. VIII, p. 603.
14. *Ibid.*, p. 604.
15. ———, *Suzanne et le Pacifique*, Grasset, Paris, 1955, *Œuvre Romanesque*, Vol. I, Chap. I, pp. 256–257.
16. ———, *Pour Lucrèce*, Ides et Calendes, Neuchâtel & Paris, 1945–53, *Théâtre Complet*, Vol. XVI (1953), Act III, Sc. 2, p. 79.
17. *Combat avec l'Ange*, Chap. IX, p. 602.

18. ———, *Amphitryon 38*, Ides et Calendes, Neuchâtel & Paris, *Théâtre Complet*, Vol. III (1945), Act II, Sc. 2, p. 62.

19. ———, *Eglantine*, Grasset, Paris, 1955, *Œuvre Romanesque*, Vol. II, Chap. III, p. 165.

20. ———, *L'Ecole des Indifférents*, Grasset, Paris, 1955, *Œuvre Romanesque*, Vol. I, "Jacques l'Égoïste," III, pp. 107–109.

21. *Ibid.*, pp. 107–108.

22. ———, *Intermezzo*, Ides et Calendes, Neuchâtel & Paris, 1945–53, *Théâtre Complet*, Vol. IV (1946), Act I, Sc. 8, p. 53.

23. *Ibid.*, Act I, Sc. 8, p. 54.

24. *Electre*, Act II, Sc. 4, p. 107.

25. ———, *Juliette au Pays des Hommes*, Grasset, Paris, 1955, *Œuvre Romanesque*, Vol. I, Chap. V, p. 291.

26. ———, *Siegfried et le Limousin*, Grasset, Paris, 1955, *Œuvre Romanesque*, Vol. I, Chap. V, p. 478.

27. *Ibid.*, Chap. VII, p. 514.

28. *Aventures de Jérôme Bardini*, "The Kid," II, p. 320.

29. *Juliette au Pays des Hommes*, Chap. VIII, p. 615.

30. ———, *Supplément au Voyage de Cook*, Ides et Calendes, Neuchâtel & Paris, 1945–53, *Théâtre Complet*, Vol. VI (1946), Sc. 4, pp. 158–159.

31. ———, *Sans Pouvoirs*, Editions du Rocher, Monaco, 1946, "Avenir de la France," pp. 144–145.

32. ———, *Provinciales*, Grasset, Paris, 1955, *Œuvre Romanesque*, Vol. I, "De ma fenêtre," I, p. 9.

33. *Juliette au Pays des Hommes*, Chap. I, p. 547.

34. ———, *Bella*, Grasset, Paris, 1955, *Œuvre Romanesque*, Vol. II, Chap. II, p. 22.

35. *Electre*, Act II, Sc. 8, pp. 150–151.

36. *Choix des Elues*, Chap. VII, p. 739.

37. ———, *Intermezzo*, Ides et Calendes, Neuchâtel & Paris, 1945–53, *Théâtre Complet*, Vol. IV (1946), Act II, Sc. 4, p. 140

38. *La Guerre de Troie n'aura pas lieu*, Act I, Sc. 6, p. 34.

39. *Ibid.*, Act II, Sc. 8, p. 93.

40. *Ibid.*, Act I, Sc. 8, p. 41.

41. ———, *Amphitryon 38*, Ides et Calendes, Neuchâtel & Paris, 1945–53, *Théâtre Complet*, Vol. III (1945), Act I, Sc. 5, pp. 38–39.

42. *Electre*, Act II, Sc. 6, pp. 118–119.

43. *Siegfried et le Limousin*, Chap. V, p. 465.

44. ———, *L'Impromptu de Paris*, Ides et Calendes, Neuchâtel & Paris, 1945–53, *Théâtre Complet*, Vol. VIII (1946), Sc. 6, p. 66.

45. ———, *Pleins Pouvoirs*, Gallimard, Paris, 1939, Chap. V, "Notre Conscience," pp. 208–209.

46. *Ibid.*, pp. 177–178.

47. ———, *Siegfried*, Ides et Calendes, Neuchâtel & Paris, 1945–53, *Théâtre Complet*, Vol. I (1945), Act II, Sc. 2, p. 59.

48. *Ibid.*

49. *Ibid.*

50. *Ibid.*, Act I, Sc. 2, p. 14.

51. *Ibid.*, Act III, Sc. 1, p. 75.

52. *Ibid.*, Act I, Sc. 2, pp. 14–15.

53. *Ibid.*, Act III, Sc. 2, pp. 59–60.

Chapter VII

1. Frédéric Lefèvre, *Une heure avec... Première Série,* Gallimard, Paris, 1924, "Jean Giraudoux," p. 149.

2. This article was reprinted in Sartre's *Situations I,* Gallimard, Paris, 1947, pp. 82–98.

3. *Situations I,* "M. Giraudoux et la philosophie d'Aristote," p. 97.

4. *Ibid.*

5. *Ibid.*

6. Claude-Edmonde Magny, *Précieux Giraudoux,* Editions du Seuil, Paris, 1945; 2nd ed. 1968, Chap. I, p. 28.

7. *Ibid.*, Chap. II, p. 51.

8. *Une heure avec... Première Série,* Jean Giraudoux, p. 150.

9. *Ibid.*, p. 149.

10. Frédéric Lefèvre, *Une heure avec... Quatrième Série,* Gallimard, Paris, 1927, "Jean Giraudoux," p. 120.

11. *Ibid.*

12. *Ibid.*, p. 117.

13. *Ibid.*, pp. 126–127.

14. Jean Giraudoux, *Amphitryon 38,* Ides et Calendes, Neuchâtel & Paris, 1945–53, *Théâtre Complet*, Vol. III (1945), Act II, Sc. 7, p. 103.

15. *Ibid.*, Act III, Sc. 5, p. 135.

16. ———, *Adorable Clio*, Grasset, Paris, 1958, *Œuvres Littéraires Diverses*, "Adieu à la Guerre," p. 264.

17. ———, *L'Ecole des Indifférents*, Grasset. Paris, 1955, *Œuvre Romanesque*, Vol. I, "Bernard, le faible Bernard," III, p. 173.

18. *Précieux Giraudoux,* Chap. V, pp. 53–81.

19. ———, *Juliette au Pays des Hommes*, Grasset, Paris, 1955, *Œuvre Romanesque*, Vol. I, Chap. VI, "Prière sur la Tour Eiffel," p. 597.

20. *L'Ecole des Indifférents,* "Jacques l'Égoïste," VI, p. 125.

21. *Ibid.*, p. 124.

22. ———, *Littérature*, Grasset, Paris, 1958, *Œuvres Littéraires Diverses*, Chap. I, "Gérard de Nerval," p. 501.

23. *Situations I,* "M. Giraudoux et la philosophie d'Aristote," p. 98.

Selective Bibliography

I. Works by Jean Giraudoux

Provinciales, Grasset. Paris, 1909; enlarged edition, 1922.

L'Ecole des Indifférents, Grasset, Paris, 1911; revised edition, 1934.

Lectures pour une Ombre, Emile-Paul, Paris, 1917.

Simon le Pathétique, Grasset, Paris, 1918; revised edition, 1926.

Amica America, Emile-Paul, Paris, 1919.

Elpénor, Emile-Paul, Paris, 1919.

Adorable Clio, Emile-Paul, Paris, 1920.

Suzanne et le Pacifique, Emile-Paul, Paris, 1921; Cercle Lyonnais du Livre (Illustrations by Daragnès), Lyons, 1928.

Siegfried et le Limousin, Grasset, Paris, 1922.

La Prière sur la Tour Eiffel, Emile-Paul, Paris, 1923.

Juliette au Pays des Homes, Emil-Paul, Paris, 1924.

Bella, Grasset, Paris, 1927.

La Première Disparition de Jérôme Bardini, Kra, Paris, 1927.

Eglantine, Grasset, Paris, 1927.

L'Orgueil (In *Les Sept Péchés Capitaux*), Kra, Paris, 1927.

Le Sport, Hachette, Paris, 1928.

Siegfried, Grasset. Paris, 1928.

Divertissement de Siegfried, Gallimard, Paris, 1928.

Fugues sur Siegfried (Divertissement de Siegfried and *Lamento)*, Lapina, Paris, 1929.

Amphitryon 38, Grasset, Paris, 1929.

209

Racine, first published in *La Nouvelle Revue Française,* December, 1929; included in *Littérature,* Grasset, Paris, 1941; published separately, Grasset, Paris, 1950.

Aventures de Jérôme Bardini, Emile-Paul, Paris, 1930.

Judith, Emile-Paul, Paris, 1931.

La France Sentimentale, Grasset, Paris, 1932.

Intermezzo, Grasset, Paris, 1933.

Combat avec l'Ange, Grasset, Paris, 1934.

Tessa, La Nymphe au cœur fidèle, Grasset, Paris, 1934.

Fin de Siegfried, Grasset, Paris, 1934.

La Guerre de Troie n'aura pas lieu, Grasset, Paris, 1935.

Supplément au Voyage de Cook, Grasset, Paris, 1937.

Electre, Grasset, Paris, 1937.

L'Impromptu de Paris, Grasset, Paris, 1937.

Cantique des Cantiques, Grasset, Paris, 1938.

Choix des Elues, Grasset, Paris, 1938.

Les Cinq Tentations de La Fontaine, Grasset, Paris, 1938.

Ondine, Grasset, Paris, 1939.

Pleins Pouvoirs, Gallimard, Paris, 1939.

Littérature, Grasset, Paris, 1941.

Le Film de la Duchesse de Langeais, Grasset, Paris, 1942.

Sodome et Gomorrhe, Grasset, Paris, 1943.

Hommage à Marivaux, Cl. Sézille, Paris, 1844.

Le Film de Béthanie (Les Anges du Péché), Gallimard, Paris, 1944.

La Folle de Chaillot, Ides et Calendes, Neuchâtel & Paris, 1945.

Sans Pouvoirs, Editions du Rocher, Monaco, 1945.

Armistice à Bordeaux, Editions du Rocher, Monaco, 1945.

L'Apollon de Bellac, Ides et Calendes, Neuchâtel & Paris, 1946.

Visitations, Ides et Calendes, Neuchâtel & Paris, 1946.

Pour une politique urbaine, Editions Arts et Métiers Graphiques, Paris, 1947.

De Pleins Pouvoirs à Sans Pouvoirs (incl. "Armistice à Bordeaux"), Gallimard, Paris, 1950.

La Française et la France, Gallimard, Paris, 1951.

Les Contes d'un matin, Gallimard, Paris, 1952.

Pour Lucrèce, Ides et Calendes, Neuchâtel & Paris, 1953.

La Menteuse, Grasset, Paris (fragments) 1958; complete text, 1969.

Or dans la nuit, Grasset, Paris, 1969.

II. Special Editions

Théâtre Complet, Ides et Calendes, Neuchâtel & Paris, 1945–53, 16 vols.

Œuvre Romanesque, Grasset, Paris, 1955, 2 vols.
Œuvres Littéraires Diverses, Grasset, Paris, 1958, 1 vol.

III. English Translations
of Jean Giraudoux's Works

Amphitryon 38. Adapted by Samuel N. Behrman as *Amphitryon 38,* Random House, New York, 1938; translated by Phyllis La Farge with Peter Judd, Hill & Wang, New York, 1964; translated by Roger Gellert, Oxford University Press, New York, 1967.

L'Apollon de Bellac. Adapted by Maurice Valency as *The Apollo of Bellac,* Samuel French, New York, 1954; abridged version by Ronald Duncan, Samuel French, London, 1957.

Bella. Translated by J. F. Scanlan as *Bella,* Knopf, New York, 1927.

Electre. Translated by Wynifred Smith as *Electra,* in Eric Russel Bentley, *From the Modern Repertoire,* Series II, Indiana University Press, Bloomington, 1952; translated by Phyllis La Farge with Peter Judd, Hill & Wang, New York, 1964.

Elpénor. Translated by Richard Howard with Renaud Bruce as *Elpenor,* Noonday Press, New York, 1958.

La Folle de Chaillot. Adapated by Maurice Valency as *The Madwoman of Chaillot,* Random House, New York, 1947.

La Guerre de Troie n'aura pas lieu. Translated by Christopher Fry as *Tiger at the Gates,* Oxford University Press, New York, 1956.

Intermezzo. Adapted by Maurice Valency as *The Enchanted,* Random House, New York, 1950; translated by Roger Gellert as *Intermezzo,* Oxford University Press, New York, 1967.

Judith. Translated by J.K. Savacool as *Judith* in Eric Russell Bentley, *The Modern Theatre,* Doubleday, New York, 1955–60; translated by Christopher Fry as *Judith,* Methuen, London, 1963.

Lectures pour une Ombre. Translated by Elizabeth S. Sergeant as *Campaigns and Intervals,* Houghton Mifflin, New York, 1918.

Ondine. Adapted by Maurice Valency as *Ondine,* Random House, New York, 1949; translated by Roger Gellert as *Ondine,* Oxford University Press, New York, 1967.

Pour Lucrèce. Translated by Christopher Fry as *Duel of Angels,* Methuen, London, 1958.

Racine. Translated by Percy Mansell Jones as *Racine,* Gordon Fraser, Cambridge, 1938.

Siegfried. Translated by Philip Carr as *Siegfried,* L. MacVeah-The Dial Press, New York, 1930; translated by Phyllis La Farge with Peter Judd, Hill & Wang, New York, 1946.

Siegfried et le Limousin. Translated by Louis Collier Willcox as *My Friend from Limousin,* Harper, New York and London, 1923.

Supplément au Voyage de Cook. Adapted by Maurice Valency as *The Virtuous Island,* Samuel French, New York, 1956.

Suzanne et le Pacifique. Translated by Ben Ray Redman as *Suzanne and the Pacific,* G.P. Putnam's Sons, New York and London, 1923.

IV. Some Articles
and Books on Jean Giraudoux

Albérès, R. M., *Esthétique et moral chez Jean Giraudoux,* Nizet, Paris, 1957.

Bourdet, Maurice, *Jean Giraudoux: son oeuvre,* Editions de la Nouvelle Critique, Paris, 1928.

Brasillach, Robert, "Le Théâtre de Jean Giraudoux," *La Revue Universell,* May 1933.

Cocteau, Jean, *Souvenir de Jean Giraudoux,* J. Haumont, Paris, 1946.

Cohen, Robert, *Giraudoux: Three Faces of Destiny,* University of Chicago Press, Chicago, 1968.

Debidour, V. H., *Giraudoux,* Editions Universitaires, Paris, 1955.

Houlet, Jacques, *Le Théâtre de Jean Giraudoux,* Pierre Ardent, Paris, 1945.

Inskip, Donald, *Jean Giraudoux: The Making of a Dramatist.* Oxford University Press, New York, 1958.

LeSage, Laurent, *Jean Giraudoux: His Life and Works,* Pennsylvania State University Press, University Park, Pa., 1959.

———, "Jean Giraudoux, Surrealism, and the German Romantic Ideal," *Illinois Studies in Language and Literature,* Vol. 36, No. 3, 1952.

Magny, Claude-Edmonde, *Précieux Giraudoux,* Editions du Seuil, Paris, 1945.

May, Georges, "Jean Giraudoux: Diplomacy and Dramaturgy," *Yale French Studies,* No. 5, Spring 1950.

Mercier-Campiche, Marianne, *Le Théâtre de Jean Giraudoux et la condition humaine,* Editions Domat, Paris, 1954.

Raymond, Agnes G., *Jean Giraudoux: The Theatre of Victory and Defeat,* University of Massachusetts Press, Amherst, Mass., 1966.

Index